PROUST and LITERATURE

The Novelist as Critic

PROUST
and
LITERATURE

The Novelist as Critic

WALTER A. STRAUSS

> . . . tous les grands poètes
> deviennent naturellement,
> fatalement, critiques . . .
>
> BAUDELAIRE

1957

HARVARD UNIVERSITY PRESS CAMBRIDGE, MASSACHUSETTS

Distributed in Great Britain by
Oxford University Press, London

Library of Congress Catalog Number 57-7618

PRINTED IN THE UNITED STATES OF AMERICA

for Lilo

ACKNOWLEDGMENTS

The publication of this study was made possible in part by a grant from the Emory University Research Committee, to whom I am sincerely grateful. I am indebted to the generous assistance given to me, and the valuable suggestions offered, by Professor Harry T. Levin and Professor Margaret Gilman, who read an earlier draft of the entire manuscript, and by Professor Herbert Dieckmann, who read the first two chapters.

I wish to thank Librairie Gallimard and Madame Mante-Proust for permission to use copyright material from Proust's *Pastiches et mélanges, Chroniques, Contre Sainte-Beuve, suivi de Nouveaux Mélanges, Le Balzac de Monsieur de Guermantes* and *Lettres à André Gide*, as well as Louis de Robert's *Comment débuta Marcel Proust*; the Mercure de France, for material from Ruskin's *Sésame et les lys*, translated by Proust; Librairie Plon, for material from Proust's *Correspondance générale* and from Barrès' *Cahiers*; Doubleday & Company, Inc., for material from the forthcoming *Pleasures and Days, and Other Writings*, by Proust, translated by Gerard Hopkins; Harper & Brothers, for material from André Maurois' *Proust, Portrait of a Genius*; Random House, Inc., for material from *The Letters of Marcel Proust*, translated by Mina Curtiss, and from *Remembrance of Things Past*, translated by C. K. Scott-Moncrieff and Frederick A. Blossom; Simon and Schuster, Inc., for material from Proust's *Jean Santeuil*, translated by Gerard Hopkins; Mr. G. W. Cottrell, Jr., for material contained in the article "Twelve Unpublished Letters of Marcel Proust," published by the *Harvard Library Bulletin*; Mr. Alexander Henderson, for material from Proust's *Letters to a Friend*, translated by Alexander and Elizabeth Henderson and published by the Falcon Press; Allan Wingate Limited, for material from *Marcel Proust: A Selection from his Miscellaneous Writings*, chosen and translated by Gerard Hopkins.

W. A. S.

Emory University, Georgia
January, 1957

ACKNOWLEDGMENTS

[illegible]

CONTENTS

I. Introduction 1

II. Proust and the Seventeenth Century 29

III. Proust as a Critic of the Nineteenth Century 49

1. The Romantic poets — Baudelaire, "poète classique" — other poets, 49
2. Balzac, inventor, 84
3. Flaubert and "la beauté grammaticale," 105
4. Other French prose writers, 123
5. Sainte-Beuve, the "poor guide," 141
6. Foreign authors, 160

IV. Proust and his Contemporaries 187

V. Conclusion 209

Bibliography 229

Notes 239

Index of Names 261

PROUST and LITERATURE

The Novelist as Critic

I

INTRODUCTION

. . . l'impulsion d'un autre esprit . . .
reçue au sein de la solitudé.
PROUST, *Sésame et les lys.*

A la recherche du temps perdu has been described as a cathedral, a symphony, even as a kind of *Summa.* Its vastness and complexity have stimulated all varieties of scholarly and critical scrutiny, often with exciting results. The Proust bibliography is constantly growing and shows signs of an increased vitality as a result of the publication of numerous letters and a number of recently discovered early works, notably the early unfinished novel, *Jean Santeuil,* and the *Contre Sainte-Beuve,* a work difficult to classify because it fluctuates between novel, autobiography, and criticism. Moreover, the new definitive edition of *A la recherche,* by offering us a new and improved reading of the text of the novel, has given us the privilege of discovering Proust all over again. It is not too rash to infer from all this that a new phase of Proust criticism has been in the making — a reëxamination of Proust's entire career from the vantage point of additional biographical information and with the aid of hitherto unknown material in Proust's own hand. This second phase in Proust criticism, which has the advantage over the first phase in that it is concerned with the examination of a recognized classic, should succeed in clarifying the pattern of Proust's evolution as a writer, his quest for a style, and his position in the history of the novel, as well as his place among the two or three greatest writers of fiction of the twentieth century.

Much of the groundwork has already been laid; the first phase of Proust criticism established him as a great literary artist, and in doing so isolated a number of elements that deserve special examination before a comprehensive synthesis — if such a thing is possible in Proust's case — can be achieved. There are studies of Proustian psychology and philosophy, and his relationships to the fine arts and music have been defined. It is strange, however, that Proust's relationship to literature — the art to which he was closest — has been neglected. The topic has been touched upon, usually in articles, but no systematic attempt has ever been made to assess the influence of other writers on Proust, or to delineate Proust's attitude toward the writers whom he read so avidly. In a recent survey of the literature on Proust, this situation is brought into sharp relief:

> First and last, it has to be remembered — as the specialist intent on a thesis often forgets or obscures — that the secret flowering of Proust's artistic vision and purpose sprang from an unusually composite soil, refined and prepared by the acutely sharpened senses and sensibilities of the invalid, cherishing every experience that fed them from sources one or all of which might at any moment be withdrawn, and for ever, nourished by beauty and the grain of human interest in scene or life, in thought or art — architecture, music, painting and, always and above all, literature. It is a queer irony that of the many streams that fed Proust's mind none has been more neglected than this. Here, as much as anywhere, there is work to be done, on the particular inspiration and the particular kind of inspiration he drew from the classic writers of antiquity, from Racine and Vigny and Baudelaire, Saint-Simon, Balzac and George Sand, Chateaubriand and Gérard de Nerval, Dostoevski and English writers other than Ruskin — George Eliot, for instance, and Hardy. Such work could scarcely fail to be illuminating.[1]

Proust's reading was so vast that some of his friends were convinced that he had read "everything." Nor is one surprised to learn from Jacques Porel that he knew by heart entire passages from Montaigne, Racine, Saint-Simon, Balzac, Stendhal, Chateaubriand, Flaubert, Vigny, Hugo, and Baudelaire, as well as from Dostoevski, Tolstoi, Ruskin, Dickens, and Meredith.[2] Proust had a way of becoming friends with art — with cathedrals, with Vermeer, with Monet, with Beethoven's last string quartets, and with his own favorite authors.

> . . . He held familiar conversation with all masterpieces. Whatever he told you about them was intimate and stimulating, being the result of a long acquaintance with the great writers. He knew them well and was not afraid of them: for *they* were his true friends.[3]

Since this experience of friendship was as vivid for Proust as any other experience which he incorporated — after a long process of examination and re-creation — into *A la recherche*, we are permitted to ask ourselves just in what sense books helped him to fashion the edifice of the novel. We have, on the one hand, reminiscences of books, and on the other, Proust's attempt to extract the essence of his literary experience — his quest for an aesthetic framework that would both justify and elucidate *A la recherche*. Thus, the great chapter in *Le Temps retrouvé* in which the Narrator outlines his aesthetics is a synthesis of all the truths that the creations of Vinteuil, Elstir, Bergotte, and Berma have made palpable to him. The ripeness of those pages presupposes a long quest, similar to that of the Narrator, for the essential values in art, a struggle with the dialectic between art and life; in other words, it forced Proust to serve a long apprenticeship as a critic. "If he had not been the greatest novelist of our time, he would have become its greatest critic," Maurois wrote in his introduction to the definitive edition of *A la recherche*.[4] It is with Proust the critic — or better, Proust the man of taste and practicing writer in his capacity as critic — that the following pages will be concerned. For Proust was a literary critic of remarkable sensitivity — which is to say that he brought the sensibility of the novelist to bear upon his critical judgment; and the result is a kind of criticism that is not only illuminating with respect to his practice as a novelist but also perceptive in itself, filled with numerous *aperçus* and discoveries that alter the reader's conceptions of the work discussed and enables him to read it with more sharply focused eyes.

> In reality, each reader reads only what is already within himself. The book is only a sort of optical instrument which the writer offers to the reader to enable the latter to discover in himself what he would not have found but for the aid of the book.[5]

The metaphor of the novelist as an optician holds true also for the critic, as will be shown later.

Proust's criticism has a tendency to be sporadic and unsystematic, since it arises spontaneously in relation to certain literary and other experiences. Yet it is sown in abundance; witness, for instance, the opinion of Jacques-Emile Blanche, Proust's friend: "In his gigantic work, carved and lacquered like a Chinese cabinet with secret drawers, one could find scattered the material with which to make volumes of articles by the most original of literary critics . . ."[6]

Literary analysis and criticism occupied Proust during his entire lifetime, serving as a technique to help him find his own style as well as his aesthetic. There is an intermittent series of critical articles stretching from Proust's first youthful contributions in *Le Banquet* (1892) to his article on Baudelaire in the *Nouvelle Revue française* (June, 1921) and to several small contributions to various literary symposia conducted by certain newspapers. The various essays are loosely built, and tend to undulate; the digressions often become more important than the thread, but the thread is never lost. This is altogether what one would expect, in view of Proust's literary style and his artistic personality in general. Since Proust never compartmentalized any datum of experience, one is not surprised at the digressions; moreover, this method is seasoned with a particular Proustian flavor, consisting of the author's special interests, which inevitably point to *A la recherche*. The essays revolve around certain figures whom Proust admired most — Balzac, Baudelaire, and Ruskin; they pay tribute to others from whom he learned much, such as Flaubert; and take to task Sainte-Beuve, whom Proust was particularly interested in castigating. The fact that all these figures belong to the nineteenth century indicates that Proust's literary criticism operates most freely and willingly on that century; as a rule, authors from the seventeenth century are brought into the discussion to serve as measuring-sticks of style and of psychological "reality."

The recent publication of *Jean Santeuil* and of *Contre Sainte-Beuve* enables us to arrive at a clearer notion of Proust's career as a creative artist. We may, for the sake of convenience, divide his development into three stages. The first of these is the period in which Proust's first sketches appeared in *Le Banquet*, and is followed by the publication of *Les Plaisirs et les jours* (1896); it is the stage in which he was still under the influence of symbolism and Anatole France. This phase culminates in the composition of a work of fiction giving evidence of certain preoccupations and interests that are not fully realized until *A la recherche*—*Jean Santeuil*, with its wealth of material that is still awaiting the suitable inner and outer framework. Proust's abandonment of *Jean Santeuil* about 1899 in favor of the Ruskin translations (culminating in *La Bible d'Amiens*, in 1904, and *Sésame et les lys*, 1905) ushered in the second phase, which looks like a temporary withdrawal from fiction and which enabled Proust to come to grips with certain problems of literary style and composition. In this instance Ruskin definitely acted as an intercessor. Following upon the heels of translation are the Pastiches, most of which appeared in 1908 and 1909 (collected in *Pastiches et mélanges*, 1919). The Pastiches were exercising what Proust likes to call a "purgative" effect on his style, and Proust showed an eagerness to do something else. According to Professor Vigneron,[7] the idea of a *new* work took shape in Proust's mind in the spring of 1908; its form, however, was not clear to him, and during 1908 and 1909 he appears to have worked on it by fits and starts. Toward the end of 1908, Proust contemplated the possibility of organizing his materials into a kind of critical essay, now known as the *Contre Sainte-Beuve*. This work is, in a sense, complete: it has a beginning, middle, and end; but in reality it is only a foreshadowing of what is to come and serves primarily to document the metamorphosis of the hesitant critic-novelist into the full-fledged novelist: the transition from the second to the final stage. By the end of 1910 Proust appears to have seen his way clearly enough to proceed with *A la recherche*; the first version of the entire work was probably complete by early 1912. The subsequent years saw a feverish attempt to fix the richness of his vision on paper, in its totality, by incorporating additions, expansions, and modifications into the original scheme.[8] If Proust had lived longer, the last volumes, and perhaps the earlier ones, would have grown even more bulky.

Even though this division of Proust's career into stages is in no way intended to mark off sharply certain preoccupations in Proust's literary activity — in his personality, as well as in *A la recherche*, all these elements coexist at any particular moment, and only their relative importance changes — it does point up two important factors which have not received the proper attention until recently. The first disposes of the mistaken notion that Proust was more or less inert artistically from 1895 to 1910, except for his work on Ruskin (about 1900–1904) and a handful of articles. The publication of Maurois' biography and of *Jean Santeuil* and *Contre Sainte-Beuve* has completely shattered that misconception and emphasized beyond the shadow of a doubt that Proust was always in quest of a literary vocation but did not discern until rather late precisely what direction his literary exploration was to take. The second factor is the one which this book is intended to demonstrate: namely, that in all these stages literary criticism plays a certain role, becoming dominant in the central stage (1900–1910), because at that juncture literary criticism was of prime importance to him; in those years Proust, already an accomplished craftsman and a viable literary artist, needed to give a form to his vision which was already in the process of being distilled out of his experience; and this necessitated the creation of a prose style that would transmit the vision faithfully. Thus the writer in Proust is always doubled by his alter ego, the critic.

The first important piece of literary criticism is the anti-symbolist pronouncement "Contre l'obscurité," first published in the *Revue blanche* in 1896 (reprinted in *Chroniques*). *Jean Santeuil* contains a number of discussions of writers such as Balzac and Flaubert, and of the problem of literary creation in general and thus foreshadows — but only to a lesser extent — the more mature reflections of *A la recherche*. The Ruskin translations brought Proust into contact with a mind and with a meandering prose style that had things in common with his own. Ruskin's remarks on art and morality stimulated Proust to a point where he felt it necessary to go beyond the translator's task, with the result that *La Bible d'Amiens* and *Sésame et les lys* actually resemble critical editions. The translations were generously enlivened with comments, most of them of considerable literary interest, and prefaces were added in each case, of which the second, the preface to *Sésame et les lys*, entitled "Journées de lecture," serves as an excellent introduction to a study of Proust's literary tastes. In this period belong also the various essays on the study of Ruskin and on subjects suggested by Ruskin's interests, collected under the title of "En mémoire des églises assassinées," reprinted in *Pastiches et mélanges*, and "La Mort des cathédrales," reprinted in *Chroniques*. After several years of intensive work on Ruskin, Proust felt the need of exorcising the English writer as well as certain other influences that were in danger of engulfing his own literary individuality. The Pastiches are exercises of just that nature. Proust thought of them as a form of literary criticism in action, and besides, these exercises served the purpose of sharpening his mastery of various prose styles, while they gave him and his readers considerable pleasure.

The precise nature and form of his other writings of that period remains somewhat obscure at this point; if Proust's notebooks are ever published, we may perhaps have some light on the subject. But the critical phase in Proust's career was only beginning: the translator of Ruskin had quite normally turned into a critic of Ruskin; the years 1907–1909 show us the critic trying to turn into a creative writer. But what kind of creative writer? Pastiche-writing was a kind of literary criticism for Proust, but its possibilities were obviously limited. At this point he became something halfway between a literary critic and a novelist, and by the end of 1909 he had turned novelist pure and simple. The metamorphosis is interesting to observe. In November, 1908, Proust was toying with the idea of writing a criticism of Sainte-Beuve. However, he was not satisfied with a straightforward treatment, "de forme classique," in the manner of Taine [9] and felt instead that he might cast the critical article into the form of a *récit* to his mother, a sort of story that would somehow involve Sainte-Beuve. In the fall of 1909 Proust writes " . . . it's very long, four or five hundred pages," and later, " . . . I will have a copy made of the untidy draft of the first paragraph of the first chapter of Sainte-Beuve (that first paragraph is almost a book) . . ." [10]

This work, the *Contre Sainte-Beuve*, is a composite of a number of manuscripts on and around the topic of Sainte-Beuve, which M. Bernard de Fallois has arranged into a sequence. It is a fascinating work in the way in which it enables us to witness the metamorphosis of Proust the critic into the novelist. A detailed study will be found in the Sainte-Beuve chapter below. For the moment, it is sufficient to point out the nuclear position of the criticism of the nineteenth-century critic's method, which is supplemented by a number of critiques of Nerval, Baudelaire, and Balzac, in which Proust takes certain positions that are radically opposed to those of Sainte-Beuve. The Balzac discussion seems to have generated the stored-up creative current in Proust, for the critic criticizing a critic of Balzac suddenly turns Balzacian himself and begins to make over Balzac in his own fashion. The two chapters on Balzac (the critical one and the creative one) had been previously published (1950) separately under the title of *Le Balzac de Monsieur de Guermantes* and had provided us with a foretaste of the *Contre Sainte-Beuve,* but its precise importance within the context of that work (or sketch of a work, to be more accurate) did not become clear until the entire text was available.

The Balzac chapters provide a point of transition between the subjective Proust — the lyrical prose-poet of childhood reminiscences on the one hand, and the Proust *à la recherche d'une vocation* on the other hand, who meditates critically on art and style — and the objective Proust, the chronicler of the *deux côtés* and the historian of the vicissitudes of the French *bourgeoisie* and of the Faubourg Saint-Germain under the Third Republic. We are witnessing in *Contre Sainte-Beuve* the fusion of the George Eliot and the Ruskin aspects, already well established by 1904, with a newly activated Balzacian aspect in Proust. Sainte-Beuve here plays the role of a pseudo-Virgil, whereas Balzac becomes a genuine Virgil to guide Proust along the path that he was to follow from then on.

As a result, the essence of *A la recherche* can already be discerned in *Contre Sainte-Beuve*: Combray, Guermantes, preoccupation with sleep and waking sensations, Sodom and Gomorrha, fascination with names. As a matter of fact, this little work is the first in which the tripartite pattern of *A la recherche* can be glimpsed. Proust intended at first to divide *A la recherche* into three volumes: *Du côté de chez Swann*, *Le Côté de Guermantes*, and *Le Temps retrouvé*. The "Swann" preoccupation is found as early as *Jean Santeuil*, reappears in the preface to *Sésame et les lys*, and takes up the early chapters of *Contre Sainte-Beuve*. The observations and meditations on aesthetics appear in the footnotes to the two Ruskin translations and specifically in the preface of *La Bible d'Amiens*. Problems of literary evaluation gain even greater significance in the Sainte-Beuve critiques and in the final chapter of *Contre Sainte-Beuve*. The inner link between the *Swann* and *Temps retrouvé* portions were to be the revelations resulting from the involuntary memory. This too has its place in *Contre Sainte-Beuve*, in concentrated from, and serves as a keynote to the work, without actually ever becoming its key, as it does in *A la recherche*. The part that is still latent prior to the Sainte-Beuve study is the Guermantes section, foreshadowed by the Réveillon portions in *Jean Santeuil*, but without the elaborations that make *A la recherche* a study of the mores of the *haut monde*, among other things. Here the critique of Sainte-Beuve's criticism of Balzac leads Proust directly to creation: what Sainte-Beuve had failed to understand in the *Comédie humaine* and what Balzac himself had accomplished only insufficiently was to be completed by Proust himself. The Guermantes become the "good" readers of Balzac (as against the "bad" reading of Sainte-Beuve); and, like Balzac's own characters, they assume a reality in their author's mind: they begin to act independently, and the world of the Guermantes is born. The pattern of *A la recherche* is by 1910, in essence, complete and awaits its realization.

With this discovery of the outer framework of the novel to be written, Proust needed also to discover the appropriate inner components. Here *Contre Sainte-Beuve* too serves as the juncture between the preparatory and the final stages of Proust's career. When he undertook the work, he was still hesitating between the classical essay form and the *récit* (to his mother). The present edition of *Contre Sainte-Beuve* is a composite of various drafts, utilizing both methods. The *récit* wins out over the more objective approach, as might be expected. But Proust undoubtedly realized the awkwardness of this technique for a canvas as vastly conceived as *A la recherche*. For his purposes, the *récit* was a step away from the subjective impressionism of *Jean Santeuil* and pointed in the right direction. Where, however, would this right direction lead him? That is the principal technical problem arising out of the *Contre Sainte-Beuve*. The first person, the "je," of the *récit* portions of that work has simply been delegated to convey Proust's ideas and feelings, but its existence is still parasitical: it draws its sustenance too noticeably from Proust himself. Accordingly, *Contre Sainte-Beuve* lacks the focus which the device of the Narrator, the "Double I," provides for *A la recherche*. This must have become increasingly evident to Proust while he was writing the Balzac-Guermantes portions of *Contre Sainte-Beuve* and probably accounts for the fact that the work was abandoned in 1910 — but only to be begun all over again, with a somewhat different perspective.

The discovery of the over-all framework of the novel to be written and the necessity of reassessing the method of procedure to fit the new conception are sufficient reason for explaining the fact that *Contre Sainte-Beuve* remained a fragment. *Jean Santeuil* had been abandoned because Proust simply did not see how he could give shape to all the dispersed material; in the case of *Contre Sainte-Beuve* the situation is reversed, because Proust sometime in 1910 did discover what he must do, and he immediately began doing it. Professor Vigneron's valuable groundwork on the genesis of *Swann* has thus been amplified and, to some extent, superseded. From the preface of *Contre Sainte-Beuve* it becomes apparent that Proust had had experiences of the affective memory before 1910 and did not have to await this new illumination (as Vigneron speculates) in order to shape his work. The catalysts are intellectual rather than affective: Sainte-Beuve plus Balzac give Proust the orientation he needed. This does not eliminate the possibility of a renewal of the involuntary memory in 1910, which — if it occurred — must have served primarily to confirm Proust's newly found vocation. But it is not really necessary to postulate such an event: Proust may have discovered the affective memory early in his life; if not, he had always been in a state of readiness, since from his early manhood he had been given to prolonged periods of concentrated contemplation, without which the affective memory is meaningless, if not impossible. In any case, by 1908–1910 the involuntary memory was a fact for him and recognized as crucial in his personal and artistic development.

By 1919 Proust had gained fame as a literary artist and had won the Prix Goncourt with his *A l'ombre des jeunes filles en fleurs*. In spite of the fact that he was feverishly working against time on his novel, he contributed two critical articles to reviews, his most mature achievements in criticism: "A propos du 'style' de Flaubert" and "A propos de Baudelaire," both republished in

Chroniques. To these two articles should be added the prefaces to Jacques-Emile Blanche's first volume of *Propos de peintre: de David à Degas*[11] and to Paul Morand's *Tendres Stocks*. The former contains a number of reflections on Sainte-Beuve; it is, however, less important than the latter, which provides a mature statement of Proust's notions about literary style. In addition to these more ambitious essays there are short contributions to a number of "enquêtes" on literary and other themes held by various newspapers. The inclusion in the *Contre Sainte-Beuve* volume of a number of short essays and sketches under the title "Nouveaux Mélanges" adds to our knowledge of Proust the critic. These pieces appear to have been written before and after the Sainte-Beuve work and attest a steady and continuing interest on Proust's part in the value and discipline of criticism.

Of considerable interest but not of equal importance from the standpoint of criticism are the literary judgments sprinkled throughout *A la recherche du temps perdu*. Since Proust the novelist is constantly aware of the fact that he is writing fiction, not literary criticism, he knows how to subordinate literary criticism to character portrayal; he uses literary references frequently to "deepen" his characters. Moreover, the Marcel of the novel is often delegated by Proust to express literary opinions and criticisms. Beginning with the Narrator as a child reading at Combray, until his final literary creed of *Le Temps retrouvé*, Proust offers proof after proof of the integral part books play in the life of the Narrator. Literature may be said to be omnipresent in the novel — whether in the form of books read by the Narrator or by the other characters; or in the form of conversation; or through re-creation, either directly, as in the case of *Phèdre* played by Berma, or more subtly, when Proust records life as imitating art, when portraits and scenes from Sainte-Simon, Madame de Sévigné, or Balzac are transposed into characters and events of *A la recherche du temps perdu*. The literary pastiche too has its place in this scheme; the first volume of *Le Temps retrouvé* contains a pseudo-fragment of the Goncourt Journal; and Proust's flair for mimetic speech gives us a number of *pastiches vivants* — Norpois, Legrandin, Françoise, Bloch, Brichot, to name but a few.

The preceding discussion, to a certain extent, sets the stage for the pages to follow. From Proust, the lover of books, the man of taste, we intend to proceed to Proust the writer of pastiches and the critic of great sensibility and intelligence; finally, all these elements will be shown to converge upon Proust's ideas on literary style; for Proust's quest for lost time is closely bound up with a quest for an aesthetic creed, since the re-creation of the experience of time recaptured requires a style that can render this experience in literary form. The following pattern emerges: Proust the lover of books, Proust the maker of pastiches, and Proust the critic are but preparatory and necessary stages to an author who, surveying his work at the close of his life, can find in it the recovery of lost time as well as the embodiment of an aesthetic ideal.

Within the web of Proust's childhood recollections the experience of reading occupies a central place. In recapturing the past, he was also recapturing the magic of books, the magic thrill of daydreaming with a book. The Narrator of *A la recherche du temps perdu* conveys to us the sweetness of afternoons spent with a book in the garden at Combray, punctuated only by the striking of the village clock, which appears irregular to the boy whom absorption in his book makes oblivious to his surroundings; and, characteristically, the absorption is likened to sleep, that contact with a profounder reality — in a certain sense, the experience into which the foundation stones of the entire work are sunk.

All these impressions are built into the general framework of the Narrator's recaptured childhood at Combray, and given a sentimental dimension by the memory of his mother's reading of the works of George Sand to young Marcel; later, his discovery of the works of Bergotte marks a certain point of maturity in his development and points toward the sharpening of his critical faculties. In the preface to his translation of Ruskin's *Sesame and Lilies,* Proust has more elaborately dealt with the importance and value of reading. Since the preface was written prior to 1905, it may be regarded, as Georges de Lauris suggests, as "a delicate prelude to his own masterpiece." [12] In it one finds Proust the avid reader and still groping writer assessing his indebtedness to books.

"No days, perhaps, of all our childhood," he begins, "are ever so fully lived as those that we had regarded as not being lived at all: days spent wholly with a favorite book." The sweetness of the experience is proportional to the amount of love that has been showered upon the book; and the memory becomes "much more precious, so we have come to think, than what we then were reading with such passion," so that such a book revisited becomes like a calendar kept with the hope of finding in it the reflection of "the houses and the ponds that are no more." [13]

In the same essay Proust comes to grips with Ruskin's ideas, as expressed in *Sesame and Lilies*, about the significance of reading. Ruskin's essential idea, as Proust points out, is the same as Descartes' — "The reading of all good books is like talking with those noble men of past centuries who were their authors" [14] — it is communication with a society of another sort,

> . . . a society continually open to us, of people who will talk to us as long as we like, whatever our rank or occupation; — talk to us in the best words they can choose, and with thanks if we listen to them. And this society, because it is so numerous and so gentle, — and can be kept waiting round us all day long, not to grant audience, but to gain it — kings and statesmen lingering patiently! — in those plainly furnished and narrow ante-rooms, our book-case shelves . . .[15]

Proust comments that the idea appears beautiful to him, since it is useful to Ruskin's notion of books as friends, but has only a symbolic significance. For it might conceivably be possible, he continues, that one can choose the friends one would like to have, and still these friendships would not replace the "friendship" of books. The weakness in Ruskin's ideas lies in his failure to distinguish the different kinds of communication which the two friendships imply. The result is that "a conversation with Plato would still be a conversation, that is to say, an infinitely more superficial activity [*exercice*] than reading."[16] In other words, Ruskin understands inadequately "the psychological activity which goes by the name of 'reading.'"[17] Proust knows that between conversation and reading there is a psychological difference:

> Our way of communicating with others implies a loss of the active forces of the soul that are, by contrast, concentrated and exalted by this marvelous miracle, reading, which is communication in the bosom of solitude. When a person reads, he receives someone else's thought, and yet he is alone; he is in the throes of thinking, of aspiration, of personal participation: he receives another man's ideas truly — that is to say, in his mind — he can make them part of himself, he becomes the other person, and still he is but developing his own self with greater variety than if he were thinking by himself; and he is thrust in his own direction by someone else.[18]

It is this particular conception of the function of books which lies behind all Proust's critical judgments. Whether Proust allowed Racine, or Saint-Simon, or Balzac, or Ruskin to communicate with him "in the bosom of solitude," the result was always the same: genuine receptivity gave rise to a kind of expansion of Proust's self ("épouser un auteur," as the French express it so well) and modified it. And it is this attitude of receptivity and contemplation that is equally relevant to Proust's mature aesthetics in *Le Temps retrouvé*.

Conversation, then, has its limitations as spiritual communication. Conversation depends on the medium of sounds and thereby constitutes a less effective spiritual catalyst:

> . . . the spiritual impact has been diminished; inspiration and profound thought have become impossible. Moreover, thought, becoming spoken thought, is falsified, as is proven by the literary inferiority of those who enjoy conversation and excel in it too much . . . One might say that in general conversation opens the way to brilliant

expressions or pure arguments, but practically never to a profound impression.[19]

This same idea had already been enunciated by Proust in *Jean Santeuil* and appears to have fascinated him for a considerable length of time. He is trying to find out why the best conversationalists (and, by extension, the best letter writers) are not necessarily the best, or the profoundest, writers. The answer he gives here may be used to answer those who deplore the quality of Proust's own correspondence. Proust simply made a distinction between the process of expressing an idea and expressing an impression: conversation is a craft only; writing is an art.

Proust concludes that Ruskin's idea about reading is conceived like "a sort of beautiful Platonic myth, with that same simplicity with which the Greeks have demonstrated almost all the great truths, leaving to modern scruples the task of investigating them."[20] A practical test of this notion is described in *Jean Santeuil* when Jean and his professor, Beulier, read jointly Michelet's *Bible de l'humanité* and then Xenophon's *Memorabilia.* Jean cannot conceal his disappointment in the seeming naïveté of Xenophon. But Beulier corrects him:

> "No . . . it is not a question of the other being better; they are two different things. Hang it all, there is room for all sorts, isn't there? Antiquity is not the nineteenth century. But this stuff of Xenophon's is, in its way, just as good. No one will ever write like that again. It is all so simple yet everything is said. That was a time when writers were not concerned to develop their ideas. They offered them for what they were worth without labouring them, without extracting from them all that they contained. The soft down upon them was preserved and the freshness."[21]

Proust is in agreement with Ruskin's belief that reading plays a preponderant part in our spiritual life. As a matter of fact, these limitations actually grow out of the virtues of reading; "and, if we ask what, precisely, those virtues are, I find the answer to lie in the kind of reading that we enjoy in childhood."

He picks up a copy of Théophile Gautier's *Le Capitaine Fracasse*, read twenty years earlier.

Two or three passages in it I loved with an especial fervor, thinking them the most original, the loveliest, in the whole volume. It was impossible for me to believe that any other author had written anything comparable. But I had the feeling that their beauty corresponded to a reality of which Théophile Gautier gave me but a few fleeting glimpses. And, since I was convinced that he *must* know the whole of it, I longed to read others of his books, books containing passages no less beautiful, and designed to give me information on all the subjects on which I wanted to have his views.[22]

In this way the work of art may hint at an author's vision and suggests to the reader that he should share it with him. In Gautier's case, Proust's reaction is similar to that of the adolescent reader, such as Jean Santeuil, to whom Gautier for the first time opens up "the permanent possibility of the loveliest phrases which the human being may be allowed to hear" — expressions such as "as Homerus said" or "Olympianly," which ring in the adolescent's imagination, for he is "closer to Gautier than we are and can better glimpse than we a beauty which no longer touches us." [23] And so the youth feels that the author who has given him a glimpse of a new reality is capable of other revelations:

For a writer whom we adore becomes for us a species of oracle whom we long to consult on a multiplicity of matters so that whenever he takes the stage and gives us his opinion, expresses some general idea, speaks of Homer or of the Gods we know, we are enchanted and listen open-mouthed to the casually dropped maxim, disappointed only that it takes so short a time to utter.[24]

But the "oracle" is often silent, and the reader likely to be disappointed, and in this disillusionment lies the difference between reading an author and conversing with him. The questions that one yearns to have the author answer are often not even touched upon, and in the long run the answer must be striven for by the reader himself.

> Indeed, the great, the marvellous power possessed by good books (which makes us realise the part, at once essential yet limited, that reading can play in our mental lives) lies in this, that what the author may treat as 'Conclusions' can, for the reader, be 'Incitements'. We have a strong feeling that our own wisdom begins just where that of the author finishes, and we want him to give us answers when all that he can offer are desires. And these desires books can awake in us only by compelling us to contemplate the final beauty to which they provide a gate, by squeezing the last drop from the art of which they are the embodiment.[25]

This singular author-reader relationship, governed by what Proust calls "a curious but providential law of our mental vision (a law, perhaps, which means that we can never receive the truth from anybody, but must always be creating it for ourselves)," [26] rests on the paradox that when the author has said all he is able to say the reader feels that he has not yet said anything. In view of all this, the author's relation to the reader is not a didactic one, but rather one of stimulation, or inspiration, even one of evoking nostalgia. This is, as might be expected, considerably at variance with Ruskin's ideas, although it can be said that the two men are actually not so far apart as they seem but rather tend to move along slightly different levels. (As a matter of fact, Proust admits somewhat later in his notes to *Sésame et les lys*, "I feel that I have contradicted him less than I thought.") [27] Ruskin is constantly aware of the moral benefit to be derived from books; for Proust, books are so essentially a factor of the spiritual life that their moral value pales before the more profound emotional and aesthetic effect which they have on receptive souls. Ruskin, on the other hand, exhorts us to listen to authors as teachers.

There is also a difference of orientation: for Proust, the author elicits love from the reader, for Ruskin, the reader offers it to the author. Proust characterizes reading as a "pure, unruffled friendship." [28] Each *good* book reflects it in its own way, in the way it mirrors the thought of its author at every point. And thus even an old childhood friend like Gautier — "a simple, decent fellow with plenty of taste (it is amusing to think that he was once regarded as a representative of perfection in art)" [29] — remains a good companion, in spite of all his lack of true artistry.

When Ruskin closes his book, the lesson is ended for him; in Proust's case, merely the overture has been completed. He will now begin to ask questions, to express desires, because works of art, he realizes, arise out of simple chance encounters between artist and subject matter, a kind of confrontation with an objective correlative: "For one of the effects of the love which the poets wake in us, is that it makes us attach a literal significance to matters which, for them, are expressive only of emotions personal to themselves." [30] The significant phenomenon, that which lifts the subject into the realm of art, is the impress of genius which the artist has left upon it. "What makes them seem to us more beautiful than the rest of the world is that they give, like some vague reflection, the effect that they produced on genius. It would appear to us just as remarkable, just as despotic, no matter what insignificant and submissive corner of the world they might have happened to paint." [31] In this sentence we have a definition of style — the "reflet insaisissable" of the spiritual activity of genius — and this definition of style will be variously formulated in other places. Moreover, Proust's concern with books quite naturally implies an equally lively concern with painting; as *A la recherche du temps perdu* shows, for Proust the arts are interrelated and inseparable from life. The characteristic of the genius is to transmute experience into art by vision. "The supreme effort of the writer, as of the graphic artist, can do no more than lift for us a corner of the veil of ugliness and insignificance which leaves us incurious before the spectacle of the universe." Although this sounds like a decadent view of art, it does not actually eliminate the universe or life itself; it is merely the prelude to a transformation in which art becomes a way of piercing the drabness of the universe, a way of getting at its secret. "[Reading] stands upon the threshold of the life of that spirit: it can show us the way in, but it is not, in itself, that life."[32] The artist's vision disperses the mist, and the spiritual life, stimulated by reading, provides the energy.

Books may yet serve other purposes — they can serve as a kind of therapeutic discipline to "pathological cases" — to batter lazy minds into activity. In a highly revealing passage Proust describes these pathological types:

> We know that there are diseases of the nervous system, as a result of which the patient, though he may have nothing organically wrong with him, becomes bogged in a sort of paralysis of the will, as in some deep rut, from which he cannot extricate himself unaided, and in which he will, at long last, perish utterly unless a strong and helping hand is stretched to him. His brain, his limbs, his lungs, his stomach, all are intact. There is no *physical* reason why he should not work, walk, endure cold, and eat as usual. But though he is perfectly capable of performing these actions, he lacks the will to do so . . . Now, there are minds of a certain type that it is possible to compare with cases of this kind, minds which a species of laziness or frivolity prevents from striking spontaneously into their own deepest regions where the real life of the spirit has its origins.[33]

Among these spirits Proust mentions Fontanes and Coleridge; he might have added that he himself was in danger of sliding into the same "deep rut," if he had not succeeded in mastering himself. There is no doubt that in his victory over indolence books exercised this same therapeutic value (in addition to the more important "spiritual" value) on him, and that Ruskin occupies a prominent place among the works "administered."

Books, then, may become interventions, setting into motion the creative activity of a mind incapable of generating this activity by itself. He points out that most minds are prone to this kind of sloth to a greater or lesser degree and that books have often served as a kind of exaltation to writers. Thus Emerson used to read a few pages of Plato before he took up the pen, "nor is Dante the only poet whom Virgil piloted to the gates of Paradise."[34]

However, reading may become dangerous, namely, when it tends to become a substitute for genuine intellectual activity, "when truth appears to us, not as an ideal which we can realize only as a result of our own thinking and our own emotional efforts, but as a material *object* which exists between the pages of a book, like honey made by others . . ." [35] But the dangers of this approach to reading, which might be called the oracular fallacy, since it expects answers from books, as though the truth could be copied into a notebook,[36] is not the worst of all. The man of letters who has come to look upon books as immobile idols — as fetishes — is more deceived than the man who thinks that truth is to be found within the covers of a book. The true substance of books remains forever out of his reach. However, Proust adds, we are all infected with this kind of fetishism, especially writers themselves — a statement which is probably more applicable to Proust himself than to most other writers. "After all, is it not for men of this kind that books are written; and do they not owe to them the discovery of a host of beauties, which remain hidden from the eyes of the vulgar?" This kind of erudition often serves to fan genius, not to extinguish it ("as a bundle of twigs will put out a small fire, but feed a big one"). Examples of writers who were "fanned on" by their erudition are Hugo, Maeterlinck, and especially Schopenhauer. ("Schopenhauer, for instance, provides an example of a temperament so vital that it can support without difficulty the burden of a vast amount of reading, because for him each new piece of information was immediately reduced to the dimensions of the fragment of living reality which it contained.") [37]

To sum up, Proust draws up what amounts to a hierarchy of readers' attitudes toward books — the inspirational, the therapeutic, the oracular, and the fetishistic. This method enables him to voice preferences without being dogmatic. He is far too honest about himself to deny the palliative influence of books on his own neurosis and their importance in helping him to overcome the paralysis of his will. (Here the inspirational aspect of reading triumphs over the therapeutic.) That the oracular approach, which makes reading a kind of sleuthing activity in which truth is tracked down and incarcerated in a file box, has its seductions, Proust does not deny. He admits that there is a certain kind of satisfaction in the pursuit and seizure of an elusive fact — the contentment that comes from the successful accomplishment of a clearly stated mission. But the truth is not so easily accessible as all this, and certainly not hidden within the pages of a book. This opinion is also consistent with his notion of the inadequate critic, the one who erects edifices around an author, without ever getting at him from within. Finally, Proust's indulgence toward the fetishists is all too understandable and reflects first of all a devotion to things beautiful and things loved. Besides, as may be seen from his discussion, the "immobile idol" — dry erudition — quickly becomes "mobile" when lively spirits begin to use it. The more intelligent the reader, the less susceptible he is to the dangers of reading (that is, substitution of reading for independent intellectual activity, book-fetishism). "An original mind can subordinate its reading to its own personal activity." Nevertheless, this process is absolutely necessary, for the mind can be cultivated only through contact with other minds. "When all is said, men of letters are the 'people of quality' in the world of the intelligence, and ignorance of this or that book, of this or that detail of literary knowledge, will always be, even in a man of genius, a mark of the intellectual plebeian."[38] At the highest level, as in the case of Schopenhauer, this idolatry becomes the handmaiden of creation, serving as an "incitation" to spiritual activity.

Proust's high regard for the function of the critic is attested in the preface to his translation of Ruskin's *Bible of Amiens*, in which he sees the critic playing the part of an "optician," not unlike the novelist. The passage deserves to be quoted in full; it is of prime significance for the present inquiry, and will be referred to frequently, particularly in our Conclusion.

> Fundamentally, some such attempt to help the reader to feel the impact of an artist's unique characteristics, to put before him those traits whose similarity with what he is reading at the moment may enable him to realise the essential part they play in the genius of a

particular writer, should be the first part of every critic's task. If *he* has felt these things, and has helped others to feel them, he has come near to fulfilling his function. And if he has not, then he may write as many books as he will about *Ruskin: The Man, The Prophet, The Artist,* about the *Extent of his Influence and the Errors of His Teaching,* yet, no matter how majestically he may raise these vast constructions, he will merely have skirted his subject. They may win for him a great reputation, but as aids to the understanding of his author's work, the subtle appreciation of its shades, they will be valueless.

In my view, however, the critic should go further still. He should try to reconstruct the peculiar life of the spirit which belongs to every writer who is obsessed by his own special view of reality, whose inspiration can be measured by the degree to which he has attained to the vision of that reality, whose talent can be estimated by the extent to which he can re-create it in his work, whose morality can be interpreted as the instinct, which, by compelling him to see life under the aspect of Eternity (no matter how peculiar to himself that life may seem, to us, to be), forces him to sacrifice to the urgency of visualising it, and the necessity of reproducing it, and, thereby, assuring a vision of it that shall be durable and lucid, [every pleasure,] every duty, and even existence itself, because existence for him has no justification save as being the sole possible medium through which he can make contact with reality, no value other than that which an essential instrument may have for a doctor engaged on an experiment.[39]

The twofold function of the critic, first of all, aims at a definition of the writer's uniqueness and originality; and all the biographical and historical and psychological explanations are merely peripheral. Here Proust is giving the first evidence of his criticism of Sainte-Beuve. And secondly, the great critic, in Proust's opinion, looks even more deeply into the writer's creative personality, discerning the writer's special vision and his method of re-creating this vision in terms of literature. Just as the novelist is not merely a technician but above all a "seer" presenting his particular vision to the reader, so the critic's task too is to help the reader to see. Proust consistently uses optical imagery to emphasize this point: in one case the novelist is an optician, in another, the style is a "reflet insaisissable"; here the critic's duty is to define the "vision durable et claire." In another instance, Proust, using another sort of metaphor of visual analysis, claims the relevance of his approach so long as one basic assumption is granted him, namely

> . . . if the words of a book are not entirely mute, if I am right in thinking that they are similar to spectrum analysis in the way they furnish us information about the internal composition of other human beings, who are like so many distant worlds . . .[40]

In his best critical essays — and this includes his pastiches — he fulfills this dual aim of the critic. In many other pieces of criticism he at least reveals the "artist's unique characteristics," with exciting results.

Proust's practice of literary criticism may be divided into three categories, all of them serving the growing or matured author in one way or another. For it must never be forgotten that Proust's criticism derives from a deeply felt response to an author or a text and cannot be treated as methodical in any sense. The Sainte-Beuve novel-essay is an excellent case in point. The two principal methods Proust employed were the critical essay — the direct, analytical method, which may also be called "the approach from without" — and the pastiche, an indirect, synthetic form of criticism, but a more subtle one, enabling the critic to work from within. The interests voiced in the critical essays are to some extent reflected in the pastiches. Here again the author's preoccupation with styles is made manifest: pastiches of Balzac, Flaubert, Sainte-Beuve; and the masterful pastiche of Saint-Simon, the most ambitious of them all. Finally, there are the pastiches that served a more or less "cathartic" function, beside the fact that they gave Proust pleasure and a kind of constructive respite from his quest for a mold into which to pour his novel — the pastiches of the Goncourts (plus the Goncourt pastiche in *Le Temps retrouvé*), of Renan, Henri de Régnier, Michelet, and Faguet.

It is not too much to say that Proust made the pastiche into a highly sophisticated literary genre. There is, of course, in the French language a tradition of pastiches of literary works, from Homer on to the present as Léon Deffoux' anthology of the pastiche [41] clearly shows; but the pastiche ordinarily resembles the burlesque more than it does serious literary criticism; by reducing an author's stylistic idiosyncrasies to an absurdity, the pastiche-writer achieves an effect similar to that of clowning. A better name for this kind of pastiche would be "parody," and its major purpose is to amuse (for example: the delightful pastiches of Reboux and Muller, *A la manière de . . .*). However, no matter how skillful, such burlesques remain more or less on the outside of the author caricatured. Proust, combining an astounding literary virtuosity with a genuine capacity for "empathy" not only recreates the essential features of an author's style but also preserves the humor of the pastiche in treating it like a brilliantly conceived exercise in imitation. "He is a sophisticated man of letters," wrote Léon Daudet. "He has gone back to the roots of the authors of the seventeenth and nineteenth centuries. He writes in the style of Michelet as Michelet did himself and can furnish you with all the Bossuet you want." [42]

This amazing proclivity for imitation showed itself in all sorts of ways in the man as well as the artist. There is ample testimony to the fact that in his days as a *mondain* he delighted the salons with his imitations, which were in some cases so "real" (". . . verbal pastiches which produced every now and then something like an auditory hallucination . . .") [43] and at the same time so amusing that he seriously offended certain "victims" (notably the oversensitive Montesquiou). "In Proust, imitation is one of the most startling manifestations of his faculty to don another person's — a *real* person's — personality." [44] The literary equivalent of this imitation is the pastiche, made possible by Proust's prodigious mastery of the literary craft in his younger years, plus his phenomenal memory. His very first work provides ample proof of his craftsmanship; it imitates the models rather than makes pastiches: there are echoes of the seventeenth-century moralists and of the symbolists in *Les Plaisirs et les jours.* In *Jean Santeuil* it is possible to discern stylistic resemblances to the symbolists and Anatole France. Then, in the stylistic-critical exercises of the Pastiches, it is as though Proust were trying to shake off some of the too-dominant stylistic influences ("the greater the affinity, the stronger the temptation," observes Jean Mouton) [45] via the pastiche in order to have *champ libre.* "The pastiches are a summing-up by a lucid and solid memory, without flaws or gaps, of all the infinitesimal elements which make up a writer's individuality." [46]

The exercise of synthesizing a writer's style by producing a literary pastiche of him underlined Proust's mimetic gifts in literature and liberated Proust's originality, so that the pastiches may be considered a kind of aesthetic purgatory through which Proust was obliged to pass. "Proust," observes Georges Cattaui, "feigning to write pastiches of others and highlighting their talents as well as their eccentricities, remained profoundly himself, constantly original (and often superior to his models) . . ." [47] But with the purification by pastiche the tendency to imitate was not abandoned, but channeled. It entered into the world of *A la recherche du temps perdu* inasmuch as it became Proust's favorite method of character presentation; as Fernand Gregh observes, "his entire work is an immense repertory of 'imitations,' from Françoise's kitchen gossip to the diplomatic monologue of M. de Norpois." [48] Spitzer observes the same mechanism: "Proust takes pleasure in making his characters speak, in what one might call a phonographic representation of their speech" [49] and summarizes: "One might say that for Proust the art of characterization consists in quoting, in reproducing the 'total speech,' in creating pastiches." [50]

Proust was, of course, aware of the depth which he was giving to the pastiche by making it an instrument of criticism. Thus he wrote to Paul Souday concerning Sainte-Beuve, ". . . you will find, in addition, in my *Pastiches* another expression of what I think of him; not more analytical, it is true, but more exact, I think."[51] And to Georges de Lauris he wrote that the pleasure one might find in these Pastiches

> . . . is due to qualities (though I shouldn't say it) of my character rather than of my intelligence. One of these 'qualities' is that in not seeking to 'shine', I liberally pack into these parodies things for which a better steward of his goods would prefer to sign himself and claim the honour. I am not afraid of putting fairly good things into the mouths of Sainte-Beuve and Régnier (these two are, I think, the least bad). Another quality of mine is that, since I never even unconsciously take other men's goods, I never make more or less involuntary parodies in my works. This gives me more abundance and light-heartedness when I make them openly.[52]

The third method which Proust uses makes literary criticism a facet in character analysis. It is a device frequently used in *A la recherche du temps perdu* whereby a criticism of a certain author is produced in terms of a character of the novel, and conversely, where a character may be criticized in terms of his response to literature. This method is exceedingly complicated and makes no claim to thoroughness, serving frequently to broaden the study of a certain character (rather than to offer highly refined literary analysis) — a practice differing widely from that used in a number of modern novels in which characters tend to become embodiments of ideas and conversations tend to become forensic exercises on some given subject (the novels of Huxley, Sartre, and Koestler, for instance). Proust knew that the appreciation of certain books by a fictitious person may illustrate a certain aspect of this person's character as well as certain actions or gestures would. He accordingly makes use of this method in order to view certain authors from another point of view, so to speak, or to criticize an author by criticizing a character of his novel. This procedure produces such interesting results as the Duc de Guermantes' fondness for Balzac, Charlus' esoteric appreciation of Lucien de Rubempré, Gilberte's opinions concerning *La Fille aux yeux d'or*, Madame de Villeparisis' attitude toward Vigny, and Monsieur de Norpois' condemnation of Bergotte. In most cases, however, such criticisms must be amplified by the opinions of the Narrator. The method had already been used with considerable skill in *Jean Santeuil*. In *A la recherche*, Marcel modifies and corrects the fragmentary canvas of literary judgments left by the other characters. Here the reader is always in the presence of Proust's own literary opinions at a certain stage of his development, as can be shown, wherever possible, by reference to Proust's correspondence and to his critical writings. This unorthodoxy led an English critic to remark: "Actually his books are filled from end to end with criticisms of music, of painting, of literature, not in the way that is unfortunately familiar in this country, as unassimilated chunks in the main stream of the narrative, but as expressions of the opinions of different characters."[53] Since this assimilation is usually so successful, it is often dangerous to draw rash conclusions with regard to Proust's own critical opinions. A knowledge of the entire *A la recherche du temps perdu* is necessary, and the relationship or comments of the Narrator to the character in question must be kept in mind. Thus, for example, Monsieur de Norpois' designation of Bergotte as a "joueur de flûte" must be checked against the Narrator's subsequent rejection of Norpois' opinion and his later idealization of Bergotte. Similarly, Jean Santeuil's admiration of *Le Capitaine Fracasse* and Marcel's admiration of George Sand can be shown to be infatuations of the child or the adolescent, having their particular value at the time, and fondly remembered but long outgrown by the mature Proust. Generally speaking, Proust and Marcel coincide on intellectual matters, though not on biographical ones; a congruence between the Narrator and Proust does not occur until the latter portions of *A la recherche* are reached. In other words, Marcel has been delegated to help Proust conquer Time: he serves as an intermediary between the author and his subject matter.

II

PROUST AND THE SEVENTEENTH CENTURY

> . . . le XVIIe siècle français
> avait une manière très simple
> de dire les choses profondes.
> PROUST, *Chroniques.*

In his essay on the pleasures of reading, Proust remarks that it is characteristic of the great writers to prefer the books of the ancients, for the specific reason that not only the language of the classics but also their very subject matter is like a mirror of life.

> And this is why we ought always to read the classic authors in full, and not rest content with selected passages. An author's famous passages are often those in which the intimate texture of language is hidden beneath the beauty, beneath the universal quality, if I may so put it, which marks the whole.[1]

Racine and Saint-Simon are singled out as specific examples:

> A Racine tragedy, a volume of Saint-Simon's Memoirs are like lovely things that are no longer being made. For they contain all the lovely forms of a vanished manner of speech, such as preserve the memory of customs or of fashions in feeling that exist no longer, persistent traces of a past which nothing now resembles, but whose color the obliterating passage of time can still revive.[2]

Proust's concept of classicism is not a historical one; for him, the word "classicism" simply denotes greatness of style — no matter what that style may be. In brief, classical art is eternal art: "I believe that all true art is classic, but the dictates of the mind rarely permit of its being recognized as such when it first appears. From this point of view, art is like life." [3] Classicism is a continuing tradition, an endless metamorphosis; on first sight it appears new and startling; on longer acquaintance it reveals itself as a recurrence. Unfortunately, this view tends to create semantic confusion because it destroys conventional labels that have by now entered our vocabulary and serve an important though limited function in the history of art and criticism. Proust never concerned himself with literary schools as such and was interested only in the works of genuine merit that emerged from them. If all great art is "classical," then the two expressions "great art" and "classical" are synonymous and no longer involve a real distinction, so that it becomes necessary to designate works of literature in terms of the century in which they originated rather than in terms of the aesthetic assumptions that their authors may have consciously or unconsciously adopted. Consequently, Racine and Baudelaire are both classical: the two poets give Proust the same kind of pleasure.

> [The] great innovators are the only real classics and present an almost continuous succession. The imitators of the classics, in their finest moments, provide us only with the pleasures of erudition and of taste which have no great value. That the innovators, worthy of one day becoming classics, submit themselves to a severe inner discipline and are, above all else, builders, cannot be doubted. But just because their architecture is novel, it may remain undetected for a long time. These not-yet-recognized classics and the old classics practice the same art to such an extent that the former are still the ones who have written the best criticism of the latter.[4]

This quotation highlights two notions dear to Proust — notions which, incidentally, Proust must have considered applicable to himself by 1921 — that the classic author is always an innovator, never an imitator, and that for this reason the innovator, having a much more immediate grasp of the secret behind artistic creation, is better equipped to be a critic of the classic author. The "modern classic" author enters the community of classic writers because he perceives the fundamental unity of the art of all times. Imitation may produce entertaining or erudite results, but never creation. Consequently the author who admires the writers of a previous age, acting more or less as a critic, learns the secret of the classics, and ends by recreating the same *art* — that is to say, an imitation or a pastiche — never the same *style*. This is the meaning of the advice which Proust gave to Martin-Chauffier:

> Be careful to avoid the pitfall of excessively long sentences . . . if they are abstract. Avoid the seventeenth-century formula, preserve only the reality of that admirable epoch, its basic vitality, of deeply felt impressions, which the apparent solemnity of its style must never conceal from us. [5]

The "reality" of the seventeenth century, as of any century, is the authenticity which its writers have managed to extract from life through "deeply felt impressions," refined by the writers' intelligence. The actual manner of rendering such impressions is a problem that each great writer has to solve for himself by bending the language to his own uses:

> And when one wants to defend the French language, one actually writes quite the opposite of classical French. For example: the revolutionaries, Rousseau, Hugo, Flaubert, Maeterlinck "hold their own" beside Bossuet.[6]

Since Proust's literary criticism is confined exclusively to the seventeenth and nineteenth centuries (up to Proust's own day), one may legitimately ask why Proust omitted the other periods in French literature. The question is a puzzling one, inasmuch as one might expect Proust to have some remarks to make about Montaigne and Rousseau, for instance. As a matter of fact, no French literature before the seventeenth century receives critical attention from Proust. We do have proof, nevertheless, of Proust's love for the Middle Ages, especially his love for the

Gothic cathedrals, amply shown in the early portions of *A la recherche*. His conception of *A la recherche* as a literary cathedral is not only a tribute to the magnificence of medieval architecture, but also a recognition that his own artistic pursuits had been a striving toward a unified vision similar to that of the thirteenth and fourteenth centuries.

It may be surmised, therefore, that Proust thought in terms of three great cultural epochs for France: the Middle Ages, about whose literature he nevertheless remains silent, the seventeenth century and its *vérité*, and the nineteenth, with its attempt to make art a vehicle for presenting comprehensive views of life. According to this hypothesis, the sixteenth and the eighteenth centuries would be regarded as transitional periods. Indeed, Proust all but slurs over the eighteenth century. Montesquieu is praised (as he is by Flaubert) for certain unexpected turns of phrase — which is to say that he happens to have in common with Proust's other favorite writers a certain boldness of style. There is no critical commentary on Diderot or Rousseau, who might be expected to figure on the list of Proust's favorites. As early as 1889, his mother wrote to him, "I am not going to say anything about what I am reading, my dear, because I am deep in Madame du Deffand, and I know that you have a poor opinion of the eighteenth century."[7] Similarly, in a letter to Madame Straus in 1908 he brushes aside the "neoclassicists": "The neoclassicists of the eighteenth and early nineteenth century, and the 'smiling candor' and the 'discreet emotion' of all epochs clash with the masters."[8] These remarks may be set alongside the portrait of Monsieur de Traves, a successful writer, in *Jean Santeuil*. Monsieur de Traves combines a lively interest in literary history and a considerable knowledge of the history of the language with a certain literary talent.

> In literature he had a fondness only for the works of the eighteenth century which Jean held to be utterly worthless, because unlike those of the nineteenth, they were not concerned to probe the mysterious truths which alone for him could provide the key to absolute truth.[9]

To sum up, Proust's attitude toward the eighteenth century appears to be governed by the feeling that it stands between a period which excelled in the revelation of "simple" truths and one which revealed, or attempted to reveal, "complex" truths. Generally speaking, this would not necessarily prevent the century from being as great as any other, but Proust's few remarks suggest that the forms of the seventeenth century became academic in the eighteenth century — neoclassical — and genuine innovation, which represents the backbone of true classicism, was scarce. Undoubtedly, behind this opinion lies Proust's temperamental incompatibility with the Enlightenment.

Proust almost regularly uses the words "réalité" and "vérité" to characterize the literature of the seventeenth century, illustrating his meaning by references to Racine. In fact, the name of Racine recurs in Proust's work, his novel as well as his critical writings, like a Wagnerian leitmotiv.

A schoolboy composition on the subject of Racine and Corneille shows the adolescent Proust's precocious appreciation of Racine's art. The theme is in itself interesting inasmuch as it affords a glimpse into the early acuity of his critical talent. The essay topic was the following: "To be a passionate lover of Corneille one must be no enemy to a certain amount of bravura. To feel passionate love for Racine is to run the risk of having, to excess, what we in France call 'taste,' a quality that may at times be highly distasteful." [10] Proust opened the treatment of the subject by expressing a certain attitude toward literature — not an original attitude by any means, but one which gives us a valuable insight into Proust's early literary opinions.

> The creations of poetry and literature are never the outcome of pure thought. They are, in addition, the expression of a personality which differs with each artist, and takes on something of his individuality.

This personality, subjected to the exigencies of art, produces such masterpieces as *Le Cid* and *Andromaque*, as well as the feebler products of the authors' early or late life, such as *La*

Thébaïde or *Attila*, respectively, in which the tenderness of Racine shows itself as "préciosité galante" or the grandeur of Corneille has developed into extravagance. "The very quality which once gave charm, life, and *newness* to his work, shows, when unduly magnified, as the error of his genius, the cause of his decadence." But this, Proust added, is no reason for rejecting it, for the temperament of the author still remains the same, even though the artistic discipline has weakened. These weaknesses, after all, are only an exaggeration of something (a "natural bent") that was adumbrated by the author in his best work but kept strictly under control. So that Corneille, in spite of his exaggeration, always offers his readers and spectators a magnificent pageant of "Les Jeux de l'Amour et du Devoir." On the other hand, Racine does not offer a pageant; he offers an exquisite veil which hides a much more violent display:

. . . And if of Racine we may say that, even when his situations are most daring, he never fails by his superb use of language to keep the action within the "tight discipline of propriety," can we be blamed for thinking that he takes rather too much pleasure in doing so, that he shows rather too much ingenuity in the handling of his theme, that he sometimes identifies his art to excess with the *over*formal, the *over*subtle? If our contemporary critics insist so loudly on directing our attention to the harsh realism that lies behind the tragedies of Racine, are we entitled to object? Is not the fact that we have made this discovery so late in the day merely a proof of the loving care with which he smoothed and fused the form of his drama? To fail to say at once what he has to say, or rather, to say it with a refinement of manner which spreads a veil of elegance (of almost sensual delight) over the underlying horror, to turn his back on a more direct method, knowing nothing of complicated half-tones—all this may not be habitual with Racine (unless we wish to regard it as his habitual defect), but the fact remains that, in other writers, it is the source of a peculiar grace which we have grown accustomed to describe, not wholly without justification, as being "Racinian."

This statement probably contains Proust's earliest pronouncement on the subject of literary style; and beyond Proust's observations on Racine's art, it is of interest because it sets up Racine as a literary model even at this early stage. Besides, the words "smoothed and fused" (*fondu et adouci*) will recur throughout Proust's future observations on style and artistic excellence, whether this quality be discovered in music, architecture, painting, or literature. The particular achievement of Racine, he finds, is his ability to be grim and "ferociously realistic" at bottom while following the dramatic conventions on the surface. In Racine this was possible only because of his extraordinary refinement coupled with his wonderful mastery of the language which enabled him to register the turbulent underside of his polished surfaces. These elements are the principal ingredients in the process of amalgamation that becomes Racine's art, and they are for that reason the things that one ought to admire in Racine, even if in *La Thébaïde* they do not exist in the proper balance that brings *Phèdre*, *Britannicus*, and *Athalie* to incandescence. To love Racine, then, is to love the profundity and subtlety of this art.

> . . . to love Racine passionately means . . . to love the deepest, the tenderest, the most painful, and the most sincere of those intuitions which he brought to the understanding of so many charming and martyred existences, just as to love Corneille means to love, in the integrity of its beauty and in the unbending quality of its pride, the highest possible realization of an heroic ideal.

Proust is actually more concerned with defining his admiration of Corneille and Racine here, not so much with a definition of style in general. In attempting to define Racine's particular attributes, his recurrent traits, he is already giving evidence of his preoccupation with a writer's distinctive characteristics. The search for the "figure in the carpet," as will be shown more precisely in the case of certain nineteenth-century writers, is Proust's favorite method of critical analysis.

In his later years, Proust's interest in Corneille seems to have waned, whereas his love of Racine increased:

> It is the living syntax of seventeenth century France — and of

customs and manners of thought now dead — which we love to find in Racine's lines. It is the very form of that syntax, stripped of all covering, made honorable and lovely by his keen, yet ever sensitive, chisel, that moves us, familiar though we are with its every oddity, its every daring turn, and whose concentrated design we see pass like a swift dart of light, or hang fire in beautiful, broken rhythms, in the gentlest and most tender passages. It is these forms of language, wrested from the past, that are offered to our eyes as might be some ancient and unruined city.[11]

To explain the "brusque dessin" that animates Racine's verse, he quotes the well-known lines from *Andromaque*:

> Pourquoi l'assassiner? Qu'a-t-il fait? A quel titre?
> Qui te l'a dit?

whose charm, he asserts, comes from the fact that the usual syntactical bonds have been severed: "A quel titre?" and "Qui te l'a dit?" both go with "Pourquoi l'assassiner?" not with "Qu'a-t-il fait?" Moreover, the last sentence of the quotation is elliptical for "Qui te l'a dit, de l'assassiner?" This is what Proust means by "the recurrent broken line," "zigzags of expression . . . which have the effect of somewhat obscuring the sense." [12] At this juncture Proust quotes the line

> Je t'aimais inconstant, qu'aurais-je fait fidèle

from the same play. The elliptical "qu'aurais-je fait fidèle" produces a special kind of pleasure here, in spite of its syntactical incorrectness. (In a letter to Madame Straus in 1908, he states that all these lines from *Andromaque* would not be accepted in a literary magazine of that day.) [13] But in this particular boldness on the part of Racine lies his principal charm.

Racine's most famous lines have become celebrated because they can produce this sense of delight by reason of a familiar piece of linguistic daring which stands like a dangerous bridge between two gently-rounded banks . . . what pleasure we derive from encountering such expressions, the almost flat simplicity of which gives to the sense, as to certain faces in Mantegna's pictures, a sweet completeness, a marvelous touch of color!

> Et dans un fol amour ma jeunesse *embarquée* . . . [*Phèdre*]
> Réunissons trois coeurs qui n'ont pu s'*accorder*. [*Andromaque*] [14]

For Proust, Racine's syntactical boldness is perhaps his finest stylistic quality — in the same way that his revelation of a "réalité farouche" is his finest achievement as an observer of the human scene. The particular pleasure Proust finds in Racine is to submit to his grace, to be carried along by it, and to find himself suddenly suspended or arrested by a stylistic "dissonance," or an insight abruptly revealed, which heightens the pleasure and discloses the profundity of the work. None of these devices is predictable: they are all abrupt discontinuities, explained only by the intuition of the author and recognizable only by a similar mechanism in the reader. These same critical opinions govern Proust's remarks on other authors, and their relevance is heightened by the fact that these devices have an integral place in Proust's own style. By observations of this type the critic in Proust is constantly revealing himself as the novelist's double.

All of Proust's favorite authors — Racine, Madame de Sévigné, Saint-Simon, Balzac, and Baudelaire — are utilized to animate certain portions of *A la recherche*, usually in terms of literary reminiscences, sometimes by an ingenious method of transpositions. *Phèdre* is the vehicle which helps the Narrator to grasp the perfection of Berma's art; and whenever Proust draws a parallel between the art of Racine and Baudelaire, the tragic queen seems to be hovering about the page. She is invoked in relation to the Narrator's own love and jealousy, and Racine's ability to register the turbulence of Phèdre's passion is underscored.[15] References to *Esther* and *Athalie* in the novel often contain touches of humor in their transposition of scenes into modern milieus, a technique which often approaches the mock-heroic burlesque.[16] Such reminiscences and transpositions of Racine illustrate Proust's conviction about the timeless "vérité" of Racine's art. Monsieur de Charlus, whose literary tastes often coincide with those of the Narrator and of Proust himself, exclaims in the course of a conversation with Saint-Loup, "There is more truth in a single tragedy of Racine than in all the dramatic works of Monsieur Victor Hugo."[17] An inane criticism of Racine is used to show the inadequacy of Bloch's literary judgment. As an admirer of the Parnassians, he is made to speak with Théophile Gautier's adolescent arrogance:

> I am bound to admit, natheless, . . . that . . . the man Racine, did . . . once in his life, compose a line which is not only fairly rhythmical, but has also what is in my eyes the supreme merit of meaning absolutely nothing . . .
>
> *La fille de Minos et de Pasiphaé.*[18]

On the subject of Racine's prose, Proust is more critical. Replying to Anatole France's suggestion that Racine's *Lettres aux imaginaires* be taken as a canon of good writing, he first of all rejects the principle of a canon ("for the very good reason that it means setting up a fixed standard of style to express thoughts that are, in fact, far from being fixed or all of the same kind"[19]); he is, of course, being consistent in his conviction that there are no absolutes in aesthetics and that each great writer has to forge his own style. Consequently, each work presents an individual critical problem, and critical labels fail to get at the individual merits of a work. Standards of taste, for Proust, are elusive: intuition and sensibility serve as determining factors, since in the realm of taste, rules or models, by definition, do not exist. If, however, Anatole France insists on choosing a canon, he continues, let it not be the *Lettres aux imaginaires*,

> . . . a piece of writing, that is so dry, so threadbare, so short-winded. It is easy for an artistic form which contains so small a quantity of thought to be light and graceful . . . Indeed these letters to the author of the Imaginaires are almost as feeble as the absurd correspondence which passed between Racine and Boileau when they set about exchanging views on medicine.[20]

Proust's argument is convincing enough. The *Lettres à l'auteur des hérésies imaginaires* are elegant, witty — often ironic — replies to certain moral objections to the theater issued by Port-Royal. Racine continually twits their author (presumably

Nicole) about his attempt to emulate the *Lettres provinciales*, whose style Racine probably had in mind when he composed his two *Lettres*. The content of these letters is meager, as Proust states, and in contrast with Pascal's brilliant irony, the two Racine letters strike the reader as being but mildly sarcastic. This quality undoubtedly appealed to Anatole France when he tried to select a model, but Proust realized immediately that France was simplifying the issue.[21]

In addition to Racine, Madame de Sévigné occupies a high position among Proust's favorite authors of the seventeenth century. His appreciation of Madame de Sévigné's style stems to a large extent from his having learned to love her simplicity, sensibility, and goodness at an early age. The fact that Madame de Sévigné's Letters were favorite reading matter in the Proust household and that a wealth of sentimental and tender memories are bound up with the Letters served only to strengthen this affection.

In connection with his argument on criteria of style in *Tendres Stocks*, Proust exalts Madame de Sévigné's epistolary style at the expense of the Boileau-Racine correspondence and of Racine's *Lettres aux imaginaires*, quoting the opening portions of the letter in which Madame de Sévigné describes to her daughter her arrival in Marseille:

> I am delighted by the singular beauty of this town. Yesterday the weather was superb, and the spot from which I discovered the sea, the country houses, and the mountains and the town is something astonishing . . . The crowd of chevaliers who came to see M. de Grignan yesterday upon his arrival — well-known names, such as Saint-Hérem, etc.; adventurers, swords, smart-looking hats — people just made to order to bring to life one's idea of war, a novel, an embarkation, adventures, of chains, shackles, slavery, captivity. You know how much I like novels: that whole spectacle delighted me.

He concludes " . . . in composition, color and variety, what a picture on the grand scale from the hand of that great writer!" [22] This same idea — that of Madame de Sévigné as a sensitive genre artist — is further developed in the novel by the Narrator, who, on the train to Balbec, picks up his Grandmother's copy of the Letters. Rejecting the stock phrases and turns of speech that are ordinarily associated with people's taste for Madame de Sévigné, Marcel remarks:

> But my grandmother who had approached that lady from within, attracted to her by her own love of kinsfolk and of nature, had taught me to enjoy the real beauties of her correspondence, which are altogether different. They were presently to strike me all the more forcibly inasmuch as Madame de Sévigné is a great artist of the same school as a painter whom I was to meet at Balbec, where his influence on my way of seeing things was immense. I realized at Balbec that it was in the same way as he that she presented things to her readers, in the order of our perception of them, instead of first having to explain them in relation to their several causes. But already that afternoon in the railway carriage, as I read over again that letter in which the moonlight comes: "I cannot resist the temptation: I put on all my bonnets and veils, though there is no need of them, I walk along this mall, where the air is as sweet as in my chamber; I find a thousand phantasms, monks white and black, sisters grey and white, linen cast here and there on the ground, men enshrouded upright against the treetrunks," I was enraptured by what, a little later, I should have described (for does not she draw landscapes in the same way as he draws characters?) as the Dostoievsky side of Madame de Sévigné's Letters.[23]

Madame de Sévigné, as Proust observes, has the same respect and feeling for "things" which he finds in many of his favorite writers, such as Balzac, Flaubert, and Baudelaire, and in painters, such as Chardin and Vermeer. It is this particular love of "things" which enriches so many of the pages of *A la recherche*, and finally becomes one of the cornerstones of the Narrator's digression on literary aesthetics in *Le Temps retrouvé*. Madame de Sévigné, like the painter Elstir, knows how to take "things" and place them in relation to each other: she offers us every now and then a literary still life. And this way of seeing things, Proust notes, has a curious correspondence to Dostoevski's way of seeing human beings — it is a synthetic vision, which combines its elements, not an analytic one, which separates them. When Albertine asks the Narrator to explain to her what he means by the "Dostoevskian" side of Madame de Sévigné, Marcel explains:

> . . . Mme. de Sévigné, like Elstir, like Dostoievski, instead of presenting things in their logical sequence, that is to say beginning with the cause, shews us first of all the effect, the illusion that strikes us.[24]

But over and above these stylistic considerations, the name of Madame de Sévigné adorns the pages of *A la recherche du temps perdu* like a garland binding the Narrator to the Grandmother and the Mother to both. After the Grandmother's death, the Narrator's Mother perpetuates the living presence of Madame de Sévigné's goodness in the family; she quotes her and meditates upon her observations, just as her own mother had done before. And the exquisite and moving way in which such quotations can be used is illustrated in the scene following the Grandmother's first attack at the Champs-Elysées.[25]

This use of Madame de Sévigné to deepen the character of his Grandmother is a good illustration of what might be termed Proust's method of "literary inspection." Counterparts to the Grandmother are Madame de Cambremer-Legrandin, who sneers at the sight of Madame de Sévigné's Letters,[26] and Madame de Villeparisis, who deprecates the Letters. She remarks to Marcel's Grandmother,

> "Don't you find it rather exaggerated, her constant anxiety about her daughter? She refers to it too often to be really sincere. She is not natural." My grandmother felt that any discussion would be futile, and so as not to be obliged to speak of the things she loved to a person incapable of understanding them, concealed by laying her bag upon them the *Mémoires de Mme. de Beausergent.* [27]

Thus, Madame de Sévigné becomes a measure of human goodness and warmth, separating the sensitive from the insensitive and the genuine from the pretentious.

The Duc de Saint-Simon occupies a prominent place among the writers to whom Proust owed most. Proust's affinity with

Saint-Simon comes into evidence most strikingly in the last pages of *Le Temps retrouvé*, when the Narrator, having at last discerned his vocation, reflects upon the nature of the work he is about to undertake. Marcel has decided to write the work that has been germinating inside of him, and to write it at night, somewhat in the manner of Saint-Simon:

> Not that I intended to reproduce in any respect the *Arabian Nights*, any more than the *Mémoires of Saint-Simon*, which likewise were written at night . . . It is quite true that, when one is enamoured of a book, one would like to create something exactly like it but one must sacrifice one's love of the moment and think, not of one's predilection but of a truth which does not ask our preferences and forbids us to give them a thought. And it is only by following this truth that one happens occasionally to come upon what one abandoned and, even while keeping them out of one's mind, to write the *Arabian Nights* or the *Mémoires of Saint-Simon* of another period.[28]

Beyond the superficial parallel that suggests itself between the court of Louis XIV and the world of the Guermantes, there are other points of congruence between Proust and Saint-Simon, notably stylistic similarities and descriptive techniques. This problem of parallels has been only touched upon by a few critics who failed to see the broader implications of the subject.[29] Albert Thibaudet, who is interested in finding Proust's place in the lineage of French prose styles finds that ". . . Among all the French styles since *Les Provinciales*, a separate category should be created for Saint-Simon and Marcel Proust alone."[30] The suggestion that Saint-Simon and Proust belong in a category apart from the main stream has a certain plausibility but leaves out of consideration the "classicism" of Proust — that is, his debt to the mainstream of the French tradition, his refinement, his careful molding of the sentences — as opposed to the natural ebullience, the extreme energy behind the sentences whose cascades Saint-Simon did not try to restrain.

The short study by Leo Spitzer of Proust's and Saint-Simon's styles clarifies and supplements Thibaudet's opinion excellently.

The material of this study is Proust's pastiche of Saint-Simon, the most extended and perhaps the best of all the pastiches which Proust created. Here one feels the joy he must have experienced when he wrote it; indeed, in 1908 he wrote to Georges de Lauris "[I] am in the midst of my Saint-Simon who entertains me very much." [31] The pastiche is the most "Proustian," embodying the best of those elements which make the pastiches genuine pieces of criticism — Proust's uncanny ability to get into the author's skin and to speak his language (often more characteristically than the author himself!) — and at the same time gently humorous. As Jean Mouton observes,

> Proust's pastiche does not aim at a caricature of the writer, as do most of the pastiche-writers more or less successfully. Proust himself does not hesitate to underscore humorously this or that characteristic, without, however, succumbing to the temptation of parody; he wishes above all to discover the mainspring of each style.[32]

Spitzer poses the problem whether one might say that Proust had adopted Saint-Simon's style, or whether he adapted his own style to that of Saint-Simon. He reconciles the two points of view by a synthesis: "The correct formulation seems to be that Proust has amalgamated Saint-Simon's style and his own." [33] The characteristics of Saint-Simon's style are all preserved in the pastiche — the use of familiar expressions, such as "le Régent craignant toujours qu'il chantât pouilles sur lui"; coinages, such as "je me licenciai à le lui dire"; elliptical expressions, such as "enchanter par une parole obligeante qui montre qu'on sait le réel et le consistant, disons le mot, l'intrinsèque des généalogies." [34] More generally speaking, Proust has recreated the excitement of Saint-Simon's flow of language, the abundant recollection and imagination that were brought into play whenever Saint-Simon sat down to write. This ebullience accounts for the "unclassical" aspect of Saint-Simon's art, and Proust managed to recapture this breathlessness, especially in a nonstop sentence stretching over two pages,[35] which outdistances his model, with its elements spliced together with commas, semicolons, dashes, and parentheses. Compare this procedure with Gaston Boissier's analysis of Saint-Simon's style:

> In every case, even if the sentences, taken as a whole, sometimes drag or are top-heavy, there is nothing more lively, more nimble, and more charming than the little elements of which they are composed.[36]

One notes that the principal stylistic difference between Saint-Simon and his imitator lies in the fact that Proust's long sentences can no longer be chopped up — the component elements are riveted together. The common denominator, however, is the delight which both Proust and Saint-Simon took in the spoken language. But Proust, the writer by vocation, imposed stricter disciplines upon himself than Saint-Simon, who was a writer by avocation. He felt that here and there Saint-Simon left something to be desired: " . . . I do believe another writer performs his duty in trying to probe into the subject matter where Saint-Simon's treatment is summary." [37] Thus he feels that the Duke should have *illustrated* what he merely refers to as "Montemart's wit," the idiosyncrasies of speech of Monsieur de Montespan, and so on. Out of this criticism grew, by his own admission (in the same letter), some of the finest pages on "l'esprit des Guermantes," and the many singularities of speech which form part of the character portraits throughout *A la recherche.* Here again the pastiche-writer has found it necessary to turn critic for the sake of his own pursuits.

Inasmuch as the living presence of the *Mémoires* has been woven into the pattern of *A la recherche du temps perdu,* frequent allusions to Saint-Simon are not surprising. Direct criticism on the part of the Narrator occurs in two places; in one, Saint-Simon's portraits written "without self-admiration" are praised above the others:

> Saint-Simon's portraits composed by himself (and very likely without his admiring them himself) are admirable, whereas what he cites as the charming wit of his clever friends is frankly dull where it has not become meaningless.[38]

In other words, Saint-Simon, who pretended not to be an artist, was an artist in spite of himself and he was at his best when he was detached, uninvolved emotionally. The second is a tribute to Saint-Simon's style and gives rise to a searching reflection on Proust's part:

> An author of memorials of our time, wishing to write without too obviously seeming to be writing like Saint-Simon, might, on occasion, give us the first line of his portrait of Villars: "He was a rather tall man, dark . . . with an alert, open, expressive physiognomy," but what law of determinism could bring him to the discovery of Saint-Simon's next line, which begins with "and, to tell the truth, a trifle mad"? The true variety is in this abundance of real and unexpected elements, in the branch loaded with blue flowers which thrusts itself forward, against all reason, from the spring hedgerow that seemed already overcharged with blossoms, whereas the purely formal imitation of variety (and one might advance the same agrument for all the other qualities of style) is but a barren uniformity, that is to say the very antithesis of variety, and cannot, in the work of imitators, give the illusion or recall other examples of variety save to a reader who has not acquired the sense of it from the masters themselves.[39]

In keeping with this "Dostoevskian" way in which Saint-Simon, too, looks at persons and things, personality is conceived of as not linear but as jagged, full of contradictions, not reducible to simple logic. Character portrayal often parallels the abrupt discontinuities of Racine's or Molière's literary style; practically all of Proust's characters in the novel are illustrations — or rather demonstrations — of the tenet of the multiform personality.

As might be expected, Saint-Simon also serves as a prism through which Proust's characters can be refracted. Thus the reader finds out that Saint-Simon is one of Swann's favorite authors; and Monsieur de Charlus has a way of looking at society as through Saint-Simon's eyes:

> With the singular amalgam that he had made of the social conceptions at once of a great nobleman and an amateur of art, instead of being polite in the same way that a man of his world would be, he would create a sort of tableau-vivant for himself after Saint-Simon.[40]

And by a sort of higher irony, Charlus' final degeneration is equated with the analogical degeneration of the "inverts," the Duke of La Rochefoucauld, the Prince d'Harcourt, and the Duke of Berry, as depicted by Saint-Simon. "He was the descendant of so many great noblemen, princes of the blood or dukes about whom Saint-Simon tells that they associated with no one who could be named." [41]

Other writers of the seventeenth century receive little critical attention from Proust. One might expect fuller treatment of La Bruyère, whom Proust admired and whose influence he underwent, at least in his early years. The relationship of a group of character portraits, "Fragments de Comédie italienne," in *Les Plaisirs et les jours* to La Bruyère's *Caractères* is evident: the same brevity of treatment, brevity of phrasing, and the final concluding word to seal off the sketch in a surprise movement. The tendency toward epigrammatic formulation of psychological *aperçus*, the desire to make moralistic reflections — these elements are more pronounced in the earlier Proust, simply because the later style, with its shifts, complexities, and multiple points of view, is yet to come. And yet, despite Proust's emphasis on faith in the impression rather than the intellect in *A la recherche*, there are a great many moralistic and psychological observations, often in the form of epigrams, imbedded in the novel. Professor O'Brien points out that Proust owes something not only to La Bruyère's lucid analysis of men's foibles but also to La Rochefoucauld's misanthropy, and that as a *moraliste* he continues the French tradition of the seventeenth century.[42]

This particular receptivity to the art and the mode of expression of the seventeenth century and the tendency to carry over some of its forms into his own work underscores Professor Curtius' remark on Proust's classical temper (*Lebensstimmung*).

> There is a typically French classicism of temper in Proust's work — which must, however, be differentiated from the classicism of artistic form. Classicism in the sense discussed here is a way of giving expression to a rich literary heritage which takes pleasure in embellishing the present moment by means of the fruit of recollection.[43]

Proust takes great pleasure in enhancing the present moment, the present impression, by a classical reference; by this method he also reveals to the reader the relevance, the perennial "reality," of his favorite authors. It should be remembered that the habit of allowing art to embellish life was a feature of Proust's home life; Proust's mother used to quote her favorite authors at appropriate moments — a practice which is carried over into the novel by means of the Narrator's Grandmother.

Moreover, as Professor O'Brien points out in the case of the "Maxims," Proust belongs to the great classical tradition — rather than to a separate category — in France, whose achievement has been from Montaigne to the present day to impose clarity on the complexity of experience. Proust's position in the mainstream of this tradition has been recognized, and this, in addition to Curtius's observation, helps to explain the real and profound affinity which he felt for the seventeenth century. Jacques Rivière pointed out this classical orientation as early as 1920:

> Proust sees all things, even external ones, from the same point of view in which he sees himself. And since he has adopted for himself the habit of refraction, his eye immediately decomposes and particularizes. Thus, by never separating any detail from the whole, he succeeds in showing us individuals always as entirely concrete, inside as well as outside, astonishing and yet familiar.
>
> In this way he is picking up the strands of the great classical tradition. Did Racine do otherwise than to seek others within himself? Having one day sent out his intelligence in quest of his sensibility, step by step, by whatever gains the former made over the latter, he became a creator. And only in this way.[44]

Rivière discerned clearly that in Proust intelligence and sensibility operated in such a way that the final result was concretion, not abstraction. As Rivière pointed out in a subsequent passage, this process leads to invention rather than creation, properly speaking. But this is perhaps equivalent to saying that all artistic creation is really invention. This sense of concreteness with which great art begins and upon which art works its characteristic alchemy is evident in a passage from one of Proust's letters to Madame de Noailles, in which Proust seeks to define the absolute beauty that resides in certain works of art.

> If one tries to discover what constitutes the absolute beauty of certain things, La Fontaine's fables, Molière's comedies, one discovers that it is not their depth, or some other virtue, which seems outstanding. No, it is rather a kind of blending, a kind of transparent unity, into which all things, giving up their primary appearance as merely "things," have gone to take their place one beside the other in a kind of order, penetrated by the same light, one reflected in the other, unmarred by a single word that has remained refractory to this assimilation.[45]

This letter, written in 1904, reads like an earlier — but already mature — draft of the second volume of *Le Temps retrouvé*. The unity of the work, its transparency — in brief, its reduction to homogeneous terms of the artist's vision — this is what absolute beauty signifies for Proust; and this is what he learned from the masters of the seventeenth century.

And for this reason, the seventeenth century always served Proust as a noble example to look back to, a repository of literary beauty, of whose profundities, he suggests, the seventeenth-century reader may not always have been aware: " . . . We are permitted to enjoy in Racine's tragedies, in his *Cantiques*, in the letters of Mme. de Sévigné, in Boileau, a beauty which is really there and which the 17th century barely perceived." [46]

III

PROUST AS A CRITIC OF THE NINETEENTH CENTURY

> . . . le XIVe siècle dont les plus grands écrivains ont marqué leurs livres, mais, se regardant travailler comme s'ils étaient à la fois l'ouvrier et le juge, ont tiré de cette autocontemplation une beauté nouvelle extérieure et supérieure à l'oeuvre . . .
>
> PROUST, *La Prisonnière.*

1. The Romantic poets — Baudelaire, "poète classique" — other poets

In a letter written in 1906 to Anna de Noailles, Proust bracketed Hugo, Vigny, and Lamartine with Baudelaire and Racine,[1] and his essay on Baudelaire opens with a number of remarks on the Romantic poets. In Hugo he admires first of all the force of the poet's expression, and in addition he notes the grandeur of conception that makes Hugo's *Légende des siècles* the counterpart of the *Comédie humaine*, a work on which unity was imposed retrospectively.

> Hugo . . . wrote a number of admirable but entirely disconnected poems, and called the result *La Légende des siècles*. The title has a beauty all its own, but the work as a whole, in spite of the excellence of its component pieces, does not really live up to it.[2]

In Proust's opinion, the over-all conception does augment the sum of its parts, even if the fusion of microcosm to macrocosm is inadequate — a point which will be elaborated somewhat further in the discussion of Balzac.

Perhaps it is as a result of a successful fusion of the single poem and the total conception of *La Légende des siècles* that Proust singles out *Booz endormi.*

> . . . There, a whole epoch of history and geology is unrolled before us on a scale, and with a vigor that nothing can contract or stop, from
>
> La Terre encor mouillée et molle du Déluge
>
> to Jesus Christ:
>
> En bas un roi chantait, en haut mourait un Dieu.
>
> This great biblical poem . . . has none of the dryness of history. It is perpetually vivified by the personality of Victor Hugo, who, in Boaz, objectifies himself.[3]

Hugo treats this magnificent canvas of history with an astonishing simplicity that disarms the critic; Proust, too, seems to feel that he can merely attempt to point out the devices that make the work vigorous. Thus he notes that the poem derives its vividness from Hugo's identification of himself with the noble figure of Boaz:

> Les Femmes regardaient Booz plus qu'un jeune homme,
> Car le jeune homme est beau, mais le vieillard est grand.

This vitality — which in these verses is like a magnificent and noble gesture — is achieved "with the most relaxed and stately syntax." An example of this are the lines which follow those just quoted:

> Le vieillard, qui revient vers sa source première,
> Entre aux jours éternels et sort des jours changeants.

Proust comments that here Hugo makes the laws of logic subservient to the laws of versification:

A prose writer would obviously have begun by saying "sort des jours changeants." Nor is he afraid to fling trivial expressions to the end of a line, where they assume a new kind of nobility.

> Laissez tomber exprès des épis, disait-il. [4]

Here are examples of what Proust has called "sauts brusques" in other authors, surprise breaches of the rules of syntax or of logical continuity to bring about particular effects. Certainly the last-quoted line achieves a grandeur and simplicity that could not be attained through any rearrangement of the words.

The poem is enriched by personal impressions and by Hugo's identification with Boaz:

> It is, I am quite sure, in one of Victor Hugo's personal impressions, and not in the Bible at all, that one must seek the origin of these wonderful lines:
>
> Quand on est jeune on a des matins triomphants,
> Le jour sort de la nuit ainsi qu'une victoire.
>
> The most closely knit thoughts are given just the necessary degree of fusion:
>
> Voilà longtemps que celle avec qui j'ai dormi,
> O Seigneur, a quitté ma couche pour la vôtre
> Et nous sommes encor tout mêlés l'un à l'autre,
> Elle à demi vivante, et moi mort à demi.
>
> The greatness of the style shows no sign of weakening even in such simple phrases as:
>
> Booz ne savait point qu'une femme était là
> Et Ruth ne savait point ce que Dieu voulait d'elle.[5]

These lines sum up what Proust pointed out before; it is, again and always, the simplicity, the grandeur, the forcefulness of the verse produced by an intelligence that imparts the "fusion nécessaire" to experience, and converts the syntax to its own uses.

Besides Hugo the syntactical magician, there is Hugo the linguistic virtuoso.

Moreover, simply by reading Victor Hugo one gets an impression of a writer who knows his language admirably well. In every instance the technical terms of any particular art are used in their exact denotation. In the poem *A l'Arc de Triomphe* alone, I can recall:

> Sur les monuments qu'on révère
> Le temps jette un charme sévère
> De leur façade à leur *chevet* . . .
> C'est le temps qui creuse une ride
> Dans un *claveau* trop indigent . . .
> Quand ma pensée ainsi vieillissant ton *attique*
> . . . Se refuse enfin lasse à porter l'*archivolte*.[6]

Hugo's lines do not utilize the vocabulary of architecture to produce a spurious local color; Proust finds these verses almost Parnassian in their precision. In this context he quotes an opinion of Fernand Gregh in his *Etude sur Hugo*, in which Gregh claimed that Hugo's genius lay in the growth of his talent through hard work. The passage quoted shows, then, how Hugo *absorbed* rather than simply *utilized* architecture. At this point, too, Proust recalls that Hugo was, like Baudelaire, a lover of the classics. In numerous instances he calls attention to the classical "diet" (*nourriture*) of the Romantics;[7] and he likes to dwell on the fact that innovators always know their classics, whereas it is the epigones of such innovators who treat them with contempt.

> As for expressions used with all their ancient vigor, encompassed by all their Latin splendor, the line which concludes one of the loveliest poems in *Les Contemplations:* "Ni l'importunité des sinistres oiseaux" can take pride in its glorious ancestor from which it is descended in a direct line ("importunique volucres").[8]

The example shows, as Proust puts it, that a great writer knows thoroughly not only his own language but also his literary predecessors. And does not the line from *Booz endormi* which he praised above, "Entre aux jours éternels et sort des jours changeants," represent a reminiscence on Hugo's part of a device known as "hysteron proteron" and frequently encountered in Vergil? But linguistic mastery does not suffice; the writer must draw his language from the storehouse of his memory:

While writing he no longer thinks of them [the dictionary and the literary predecessors] but of what he is trying to express, choosing those words which serve his purpose best, most forcefully, most colorfully, and most harmoniously. He chooses them from an excellent vocabulary, because that is the one which is at the disposition of his memory, his studies having solidly established the suitability of each term. But while he writes he does not think of this. His erudition is subordinated to his genius . . . His language, no matter how erudite or how opulent, is only the keyboard on which he improvises. And since he is not thinking of the unusual quality of the expression while he is writing, his work does not show any trace, any blemish, of affectation.[9]

Here, then, is Proust's view of how this fusion of the various elements takes place; it is interesting to note that the process is mainly unconscious. For Proust, the truly discerning critic — the critic who wishes to go beyond an analysis of the essential features of the writer — attempts to reconstitute the "special reality which haunts" him. This often necessitates the critic's delving into the aspect of an author that is more or less unconscious, without, however, psychoanalyzing him. The unconscious structure of the *vision,* not of the personality, must be analyzed. "In a writer we try to find the man when that man was only striving to lift himself to the level of the writer," Proust said in one of his profoundest aphorisms.[10] Furthermore, the subordination of the writer's intelligence to his sensibility is typically Proustian here: the *recherche,* the precious effects, must be eliminated by the free movement of sense and sensibility.

Proust concludes that in Hugo the result of this process in which erudition becomes subservient to the exigencies of literary art produces such verses as

Rêve à l'artiste grec qui versa de sa main
Quelque chose de beau comme un sourire humain
  Sur le profil des propylées

from *A l'arc de Triomphe.* And linguistic virtuosity leads to brilliant alliterations such as

Les souffles de la nuit flottaient sur Galgala

in the poem just mentioned, where six l's produce "that impression of airy lightness that the author aimed for." [11]

In *A la recherche du temps perdu* Hugo serves as the subject of literary discussion in a number of instances. Marcel finds it strange that practically all the authors whom he admires are treated slightingly by Madame de Villeparisis, who had known most of these men personally in her youth; she rejects Hugo as "that talented but extravagant writer who had acquired the title of 'Major Poet' only by virtue of having struck a bargain, and as a reward for the not disinterested indulgence that he shewed to the dangerous errors of the Socialists." [12] Madame de Villeparisis is here reflecting the judgment of her father, who handed it down to her. The pointlessness of this kind of "literary" judgment is not directly commented upon by the Narrator, but it is clear that Madame de Villeparisis has the unfortunate tendency to assess writers by their social standing or by the figures they cut in the *salons* of her youth. The use of this kind of criticism in the novel is satirical, serving to show the prejudices of Madame de Villeparisis — and to emphasize her final degradation in Venice, as described in *La Fugitive* (*Albertine disparue*).

In the drawing room of the Guermantes Hugo is also under fire. Madame d'Arpajon accuses him of being "difficult" and incapable of distinguishing the beautiful from the ugly; she uses the poem "Lorsque l'enfant paraît" from *Les Feuilles d'automne* as an example, charging that the poem is unreadable because it contains

> . . . some ridiculous things, quite unintelligible, errors of taste, that it is difficult to understand, that it's as much trouble to read as if it was written in Russian or Chinese, for of course it's anything in the world but French, still when one has taken the trouble, how richly one is rewarded, it's so full of imagination! [13]

The Narrator makes the reflection that Madame d'Arpajon is old-fashioned but essentially sincere: she has the difficulty which people often have with new works of literature, with the difference, of course, that *Les Feuilles d'automne* are anything but new. The case of the Duchess of Guermantes is more complicated. She voices this opinion about Victor Hugo:

> What is utterly detestable is the Victor Hugo of the last stage, the *Légende des Siècles*, I forget all their names. But in the *Feuilles d'Automne*, the *Chants du Crépuscule*, there's a great deal that's the work of a poet, a true poet! Even in the *Contemplations* . . . there are still some quite pretty things. But I confess that I prefer not to venture farther than the *Crépuscule*! And then in the finer poems of Victor Hugo, and there really are some, one frequently comes across an idea, even a profound idea.[14]

Judging from what Proust has admired in Hugo in his essay, it becomes evident that Oriane's criticism is unjustified and even unfounded. The two works of Victor Hugo which he had singled out were *La Légende des siècles* and *Les Contemplations*; these represented to him the highest attainment of Hugo's art, the full maturing of his power, and he offered numerous examples to prove his point. The peculiarity of Oriane de Guermantes' statement lies in her juxtaposition of two ideas about Hugo's work which are basically inconsistent; if she appreciates Hugo's ideas, she is more likely to find them in the later poetry. But apparently she does not wish to take the trouble to enter into Hugo's more complex frame of thought and prefers to restrict herself to the early Hugo, contenting herself with the ideas she finds in the early poems.

The reaction of the Narrator to Madame de Guermantes is interesting at this juncture; it throws a certain amount of light on how the Narrator operates in the novel as an intermediary stage in Proust's criticism. After leaving the Guermantes *soirée*, he reflects on the events of the evening, among them the discussion of Hugo; and he decides to reread the early volumes of poetry.

> . . . The lines of Victor Hugo which I had heard her quote were, it must be admitted, of a period earlier than that in which he became something more than a new man, in which he brought to light, in the order of evolution, a literary species till then unknown, endowed with more complex organs than any then in existence. In these first

poems, Victor Hugo is still a thinker, instead of contenting himself, like Nature, with supplying food for thought. His 'thoughts' he at that time expressed in the most direct form . . . Well, it was these 'thoughts' of Victor Hugo (almost as entirely absent from the *Légende des Siècles* as 'airs,' as 'melodies' are from Wagner's later manner) that Mme. de Guermantes admired in the early Hugo.[15]

This statement parallels a remark Proust makes elsewhere[16] concerning those people who like the early pieces of Wagner, such as *Tannhäuser*, because they sense in them the beauty of the later works, without having to make the effort which the later works demand. It is not that Madame de Guermantes is exactly lazy or incapable of the mental effort; she merely fails to see the relationship between the early poems and the late poems of Hugo and to place the differences in the proper perspective, which would enable her to assess Hugo the total man correctly. Within her own limited criteria Madame de Guermantes is consistent; it is, for instance, altogether right that she should find an occasional venture into the *Contemplations* rewarding (although in the long run she prefers to steer clear of it); for *Les Contemplations* is the exact point of juncture between the Hugo of the *Crépuscule* and of the *Légende*. Marcel defines the difference more precisely; speaking of the early "thoughts," he observes:

> They were touching, and already round about them, without their form's having yet the depth which it was to acquire only in later years, the rolling tide of words and of richly articulated rhymes put them beyond comparison with the lines that one might discover in a Corneille, for example, lines in which a Romanticism that is intermittent, restrained and so all the more moving, nevertheless has not at all penetrated to the physical sources of life, modified the unconscious and generalizable organism in which the idea is latent. And so I had been wrong in confining myself, hitherto, to the later volumes of Hugo.[17]

The result of this discovery, for the Narrator, is the same as that of a document which throws additional but not essential light on a known fact. For Proust, the mature works of Hugo represent his noblest achievement; yet he discovers also that the early ferment of the later product is admirable. In this particular instance, the Narrator has served to illustrate a phase in the development of the author's critical judgment.

On Alfred de Vigny, even though Proust places his poems on a level with Baudelaire's, the critical material is sparse. Among the finer poems of Vigny, Proust singles out *La Colère de Samson* (see below, the discussion of Gomorrha under Baudelaire) and *La Maison du berger*. He notes an "extraordinary tension" in Vigny's poems and a certain mysterious quality that is hard to define. "Even in his quiet poems, Vigny remains mysterious. The source of the quietness and of its ineffable beauty escapes us." Whereas Victor Hugo accomplishes his poetic task brilliantly, nevertheless he always remains, so to speak, translucent. "But the fabrication — even when it is fabrication of the impalpable — is always visible." [18] And thus the moment that should be mysterious always passes by without being *approfondi*. In Vigny, on the other hand, Proust takes at random four verses from *La Maison du berger*, to show how the mystery is presented but not to explain how it is created:

> Dans les balancements de ta taille penchée
> Et dans ton pur sourire amoureux et souffra [*sic*]
> Pleurant comme Diane au bord de ses fontaines
> Ton amour taciturne et toujours menacé.[19]

It is a shortcoming of Madame de Villeparisis' literary tastes that she shows herself insensitive to quotations such as the above, charging Vigny with dullness and objecting, besides, to his priding himself on being a count.[20] Just as she gave evidence of a lack of sensibility in the case of Madame de Sévigné, she lacks literary judgment here. And so the young Narrator is led to the following reflection:

> After dinner, when I had retired upstairs with my grandmother, I said to her that the qualities which attracted us in Mme. de Villeparisis, her tact, her shrewdness, her discretion, her modesty in not

referring to herself, were not, perhaps, of very great value since those who possessed them in the highest degree were simply people like Molé and Loménie, and that if the want of them can make our social relations unpleasant yet it did not prevent . . . Chateaubriand, Vigny, Hugo, Balzac, [from becoming] a lot of foolish fellows who had no judgment, at whom it was easy to mock . . .[21]

Musset had been one of Proust's childhood favorites.[22] In his later years, Proust outgrew him, while retaining a fondness for certain of Musset's later poems. The Narrator of *A la recherche* traverses the same ground. In *Du côté de chez Swann*, Bloch, *Parnasse*-oriented, pontificates to Marcel:

You must conquer your vile taste for A. de Musset, Esquire. He is a bad egg, one of the very worst, a pretty detestable specimen. I am bound to admit, natheless, . . . that he . . . did . . . once in his life, compose a line which is not only fairly rhythmical, but has also what is in my eyes the supreme merit of meaning absolutely nothing. One is

La blanche Oloossone et la blanche Camire . . .[23]

A few years later Marcel has overcome his admiration for Bloch's literary judgments (which had been equally sophomoric on the subject of Racine's verse) and outdistanced his master. Thus he criticizes Bloch and his ilk for admiring inane lines such as

A Saint-Blaise, à la Zuecca
Vous étiez, vous étiez bien aise. (*Chanson*)

or in *La Nuit de Décembre*, such claptrap as

Au Havre, devant l'Atlantique
A Venise, à l'affreux Lido,
Où vient sur l'herbe d'un tombeau
Mourir la pâle Adriatique.[24]

Proust's mature opinion about Musset is expressed in a paragraph of the essay on Baudelaire. He writes:

Musset, all things considered, remains a poet of the second order, and his admirers are so well aware of this fact, that they habitually ignore one whole side of his work, and return to it only when they have tired of the other. Wearied by the declamatory tone of *Nuits* — which, however, embodies the style to which he was always logically tending — they ring the changes on his lesser verse:

> Plus ennuyeuse que Milan
> Où du moins deux ou trois fois l'an Cerrilo danse.

But they become discouraged a little further on in the same poem when he writes of Venice where he left his heart. So they turn for relief to those purely documentary pieces which paint for us the fashionable balls of Musset's day. Such trivia do not make a poet (in spite of the laughable enthusiasm with which Monsieur Taine has spoken of the music, the color, etc., of the poems). Finally, they return to *Nuits*, to *l'Espoir en Dieu*, to *Rolla*, which, in the meantime have assumed a degree of freshness. Only such delicate poems as *Namouna* are still full of life, and put forth their flowers all the year round.[25]

Proust's condemnation of Musset the versifying dandy and romantic *échevelé* is altogether justified; the little ditties of Musset are entertaining but no more; they amuse by their impertinence. Proust pointed out another characteristic of Musset in a letter to Madame Straus, saying ". . . You may have the feeling in Musset, for instance, that you like him for the poetry in him, when in reality it is only eloquence and passion . . ."[26] Since this letter is dated 1892, it is clear that Proust, seeing through Musset's rhetoric and sentimentality, had by that time left him behind. He does, however, give him credit for raising himself to the stature of his later poems, as he indicates in the phrase quoted above, for reaching the goal he had been striving toward, *Les Nuits*. In a letter to Jacques-Emile Blanche, dated 1919, Proust takes Sainte-Beuve to task for preferring first versions of a work to subsequent treatments, claiming that he did not "find the flame of inspiration in subsequent editions, etc." Proust goes on to defend against such unreasonable claims authors who revise, or better themselves:

It really amounts to ignoring the organic way in which an atom develops and prospers. It would therefore be silly to call second versions inferior. This would amount to putting on the same airs as people who like Molière for *L'Etourdi*, not for *Le Misanthrope*, Musset for "La Ballade à la Lune," not for *Les Nuits* — in other words, all the things that Molière and Musset tried to surpass.[27]

An interesting reversal of this situation occurs when a talented poet begins to write prose. Then it is as though he abandoned his genius, which nevertheless has a way of making itself felt every now and then.

A poet who writes in prose (except, of course, when he deliberately adopts the verse form, like Baudelaire in his *Petits Poèmes* and Musset in his plays). Musset in his stories, his critical essays, his academy discourses, is a man who has turned his back on his genius, who has ceased to draw from his inner consciousness those forms which he finds in a supernatural world which is his own exclusive experience. But he still has a lingering recollection of these things, and the power to prevent us from forgetting them. At some turn in the writing, we find ourselves thinking of certain celebrated "lines." They are invisible, they are not there at all, but in some vague way they seem to show behind phrases which anyone might produce, and to give them a sort of grace, a kind of moving and allusive majesty. The poet has withdrawn, but the diffused light of his genius still hovers behind the clouds. Nothing of it remains in the social figure, the diner-out, the ambitious climber, yet it is in that aspect of the man that Sainte-Beuve thinks he can discover the essential truth of the absent poet.[28]

One is constantly aware of Proust's desire to correct the error in Sainte-Beuve's approach to criticism. Hence the somewhat too generalized heading of "a poet who writes in prose," with the subsequent reservation applying to poets who write poetic prose, such as Baudelaire in his *Spleen de Paris*, and Musset's *comédies-proverbes*. The answer to the problem is surely that each poet who writes prose, and each prose writer who writes poetry, needs to be judged individually — how else to account for such disparate phenomena as Rimbaud, Mallarmé, Valéry, and Gide? Proust's grievances with relation to Sainte-Beuve will be dealt with later; for the time being it suffices to note that he considered the personality of Musset the poet vastly more significant to an appreciation of Musset the artist (even when he is an artist *manqué*!) than Sainte-Beuve's harping on Musset the man-about-town.

Proust's references to Baudelaire in his correspondence are numerous; in almost all instances, these references hold up Baudelaire as an example of literary excellence; significantly enough, Baudelaire's name is usually linked with Racine's. Secondly, Baudelaire is the only poet to whom Proust devotes a major critical article ("A propos de Baudelaire," in *Chroniques*). This article is an elaboration of the chapter "Sainte-Beuve et Baudelaire" in *Contre Sainte-Beuve,* beginning with a very detailed exposé of Sainte-Beuve's misdemeanors toward his friend Baudelaire, which will be discussed in the Sainte-Beuve chapter. The essay then launches into a demonstration by Proust of Baudelaire's greatness and uniqueness as a poet, in an effort to persuade his mother that Baudelaire is a great poet *despite* his sadism. Finally, in the essay, "A propos de Baudelaire" and in *A la recherche* itself, Proust accords Baudelaire a prominent place among his predecessors who show a special sensitivity regarding the importance of memory in personal experience.

These points will be discussed in detail. The problem of Baudelaire's influence on Proust will not be discussed here, being outside the scope of this study; and the psychological and biographical affinities between the two writers will be touched upon only whenever relevant. Moreover, all these aspects have been treated in a recent article.[29] The tendency of such treatments is to strain the parallel between Baudelaire's and Proust's Oedipus complexes, and to overstress the symbolist element in both writers. A critical comparison between the styles and aesthetics of the two men would reveal a great deal more, for there are certain similarities as well as differences in the role which criticism played in the career of both writers, inasmuch as both were critics of literature, music, and art.[30]

In his reply to Anatole France's dictum that "writers have been writing badly since the end of the eighteenth century,"

Proust uses Baudelaire's poetry as the prime example to refute Anatole France's assertion. He calls attention first of all to the sheer "force" of Baudelaire's poetry; quoting by way of illustration several lines from *Le Rebelle*:

> There is often, in Baudelaire's style, something objective and startling: but for sheer power I very much doubt whether it has ever been equalled. It would be difficult to find anything ever written on Charity that is at the same time so lacking in charity yet so powerful as the following lines:
>
> Un ange furieux fond du ciel comme un aigle
> Du mécréant saisit à plein poing les cheveux
> Et dit le secouant: "Tu connaîtras la règle . . .
> Sache qu'il faut aimer sans faire la grimace,
> Le pauvre, le méchant, le tortu, l'hébété,
> Pour que tu puisses faire à Jésus quand il passe,
> Un tapis triomphal avec ta charité." [31]

Although in the preface to *Tendres Stocks* Proust offers no further commentary on these lines, in *Contre Sainte-Beuve* he makes the context clear. Baudelaire, he explains to his mother, is cruel and sensitive simultaneously — so cruel, in fact, that sadistic people can read his lines in support of their own cruelty — for example the line

> Débris d'humanité pour l'éternité mûrs

from *Les Petites Vieilles*, or

> Le violon frémit comme un coeur qu'on afflige

from *Harmonie du soir*. The violence of these lines, the exaltation that accompanies most of Baudelaire's sadistic and satanic poems, were not lost on Proust. But he saw in this practice the result of an ascetic discipline which forced the poet (unlike Hugo) to fling the sordid truth at his readers, rather than beckoning them to share a sentiment *about* the sordid truth. "Perhaps this subordination of the sensibility to truth and to expression is at bottom a proof of genius, of the power of art as being superior to individual pity." [32] In this connection Proust quoted the lines from *Le Rebelle*, and several lines from *Les Petites Vieilles*, commenting that Baudelaire fully comprehended the virtues of charity and compassion but seems to "banish their essence" from his lines.

> It seems that by means of the extraordinary, unheard-of power of the word . . . he eternalizes a sentiment which he makes an effort not to feel at the moment he names it, where he paints, rather than expresses it

with the result that he gives us the impression that he is only enunciating, "although one feels that he has gone through it all himself, understood everything, that he is the most vibrant sensibility and the deepest intelligence." [33]

Proust was, however, aware of certain cases in which Baudelaire's imagery had a deliberate, often sensational, flavor (this could possibly be charged against the poem *Au lecteur*). In a letter to Cocteau, he speaks of "that Baudelairean harshness, which, for my taste, makes certain metaphors stand out too much and fails to amalgamate them sufficiently with the style." [34] The opening remarks of his essay on Baudelaire throw additional light on this "power" Proust discerned in the poet of *Les Fleurs du mal.*

> . . . I hold Baudelaire — together with Alfred de Vigny — to have been the greatest poet of the nineteenth century. I do not mean that if one had to choose the most beautiful *poem* of the nineteenth century one would be best advised to look for it in Baudelaire. I do not believe that in the whole extent of *Les Fleurs du Mal*, that sublime but grimacing book in which pity shows a sneering face, in which debauchery makes the sign of the Cross, where it is Satan on whom the task devolves of preaching the most profound theology, there is a single poem that is the equal of *Booz endormi.*[35]

However, when he compares the whole of *La Légende des siècles*, even Hugo's entire work, with *Les Fleurs du mal*, "how soft, vague and unaccented seems to be the general run of Hugo's output." [36]

Proust paid Baudelaire an even greater compliment when he wrote to Montesquiou in 1893, in the tone of flattery which he habitually used in addressing the Count, "I believe . . . — and not just for the sake of playing with a paradox — that it could be shown how you and Baudelaire derive from the seventeenth century the taste for maxims, the lost habit of thinking in verse." [37] It would have been interesting to see Proust elucidating this statement; did he mean perhaps that for the first time since Racine, Baudelaire was able to transform poetry into an instrument of cognition, rather than a means of adornment? The statement implies that a great poet, who manages to transform his vision of life, must be capable not only of thinking in images, but in rhythmic images. It is presupposed that the poet or the prose writer, without necessarily writing philosophical poems or novels, begins with reflection or contemplation; art results from an encounter of the artist's mind and sensibility with reality. Proust described Baudelaire accordingly as being "of a philosophical turn of mind" [38] and couples him with Vigny, rather than with Hugo. Vigny had a more genuine predisposition for philosophy, one might say, a more highly developed faculty of "thinking in verse" than Hugo, whose philosophizing represents rather a series of sweeping rhetorical gestures.

Linking Baudelaire with the seventeenth century entails a discussion of what Proust considers Baudelaire's classicism. For Proust, Baudelaire and Racine produce the same kind of pleasure. "Taking difference of period into account, nothing is more Baudelairean than *Phèdre*, nothing more worthy of Racine, even of Malherbe, than *Fleurs du Mal*." [39] In another place he is more explicit:

> Baudelaire does not know how, or does not wish to finish a work and, also, perhaps, in no one piece of his can one find the accumulated truths which succeed and verge upon one another with such great richness, in Phèdre's single declaration. But the style of the condemned poems, which is exactly that of the tragedies, surpasses them, perhaps, in nobility of feeling. [40]

What Proust means by Baudelaire's inability to finish a poem is an allusion to the fact that often the last line or lines of Baudelaire's poems produce a let-down as if Baudelaire's inspiration had been lagging, or sagging — a problem which will be further commented upon below. The observation about the correspondence of the style of the condemned poems and of Racine's tragedies is perceptive. In each case, an extremely polished, refined style acts as a thin veneer over the poet's observation of the cruel and disintegrating aspects of vicious passions and his impulse to express them forcefully. Proust notes that in Baudelaire's case the greater the vice, the purer the expression:

> Baudelaire is a great classical poet, but the curious thing about him is that the classicism of his form increases in proportion to the licentiousness of his painting. Racine wrote a great deal of much profounder poetry than Baudelaire ever did, but he never achieved a purer style than that of the sublime *Poèmes condamnés*. These two lines from the piece that caused the most violent sense of scandal:
>
> Ses bras vaincus, jetés comme de vaines armes,
> Tout servait, tout parait sa fragile beauté.
>
> might have come straight out of *Britannicus*.[41]

In *Chroniques*, quoting the same lines of *Femmes damnées: Delphine et Hippolyte*, Proust comments: "We know that these last lines refer to a woman exhausted by another woman's caresses. But had they been designed to show Junia before Nero, would Racine have expressed himself differently?"[42]

Moreover, Baudelaire's classicism is augmented by his knowledge of the classics and his familiarity with classical mythology. The frequency of classical allusions, introduced into the poems without artifice, is surprising in a cycle of poems revolving primarily about urban life. Proust points out that a typical Parisian poem such as *Les Petites Vieilles* contains several classical allusions. And in *Le Voyage* the story of Electra is alluded to "as it might have been by Racine in one of his Prefaces."[43] Finally, he finds that Baudelaire often surpasses the classics at the very moment when he finds inspiration in them:

> If Baudelaire sought inspiration from Horace . . . , he goes, in fact, far beyond him. Instead of *animae dimidium meae* (of which

I can't help believing that he was thinking) he wrote: *mon tout et ma moitié*.[44]

In general, he finds Baudelaire's short poems more successful than the longer ones. He contrasts the perfection of a short poem like *La Pipe* with the long *Voyage*:

> The long poems, even *Voyage*,
>
> Pour l'enfant, amoureux de cartes et d'estampes,
> L'univers est égal à son vaste appétit.
> Ah! que le monde est grand à la clarté des lampes!
> Aux yeux du souvenir que le monde est petit!
>
> . . . even that sublime *Voyage*, which opens so well, is sustained only by an effort of rhetoric.[45]

Finding the same weakness in *Le Cygne*, which ends, after about fifty lines, with

> Aux captifs, aux vaincus! . . . à bien d'autres encor!

Proust remarks: "These simple endings are perhaps intentional. Nevertheless, there is something curtailed about them, a quality of being short of breath."[46]

Proust is willing to admit that Baudelaire's flat endings are often intentional, realizing that in some instances it was better to end the poem "not with a bang but a whimper," or, after reaching the climax, to allow the poetic subject matter to vanish. This is true of *Le Cygne*, as Professor Hubert notes;[47] and it is difficult to share Proust's condemnation of the last line ("Au fond de l'Inconnu pour trouver du *nouveau!*") of *Le Voyage*, a poem which Proust admits is "sublime." The line has the dull ring of the *ennui* of Baudelaire and is therefore completely effective and it marks precisely the point toward which Baudelaire's "voyage" has been aspiring.

On the other hand, what Proust often finds missing in the last lines he finds achieved elsewhere; and this fact should be kept in mind by anyone trying to assess accurately his relationship to Baudelaire. "Yet no poet ever had, to the same degree, such a feeling for *renewal*, even in the middle of a poem. Sometimes it shows by a sharp change of tone." [48] Examples of this "sens du renouvellement" are to be found in the poem *L'Imprévu*, one of the satanic poems with a marvelously abrupt change of tone at the end:

Un ange sonne la victoire

De ceux dont le coeur dit: "Que béni soit son fouet,
Seigneur! que la Douleur, ô Père, soit bénie!
Mon âme dans tes mains n'est pas un vain jouet,
Et ta prudence est infinie."

Le son de la trompette est si délicieux,
Dans ces soirs solennels de célestes vendanges,
Qu'il s'infiltre comme une extase dans tous ceux
Dont elle chante les louanges.

Another example which Proust cites is the *Chant d'automne*, which shifts from the autumnal landscape ("Bientôt nous plongerons dans les froides ténèbres") to "J'aime de vos longs yeux la lumière verdâtre." Or the poem *Causerie*, in which the poet interrupts himself brusquely with "Mon coeur est un palais flétri par la cohue," whereupon

a renewal of desire lays hold of him; the woman drives him into a fresh spasm, and the poet, intoxicated by the delights proffered him by the moment, yet, at the same time, thinking of the weariness that will come when all is over, cries:

Un parfum nage autour de votre gorge nue! . . .
O Beauté, dur fléau des âmes, tu le veux!
Avec tes yeux de feu, brillants comme des fêtes,
Calcine ces lambeaux qu'ont épargnés les bêtes![49]

In another place Proust finds occasion to admire the last line of *Femmes damnées*, "Et les urnes d'amour dont vos grands coeurs sont pleins." A line of this type is particularly surprising in a poem beginning "Comme un bétail pensif sur le sable couchées . . ." which proceeds, in typical Baudelaire fashion, to evoke a picture of vice and torment, only to soften its tone toward the end ("Tantôt pleines de cris, tantôt pleines de pleurs," and still later, "Pauvres soeurs, je vous aime autant que je vous plains"), and to find this veritable expansion in the last line. Proust makes the following comment on the art of this last line: "A good writer who is merely a good writer would have compared the heart to a love-filled urn . . . Only the great poet dares to fill the heart with urns . . ." [50]

The Baudelaire chapter in *Contre Sainte-Beuve* is noteworthy among other things, for the first incidence of what Proust was to call in *La Prisonnière phrase-type* analysis: "It seems to me that I might begin by evoking for you, form by form, that world of Baudelaire's thought, that homeland of his genius of which each poem is but a fragment, and which, upon being read, joins with the other fragments which we are familiar with." [51] He goes on to point out the frequency of ports and porticoes in Baudelaire's poetry, the use of sunset colors and of white sails outlined against blue horizons — "warm and colored shapes" and "great torch-lit lines," he had called Baudelaire's poems in a slightly different context.[52]

Closely related to this inner landscape of the poet is his ability to make it poetically accessible "by a symbol, and always one which is so material, so striking, so unabstract, using the most powerful, the most ordinary and the most dignified words," [53] such as in *Les Litanies de Satan*:

Toi qui fais au proscrit ce regard calme et haut
Qui damne tout un peuple autour d'un échafaud . . .
Bâton des exilés, lampe des inventeurs . . .

Within Baudelaire's world of colors, Proust observes, there is another one made up of perfumes; and within his poetry there are verses that may strike the reader as reminiscent of Hugo, Gautier, Sully Prudhomme, Racine, Mallarmé, Sainte-Beuve, and Nerval — next to "matrix" lines such as

Beaux écrins sans joyaux, médaillons sans reliques [54]
(*L'Amour du mensonge*)

Turning to an observation of a more technical nature, Proust calls attention to the powerful "turning" (tournant) of the hemistich, as in *Le Cygne*

> Ce petit fleuve,
> Triste et pauvre miroir ou jadis resplendit (tournant)
> L'immense majesté de vos douleurs de veuve

where the poet "with those great lines which his genius, swept along the turning of the preceding hemistich, gets ready, with full force, to fill up their gigantic course and which thus give the greatest idea of the richness, eloquence, unlimitedness of genius." [55] These observations clarify Proust's notion of "renouvellement" in Baudelaire.

Proust sees Baudelaire as the poet of human suffering and Hugo, as the chronicler of human suffering.

> The feelings about which I have been speaking, the sense of suffering and of death in a humble fraternity, leads us to this conclusion, that no one has ever written *better* of the People and of the Beyond, and that Victor Hugo remains merely the poet who has written of these things *at greatest length.* All Hugo's bombast and noise, all his dialogues with God, fade into insignificance when set beside what poor Baudelaire found in the intimacy of his own mental and bodily suffering. Nor was Baudelaire's inspiration at all indebted to Hugo. Of the two, it is not Hugo, with his sham medievalism, who might have been a carver of images in a cathedral, but Baudelaire, the impure man of faith, the casuist kneeling with a grimace upon his lips, and destined for damnation.[56]

An illustration of this difference is the poem *Les Petites Vieilles,* one of Baudelaire's finest longer poems, in Proust's opinion, and dedicated to Victor Hugo himself. In this poem Baudelaire's procedure is unusual for the subject matter; the poem "[leaves] on the reader a painful impression of cruelty." [57] Proust finds that Baudelaire wanted to suppress his pity rather than show it, and to extract from the spectacle of these miserable old women a tableau that would impress itself on the reader by its very grandeur as well as its violence. Thus he records a series of caricature-portraits, as unforgettable as those of Leonardo da Vinci, such as the following:

> Celle-là, droite encor, fière et sentant la règle,
> Humait avidement ce chant vif et guerrier;
> Son oeil parfois s'ouvrait comme l'oeil d'un vieil aigle;
> Son front de marbre avait l'air fait pour le laurier.

Moreover, certain lines in the poem convey "a terrible and malicious beauty":

> Ou dansent, sans vouloir danser, pauvres sonnettes . . .

> Je goûte à votre insu des plaisirs clandestins . . .

and Proust concludes:

> The truth is, I think, that Baudelaire's poems were so strong, so vigorous, so lovely, that he overstepped the limits without realizing what he was doing. He wrote, on the subject of these miserable little old women, lines which, for sheer vitality, have never been equalled in the French language. But it no more occurred to him to soften the sharp edge of his phraseology, so as not to turn the knife in the wound of those already on the point of death, than it occurred to Beethoven, imprisoned in his deafness and intent on writing the *Ninth Symphony*, that the music was not uniformly suited to the capabilities of the human voice, with the result that, when sung, it always sounds slightly out of tune.[58]

This statement can perhaps be applied in a larger sense to Baudelaire. Baudelaire, seeing cruelty and suffering inextricable from the structure of human life, and wishing not to soften his treatment of it, gave it back in verse essentially unchanged. This accounts for the fact that in some of his most "licentious" poems violence and pathos remain coexistent, and that a poem as abhorrent as *Une Charogne* is for Baudelaire but an "objective correlative" for the ugliness of life and its decomposition. Hence the apparent impassivity, the cruelty, which is, as Professor Hubert observes,[59] a way in which certain artists, including Proust, confront (or affront) the spectacle of life. The same thing is true of *Bénédiction*, which Proust analyzes in *Contre Sainte-Beuve* along with *Les Petites Vieilles*, commenting particularly on the pictorial rather than emotive beauty of the images taken from Catholic theology.[60] Here is the way Proust sums up to his mother this particular impassivity of Baudelaire:

> Cruel he is, in his poetry, with a cruelty that is linked with an infinite degree of sensibility. His hardness is all the more astonishing because one gets the impression that he, too, has felt the sufferings that he describes and presents in so unmoved a fashion, that he has felt them in the very fibers of his being. Certain it is that in his wonderful poem, *Les Petites Vieilles,* there is not a single one of those old women's pains that has escaped him. [61]

The basic difference in attitude toward human beings between Baudelaire and Hugo also accounts for an essential disparity in the way in which the two poets treat the theme of love. Proust admits that in this respect Hugo is superior. Baudelaire's treatment of love has its peculiarities, since it tends to be fetishistic, occasionally sadistic (*La Chevelure, Le Balcon,* and *Chant d'automne* are cases in point); love in Baudelaire's poetry gravitates toward *volupté* or *immondicité*. These two conceptions of love are interchangeable, having sterility as a common denominator. This explains, perhaps, Baudelaire's interest in sterile love, his fascination with Lesbianism (Gomorrha) — and of course, Proust's interest in Baudelaire's Gomorrha. Nor is it surprising to find Proust's emphasis on the centrality of Gomorrha in the scheme of *Les Fleurs du Mal,* by recalling its original title *Les Lesbiennes*. (It should be added that this title was in Baudelaire's mind in the year 1846 and was replaced by *Les Limbes* in 1848.) Proust concludes that though the title *Les Lesbiennes* had its relevance originally, the final title of *Les Fleurs du Mal* to cover the wider range of subject matter and emotion was a felicitous one, particularly since it preserves the centrality of Gomorrha in Baudelaire's scheme of things:

> The reader's emotion is still further increased when he learns that these poems were not merely included on equal terms with the others, but were, for their author, actually the key pieces, so that he at first intended to call the volume, not *Les Fleurs du Mal,* but *Les Les-*

biennes. The more appropriate and more general title, *Les Fleurs du Mal* — a title which, today, we can no longer tease out from the history of French literature — was not found by Baudelaire at all, but was suggested to him by Babou. The collection includes a great deal more than lesbians, though it does not exclude them, because, seen in the light of Baudelaire's moral, no less than of his aesthetic, standards, they are essentially *Fleurs du Mal*.[62]

At this point Proust quite naturally thinks of Vigny. Quoting the epigraph for his own *Sodome et Gomorrhe* from Vigny's *Colère de Samson*, "la Femme aura Gomorrhe et l'homme aura Sodome," and continuing with the following lines from the same poem,

Et se jetant de loin un regard irrité,
Les deux sexes mourront chacun de son côté,

he distinguishes this notion of the irreconcilability of the sexes from Baudelaire's conception of Gomorrha as a sort of ritual:

Car Lesbos entre tous m'a choisi sur la terre
Pour chanter le secret de ses vierges en fleurs
Et je fus dès l'enfance admis au noir mystère
Des rires effrénés mêlés aux sombres pleurs . . .
(*Lesbos*)

Besides the fact that the phrase "vierges en fleurs" recalls Proust's own "jeunes filles en fleurs" and their admission to the rites of Lesbos, his commentary shows here how closely affiliated his own work is to that of Baudelaire's:

This "connection" between Sodom and Gomorrha is what, in the final section of my novel . . . I have shown in the person of a brutish creature, Charles Morel (it is usually to brutish creatures that this part is allotted). But it would seem that Baudelaire cast himself for it, and looked on the role as a privilege. It would be intensely interesting to know why he chose to assume it, and how well he acquitted himself. What is comprehensible in a Charles Morel becomes profoundly mysterious in the author of *Les Fleurs du Mal*.[63]

This passage not only shows the affinity between Proust's world and Baudelaire's but also warrants the conclusion that certain portions of *A la recherche du temps perdu*, especially *Sodome et Gomorrhe*, are Baudelairean rather than Balzacian.

In *Le Temps retrouvé* Proust includes Baudelaire in the list of predecessors whose treatment of memory is analogous to his own. Here Baudelaire is accorded a place along with Chateaubriand and Gérard de Nerval:

> And finally, in Baudelaire, these reminiscences are still more frequent and obviously less incidental and therefore, in my opinion, decisive. Here it is the poet himself who, with more variety and more indolence, purposely seeks in the odor of a woman's hair or her breast, for example, inspiring resemblances which shall evoke for him
>
> *L'azur du ciel immense et rond*
>
> and
>
> *Un port rempli de flammes et de mâts.*[64]

The important difference between Baudelaire's and Proust's treatment of memory — as Proust realizes — lies in the observation that for Baudelaire the reminiscence is more or less voluntary, or at least evoked at will ("Je sais l'art d'évoquer les minutes heureuses" — *Le Balcon*). It is limited, of course, to sense experiences, primarily tactual and olfactory ones, and tends to create reminiscences of the sea or of tropical islands, centering about the nostalgia for a voluptuous indolence. But primarily these memories are *accessible*, that is, they may be evoked under certain given circumstances to establish contact with a transcendent universe. It is not quite the same with Proust: his reminiscences are involuntary, completely fortuitous, and show no predilection for any particular sensory experience. He calls Baudelaire's kind of evocation "static," as distinct from his own: "In Baudelaire, reminiscence has a static quality; it is already in existence when the poem opens ('Quand les deux yeux fermés,' etc., 'O toison moutonnant,' etc., etc.)."[65] "Static" is perhaps a misleading word here; it might have been better to say that the particular situations at the beginning of these two poems are "pregnant" with *souvenirs*; it is merely up to the poet to set the *correspondances* into motion. On the other hand, in

Proust any object or fragment of experience is potentially charged with reminiscences.

Nevertheless, despite certain differences in their conception of the affective memory, both writers place the highest value upon the *souvenir* as a means of getting outside of Time. Proust's affinity with Baudelaire's sense of Time leads him to observe: "His world is a strange dividing up of time, in which only the red-letter days are shown. This explains such frequent expressions as, '*Si quelque soir*,' etc."[66] This "sectioning of time"—although Proust does not specifically say so—adds to the "static" quality of *Les Fleurs du Mal*. Similarly, he observes that Baudelaire's interiors are drab, ill-lit—as if only part of them were visible. And then, at a privileged moment this interior is transfigured:

> Baudelaire's world is a place to which, at rare moments, a perfumed breeze from the outer air brings refreshment and a sense of magic, sometimes on the wings of memory (*La Chevelure*, etc.), sometimes in actual fact, thanks to those porticoes which are so frequently described in his poems "ouverts sur des cieux inconnus" (*La Mort* [*des pauvres*]) or "que les soleils marins teignaient de mille feux" (*La Vie antérieure*).[67]

The situation remains static (the word seems more appropriate here); the porticoes emphasize this stateliness, the reminiscences only transpose it to a brightly-lit tropical atmosphere:

> Je vois se dérouler des rivages heureux
> Qu'éblouissent les feux d'un soleil monotone.
> (*Parfum exotique*)

It might be added that even here the dazzle of the sun is made static by the adjective *monotone*; and in this languorous *ambiance* a sort of timeless essence reigns—the "Luxe, calme et volupté" of *L'Invitation au voyage*.

In seeking an explanation for this particular sectioning of time, Proust remarks that for a sick artist, such as Baudelaire, Time is particularly crucial. Replying to Valéry's statement in *Eupalinos*, "Enlightened deeds shorten the course of nature. Thus one can say with all possible assurance that an artist is worth a thousand or a hundred thousand centuries, or indeed even more,"[68] Proust exclaims that such artists

> may . . . represent a thousand centuries when compared to the blind working of nature, but they do not — men like Voltaire, for instance — constitute in themselves an infinity of time by comparison with an invalid, a Baudelaire, better still, a Dostoievsky, who, in thirty years, between their crises of epilepsy, or whatever, can create work of which a long line of healthy writers could not have produced a single word.[69]

Here one hears, of course, the personal voice of the author, who himself belongs to this lineage. The same idea is voiced by the Narrator in the novel. The sick — or neurotic — artist is forced to make his moments of comparative health, or absence of suffering, particularly fruitful, channeling his nervous energy into the frenzied act of creation. It is needless to carry this discussion too far into Proust's or Baudelaire's creative activity. Both writers, as well as a host of others, have made the issue crucial to any evaluation of modern literature. The important fact remains that the physically or nervously unstable artist has a totally different attitude toward Time: he is forced to struggle with it at every moment of his life; this explains Proust's appreciation of Baudelaire's struggle. A corollary to this struggle is the struggle with death. Proust compares Hugo (a "healthy" poet) with Baudelaire:

> Hugo was forever talking of death, but with the detachment of a great eater, a great sensualist. It may, alas! be that only when one carries consciously in the body the dull weight of death, only when, like Baudelaire, one is threatened with aphasia, can one achieve the genuine lucidity of suffering, the religious tone, which sounds in the Satanic poems:
>
> Il faut que le gibier paye le vieux chasseur
> . . . Avez-vous donc pu croire, hypocrites surpris
> Qu'on se moque du maître et qu'avec lui l'on triche,
> Et qu'il soit naturel de recevoir deux prix,
> D'aller au ciel et d'être riche.
>
> [*L'Imprévu*]

One must, perhaps, have felt the mortal weariness that is death's immediate herald, to be able to write music on that theme sweeter than any that Victor Hugo could ever have achieved:

> Et qui refait le lit des gens pauvres et nus.
> [*La Mort des pauvres*][70]

Proust knew from his own experience that it is one thing to poetize about death, and another to speak of death movingly, sincerely. Only a man who has himself experienced the threat of death can write *La Mort des pauvres* ("C'est la mort qui console, hélas! et qui fait vivre") — not Hugo, not even in his later poetry, where Death becomes a rhetorical device to propel man from one level of incarnation to another (*La Bouche d'ombre*). One might say that Baudelaire, Proust, and Dostoevski are artists whose physical and spiritual condition forced them to "cohabit" with the idea of death; whereas Hugo shouts about death, knowing it is not within hearing distance, with the "detachment of a heavy eater," as Proust so delightfully puts it.

After discussing Baudelaire in the "A propos de Baudelaire" essay, Proust turns to a consideration of some of Baudelaire's contemporaries, giving brief mention to Sully Prudhomme and more extended treatment to Leconte de Lisle.

In Sully Prudhomme he admires "a pensive brevity" [71] which is only occasionally moving. In the poem *La Voie lactée*, for example, the beginning is good:

> Aux étoiles j'ai dit un soir
> Vous ne me semblez pas heureuses

but the next two lines have "quelque chose d'affreux":

> Vos lueurs dans l'infini noir
> Ont des tendresses douloureuses.[72]

The same unsavory mixture is pointed out in the poem *Les Vieilles Maisons*:

> Je n'aime pas les maisons neuves
> Elles ont l'air indifférent

followed by

> Les vieilles ont l'air de veuves
> Qui se souviennent en pleurant.[73]

Proust recognized that Sully Prudhomme was out of fashion, but considered certain of his lines charming and liked to quote them, often in a sentimental context.[74] Still, the brief discussion of Sully Prudhomme in the Baudelaire essay amounts to no more than a tacit bow of recognition. Proust knew that no amount of resuscitation would successfully bring Sully Prudhomme back to life; consequently he gives up the effort and turns to Leconte de Lisle.

> One man, and one man alone (before the coming of the Parnassians and the Symbolists) continued, though in a very much diminished form, the tradition of the Great Masters — Leconte de Lisle.[75]

Leconte de Lisle was primarily reacting against a laxity in the use of language for which the Romantics had been responsible, Proust observes. Yet Leconte de Lisle is not so different from his predecessors. To illustrate the similarity, Proust quotes the line

> La neige tombe en paix sur tes épaules nues

from Alfred de Musset's *La Coupe et les lèvres* and

> L'aube aux flancs noirs des monts marchait d'un pied vermeil

from his favorite poem by Leconte de Lisle, *La Fontaine aux lianes.*

> Leconte de Lisle set himself to purify the language. He showed no mercy to flat and stupid metaphors, and pruned them drastically. For all that, he could make use of the phrase (and with very happy effect) *aile du vent*, and elsewhere could speak of *rire amoureux du vent; gouttes de cristal de la rosée; robe de feu de la terre; coupe du soleil; cendre du soleil* and *vol de l'illusion.*[76]

Proust does not explain the "very happy effect" but it becomes clear from reading a number of Leconte de Lisle's poems that his use of these metaphors makes sense, since he uses them precisely, rather than vaguely or rhetorically, as the Romantics had done. Certainly in the landscape poems *Midi* and *La Fontaine aux lianes*, in which a number of these metaphors occur, such images account for the plasticity of the whole and are often used to steep that particular portion of the word-canvas in an intense monochrome.

In connection with Leconte de Lisle's plasticity, it is worth remembering that Bloch, in *A la recherche*, serves as the spokesman of Marcel's boyhood acquaintances who fell under the spell of Gautier and Leconte de Lisle. The youthful adulation of poetic impassivity appears to have been shared by young Proust; at least he records Jean Santeuil's adolescent preference of Leconte de Lisle and Verlaine over Corneille, Racine, and La Fontaine:

> . . . The great spreading poems of Leconte de Lisle which juggled with Time and put into words of shattering power the conception of Life as a dream, and the nothingness of things, were more alive for him, more profound, more stimulating than those classical works from which such mental unease is absent.[77]

Of course, even in *Jean Santeuil* this illusion — which, too, is a romantic carry-over very similar to the one Proust pointed out above — has been dispelled. Just as in *A la recherche* Bloch's aesthetic snobbery is ridiculed, so in *Jean Santeuil* an earlier incarnation of Bloch, the poet Rustinlor, utters insipid remarks about the excellence of Leconte de Lisle over and above Hugo and Racine. Speaking, for instance, of *Les Contemplations*, Rustinlor perorates:

> "H'm, Hugo at his worst . . . much inferior to his plastic and wholly . . . [external] compositions. If it comes to that . . .[external] poetry is always infinitely superior to poetry that sets out to *mean* something. Leconte de Lisle is superior to Daddy Hugo just because he is not overburdened with tiresome metaphysical considerations . . ."[78]

In spite of such eccentricities as the lengthy epithets applied to animals (the tiger = "Seigneur rayé," the shark = "sinistre rôdeur des steppes de la mer,") and even to inanimate objects (high noon is "Roi des Etés"), Proust finds in Leconte de Lisle "a new and delicious *spring* of poetry, a feeling of freshness, brought, no doubt, from the tropical countries in which he had lived."

> Leconte de Lisle had lived there, and caught and tasted every aspect of the scene. When he speaks of watercourses, we feel that his use of such words as *germer*, *circuler*, *filtrer*, is something more than merely rhetorical. Even so simple a word as *gravier* is not introduced at random.[79]

And for this reason poems like *La Ravine Saint-Gilles* and *La Fontaine aux lianes* retain a freshness that derives from their having been "reserved" by the poet for himself and observed with a love of detail — the same love of detail that Proust himself showered on places and things close to him.

The Symbolists are not discussed. One wishes that there were more on Mallarmé than an appreciative reference to the poet in a letter of 1892 to Madame Straus in which Proust quotes *Soupir*, commenting that these verses, even though they are Mallarmé's, are clear and that "the clarity does not shatter their mystery."[80] On the subject of *fin de siècle* poetry Proust is more explicit. On July 15, 1896, he published an essay in the *Revue blanche* entitled "Contre l'obscurité" (included in the posthumous *Chroniques*). This article defined his attitude toward the kind of symbolism rampant in the 1890's — the excessively esoteric, decadent type of "deliquescent" verse that went under various names and appeared in various short-lived "little magazines." In view of the fact that Proust grew up in that atmosphere — and *Les Plaisirs et les jours* shows the influence — it is interesting to note that he vigorously condemned "obscurity" at about the time when his first book actually came out. The tone of the essay reveals his malaise at having to rebuke his own generation for an esotericism that, to his own mind, was totally incompatible with genuine poetry; and he begins and ends apologetically by saying that the criticism offered in the essay would sound more authoritative in the mouth of an older man.

"Contre l'obscurité" sounds like a preliminary draft of Proust's aesthetics and actually marks the first stage in his search for criteria of literary excellence. It is also an indication of his progress in overcoming the *préciosité* of *Les Plaisirs et les jours* and looks forward to (or possibly coincides with, at least in its initial stages) the reflections on literature in *Jean Santeuil*, and the more concise and better consolidated remarks on literary art inspired by Ruskin. Proust's method here is not to condemn symbolism wholesale, but merely the affectations and obfuscations that came to characterize the Symbolist movement. To deny the lasting influence of symbolism on Proust would be incorrect; many of the passages of *Jean Santeuil*, especially nature descriptions, even certain passages in *A la recherche*, are in the best symbolist ("superimpressionist," as Crémieux put it) [81] manner, but Proust went far beyond symbolism. Nevertheless, it was evident to Proust as early as 1896 that the business of the writer was to be as clear and precise as possible, even if the effort required a recourse to certain new techniques that might at first *seem* obscure to his readers. It is this dilemma whose nature he is trying to define in "Contre l'obscurité."

The essay begins with a denial of the assertion current in 1896, that "today everybody has talent." On the contrary, replies Proust, this "talent" is little more than technical skill:

> Indeed I believe that poetry, like all other mysteries, has never been completely penetrated without initiation and even without election. Although talent has never been very widespread, it seems that rarely has there been less than nowadays. Of course, if talent consists of a certain rhetoric which is in the air and shows people how to write "free verse," as formerly it showed people how to write "Latin verses," verses having a stock supply of "princesses, melancholies," "leaning upon their elbows" or "smiling," or a supply of "beryls"

for everybody's use, then it might be said that nowadays everybody is talented. But those things are only useless shells, full of sound but devoid of content, pieces of rotten wood or rusty iron thrown ashore. Anybody is welcome to pick them up, if he chooses, since the past generation did not take them along with it. Yet what is one to do with rotten wood, which is often all that remains of a beautiful old fleet — the unrecognized likeness of Chateaubriand or Hugo . . . [82]

Out of this situation the younger symbolists have produced a double obscurity — an obscurity of ideas and images and an obscurity of grammar. Obscurity of this sort is not justifiable; it is not identical with the quality that makes all new works hard to approach or the strangeness that made Racine's and Hugo's first works difficult for their readers. Nor is it the obscurity that attaches to new and complicated philosophies; for the latter is of a totally different sort,

thoroughly worth investigating but for which it is despicable to make the inquiry impossible by using obscure language or style.

Since the poet does not appeal to our logical faculties, he cannot make use of the privilege that every profound philosopher enjoys — that of seeming obscure at the outset. [83]

In other words, literature and philosophy are not interchangeable; they originate in different sources; their appeals move along different channels. This does not prevent certain works from being philosophical, but this result is not achieved by the philosophical method:

Macbeth is, in its own way, a philosophy, not because of its philosophical method, but because it has a sort of instinctive power. The core of such a work, like the core of life itself, which the work reflects, undoubtedly remains unknowable even to a mind that probes it more and more deeply.[84]

The trouble with the "jeune école," Proust notes in another place, is that they have nothing to say because they do not think. Why, he wonders, does not someone of their own generation bring this sad fact to their attention?

> Never has the sense of duty been so feeble, the contempt for tradition so complete. Since the intelligent young men are not concerned about a moral life, since they do not work, since they read nothing but contemporary short stories, they learn their rhetoric from Mendès or Moréas and take from it a varnish which is as external as the varnish which the schoolboys of bygone days used to take from the classics, which no longer fools anyone. Will the vogue of the good student in contemporary literature last much longer? That would be unfortunate indeed.[85]

It is interesting to see Proust fancying himself the spokesman of tradition and "concern for the moral life" against his contemporaries. More important, he cautioned his fellow writers against facile imitation and the easy acquisition of a modern polish. In this context the mention of the neoclassicist Moréas may seem strange at first, since Moréas was certainly respectful of one kind of tradition. But in *Contre Sainte-Beuve* Proust states flatly that "archaicism is made up of many insincerities," one of the major ones being the tendency to copy some external trait from the ancients, one which the ancients were not aware of, because their style did not "have that ancient ring" to it. A contemporary example of this tendency, which results in something like pastiche-writing, is Moréas. Proust grants that his *Eriphyle* has charm, but he adds that this is its only quality and hides but inadequately the emptiness of the work and the absence of originality. Moréas' famous *Stances* "are saved only because their incompleteness and a kind of banality and lack of staying power in them are intentional and since in any case they would be present unintentionally, the poet's shortcomings actually are in conspiracy with his purposes." And when Moréas does want to say something, he produces no more than the inanity of the poem "Ne dites pas: la vie est un joyeux festin." [86]

Obscurity, Proust maintains in "Contre l'obscurité," must not be pursued as a result of private interests — since it is the poet's function to make obscure sensations clear; nor out of a desire to safeguard one's work from the "profanum vulgus" — which does not tamper with works of art anyway. ("If the mob could touch it, it would not be the mob."[87]) Instead, it is the poet's function to use the language as he finds it. This does not prevent the symbolists from exploiting the hidden resources of their language, but it should discourage esoteric language and neologisms.

The symbolists will be the first to grant us that how much magic each word, taken by itself or in its harmony with other words, retains from its origins or from the grandeur of its past, it has on our imagination and sensibility a power of evocation which is at least as great as its power of strict denotation. These age-old mysterious affinities between our mother tongue and our sensibility — as distinguished from a conventional language, such as a foreign tongue — constitute a sort of latent music which the poet can cause to resound in us with unparalleled sweetness. By rejuvenating a word which he uses in its old meaning, by making forgotten harmonies vibrate between two disjunct images, he allows us at any moment to inhale with pleasure the perfume of our native soil. Therein lies for us the native charm of French speech . . .[88]

This poetic creed of Proust is basic to his entire criticism of the poetry of the nineteenth century — and by extension to all literature, since for Proust poetry and prose are but diverse aspects of literary art, and since every century has its own classics. In the great poets of the nineteenth century he appreciates the ability to treat their language with love and insight, drawing new effects from its endless resources; an ability to render experience in terms of well-conceived poetic images; a classical sense of form in which the framework serves to hold in check the brimming content; and an awareness of the mystery that resides behind each discovery in nature or in the sphere of intellectual activity — a mystery that must be preserved or deepened because it is the very essence of life.

The nature of that mystery was defined at about the same time, or somewhat later, in *Jean Santeuil* when Proust, attempting to understand the creative side of the Viscountess Gaspard de Réveillon, calls poetry

> the commemoration of our inspired moments which in themselves are often a sort of commemoration of all that our being has left of itself in moments past and gone, the concentrated essence of ourselves which we exude without realizing that we are doing so, which a perfume smelled in that past time, a remembered light shining into our room, will suddenly bring back so vividly, that it fills us with a species of intoxication, so that we become completely indifferent to what is usually called "real life," in which it never visits us. [89]

This quotation shows the close bond between poetry and the recovery of the "privileged moment": Proust's art as well as the aesthetic ideal which inspired it are here manifest in a nutshell. (For the sentence already has the typically Proustian "tension," building up to the word "intoxication," and then discharging its tension quickly in the word "indifferent.")

Whenever Proust felt that a poet had in some such manner recaptured his essence, he felt that the mystery of art had been consummated. He admired Baudelaire's chiseled shapes which contain, in condensed form, so much thought and sentiment; Hugo's grandeur that reflects the rhythm of lived experience; Vigny's tensions, and Leconte de Lisle's refusal to be rhetorical. After all, these qualities also had their place in the creative personality of the author of *A la recherche du temps perdu.*

2. Balzac, inventor

Despite his sense of filiation with certain poets of the nineteenth century, Proust's keenest concern is with the great masters of realistic fiction. Here the name of Balzac looms large in his critical writings. First of all, the two chapters on Balzac in *Contre Sainte-Beuve* (which, except for a few small omissions, had been published previously as *Le Balzac de Monsieur de Guermantes*) illuminate the author of *La Comédie humaine* from many aspects; then there is the brilliant Balzac pastiche which sets the pace for the subsequent eight pastiches; and, finally, there are numerous allusions to Balzac in *A la recherche du temps perdu*, both by the Narrator and by various characters. The relationship of Proust to Balzac has been studied, and

Proust's debt to Balzac assessed, first somewhat summarily by Pierre Abraham,[1] and more recently in a perceptive essay by Harry Levin.[2] The introduction, by Ramon Fernandez, to the *Répertoire* which compares Proust's social world to Balzac's should be listed here too.[3] This essay is appropriately placed, inasmuch as the most Balzacian treatment of Proust's novel occurs in the *Répertoire des personnages de "A la Recherche du temps perdu,"* which was inspired by the Balzacian *Répertoire* of Cerfberr and Christophe.[4]

In attempting to assess his debt to his great precursor, Proust scrutinized Balzac from several viewpoints, letting Balzac as it were, look at himself; letting Sainte-Beuve criticize him; making Balzac a sort of patron saint of the world of the Guermantes; in *Jean Santeuil*, the novelist C., whom Proust utilizes as an intermediary between himself and the hero of the novel, voices certain opinions about Balzac; and finally, Proust passes judgment on him either through Marcel, destined to become a novelist, or directly, through himself as moralist-critic. This pattern of multiple viewpoints enables one to view Balzac critically in a typically Proustian fashion.

In an extraordinary passage of *La Prisonnière* the Narrator, in connection with certain reflections on Wagner's art, describes the nineteenth century as an era of self-contemplation, which added a new exterior beauty to its works by imposing upon them a unity which these works did not actually contain:

> But notwithstanding the richness of these works in which the contemplation of nature has its place by the side of action, by the side of persons who are something more than proper names, I thought how markedly, all the same, these works participate in that quality of being — albeit marvelously — always incomplete, which is the peculiarity of all the great works of the nineteenth century; with which the greatest writers of that century have stamped their books, but, watching themselves at work as though they were at once author and critic, have derived from this self-contemplation a novel beauty, exterior and superior to the work itself, imposing upon it retrospectively a unity, a greatness which it does not possess.[5]

As examples of this "self-contemplation" Proust points out *La Comédie humaine*, *La Légende des siècles*, Michelet's *Bible de l'humanité*, in addition to Wagner's works; naturally the examples could have been multiplied. The new cyclical and leitmotiv devices in music are further examples of imposing form from without. Romantic nostalgia for unity, the yearning to fuse the divided soul of the Romantics, led writers in the direction of new syntheses. Proust, as a novelist whose work is intended to project a total vision, belongs to this lineage.

The problem that arises here is that of the validity of the synthesis. What the classics did *naturally* — express a more or less uniform view of their experience — without amalgamation or synthesis, the moderns often did deliberately, sometimes even retrospectively. In the latter case, the writer tended to resemble a sorcerer, who convinced his readers that the *disjecta membra* really make one whole. This is true of Wagner, when he made four operas into a tetralogy, and it is true of Balzac, when he saw that his novels were actually part of one world. Proust expresses it this way:

> . . . Wagner . . . must have felt something of the same exhilaration as Balzac, when, casting over his works the eye at once of a stranger and of a father, finding in one the purity of Raphael, in another the simplicity of the Gospel, he suddenly decided, as he shed a retrospective illumination upon them, that they would be better brought together in a cycle in which the same characters would reappear, and added to his work, in this act of joining it together, a stroke of the brush, the last and the most sublime. A unity that was ulterior, not artificial, otherwise it would have crumbled into dust like all the other systematisations of mediocre writers who with the elaborate assistance of titles and sub-titles give themselves the appearance of having pursued a single and transcendent design. Not fictitious, perhaps indeed all the more real for being ulterior, for being born of a moment of enthusiasm when it is discovered to exist among fragments which need only to be joined together.[6]

Proust sees that the process of discovery is more or less intuitive — a sudden recognition of a profound relationship between isolated parts. In Balzac the discovery of the all-embracing framework is the more astonishing in view of the fact that Balzac's judgment of his own works was anything but genuinely critical ("the purity of Raphael," "the simplicity of the Gospels"). Nevertheless, critical criteria are absent from this autocontemplation. Proust does not tell us here how to distinguish the artificial systems of mediocre writers from the kind of unity whereby good writers add another dimension to their work. All that needs to be said is that in this case — as in the other works which he groups as representative of the nineteenth century search for "totality" — the whole is greater than the sum of its parts, a fact which Henry James recognized as well when he said ". . . what is most interesting in Balzac is not the achievement but the attempt."[7]

The second perspective which Proust finds helpful in his effort to arrive at the essence of Balzac is that of Sainte-Beuve. Whereas Balzac had been wrong as far as details were concerned and right with respect to the whole of *La Comédie humaine*, Sainte-Beuve is, in Proust's opinion, usually wrong with respect to his contemporaries. "One of the writers of his day whom Sainte-Beuve misunderstood is Balzac."[8] He points out that Sainte-Beuve neither showed a just appreciation of Balzac's style, nor did he comprehend the significance of the *retour des personnages*, and in his essays on Balzac he commits his usual errors of talking about matters that have no critical relevance to a study of Balzac's works. "Dilettantism has never created anything."[9] Proust's detailed grievances will be taken up in a later chapter. For the moment it is sufficient to say that Sainte-Beuve's perspective on Balzac is inadequate for Proust in all respects; Proust is interested not only in clarifying what is genuinely artistic in Balzac's work, but also in establishing his own roots in the past. As Proust's essay on Sainte-Beuve progresses, Balzac's stature as a great novelist grows, possibly beyond his actual dimensions, to become a sort of ideal novelist, or, as Fallois puts it in his preface to *Le Balzac de Monsieur de Guermantes*:

> Occasionally, especially at the beginning of his work, Proust remembers his task as a critic and analyzes Balzac himself. But before long, bypassing his subject, or reacting against it, he betrays different aspirations. Thus, by comparing Flaubert's style with Balzac's, referring to the return of characters, to cyclical composition, he outlines the portrait of the ideal novelist, and Balzac becomes merely a testing-ground, a pretext for an advance "essay" of the theory underlying his own work.[10]

This shifting of viewpoint to which Fallois alludes here, the tendency of the analyzing novelist to vacillate between criticism and creation, is altogether characteristic of Proust: he was, among other things, trying to clarify his notions about form and style. If he had never written his novel, his critical essays would now be regarded as analyses and criticisms on highly interesting aspects of certain writers, with no attempt made by Proust to "embrace" the writer wholly; the novel places his critical work into a different focus — that of a necessary apprenticeship and a valuable literary exercise to sharpen his own ability to deal with literary problems. Balzac actually exceeds his role of master for Proust: he becomes a mediator.

Since the critic in Proust is constantly tempted to turn into the novelist, one need, conversely, not be surprised to find echoes of Balzac in *A la recherche du temps perdu*; the link between the two worlds is provided by the Guermantes, who are prefigured in "Le Balzac de Monsieur de Guermantes." The chapter is the first point of orientation for Proust's third perspective on Balzac, that of looking at the author of *La Comédie humaine* through the eyes of the characters in *A la recherche*. The name of Balzac is inextricably linked with the Guermantes family: they read him, they have a certain esoteric insight into his "hidden" intentions: they *possess* Balzac, keep him alive; and by a shrewd device of the novelist-psychologist, Proust lets Balzac possess the Guermantes, even to the point where they unconsciously enact certain scenes and certain characters in Balzac.

Character analysis by means of examining an individual's

library is a favorite one with Proust, and "Le Balzac de Monsieur de Guermantes" begins, characteristically, with an inspection of Monsieur de Guermantes' library, where one finds "Balzac complete, in gilded calf-skin binding with green leather labels . . ." [11] Fallois observes here:

> This method of getting at the truth of a character, of conducting an inquiry about him by first inspecting his library, or listening to his conversation, contains the nucleus of one of the most important laws of Proustian psychology.[12]

Proust's allusions to books in Swann's library at various points of *A la recherche* bear out this remark. "Le Balzac de Monsieur de Guermantes" continues with what can be regarded as a summary of the Guermantes' attitude toward their favorite novelist:

> Naturally, Balzac, like all other novelists, and even to a greater extent than they, has had a type of reader who did not seek for literary values in his novels, but simply read him because he was interested in his imagination and his observation. The faults in Balzac's style did not act as deterrents . . .[13]

If their interest in Balzac were simply sociological or historical, there would be no excuse for dwelling on their point of view. In this category belong Charlus' compliment on Albertine's dress by a comparison with the robe of the Princesse de Cadignan, and his pride in being acquainted with the actual garden in which the Princess used to walk.[14] Transpositions of this sort have a tendency to lend solidity to the Guermantes and to define the parallels between *A la recherche* and the *Comédie humaine*. As a direct consequence of this literary family tie between Proust's and Balzac's *mondes*, the Guermantes have a certain recondite knowledge of Balzacian details: Monsieur de Guermantes can tell you where each landscape and so on comes from. Or the Guermantes take a particular delight in quoting from the less-known works of Balzac.[15] But on a much higher level is the appreciation of Balzac by a Guermantes with taste — Monsieur de Charlus, who does not appear in "Le Balzac de Monsieur de

Guermantes." As a number of excerpts given in Maurois' biography of Proust indicate,[16] Charlus does appear in the early *Cahiers* as Monsieur de Norpois — a curious step in the evolution of the Baron. In an early sketch of a conversation with the Narrator, this Norpois makes the following statement:

"There can be no doubt that a work like *Splendeurs et misères des courtisanes*, for example, does reveal the underlying reality of a great truth, and I, for one, can never read certain passages in that book without feelings of admiration. But I defy you, and with you three-quarters of its readers, to guess what that truth is." [17]

Norpois does not reveal the substructure of truth of *Splendeurs et misères* but Monsieur de Charlus in *Sodome et Gomorrhe* clarifies the allusion. Expressing a preference for the miniatures of *La Comédie humaine*, such as *Le Curé de Tours*, as well as for the "grandes fresques," such as the series *Les Illusions perdues* and *Splendeurs et misères des courtisanes*, he explains:

". . . It's wonderful. The scene where Carlos Herrera asks the name of the château he is driving past, and it turns out to be Rastignac, the home of the young man he used to love. And then the abbé falls into a reverie which Swann once called, and very aptly, the *Tristesse d'Olympio* of paederasty. And the death of Lucien! I forgot who the man of taste was who, when he was asked what event in his life had most distressed him, replied: 'The death of Lucien de Rubempré in *Splendeurs et Misères*.' " [18]

Charlus' "man of taste" is Oscar Wilde, who had caught the homosexual undertones in Vautrin-Herrera's behavior. Charlus could have gone on to enlarge his list by citing Vautrin's relationship to Theodore Calvi in the concluding section of *Splendeurs et misères* ("La Dernière Incarnation de Vautrin"). The element of homosexuality no longer appears in undertones there; in the passage in which the argot expression "tante" is explained by means of an anecdote involving Lord Durham, it becomes explicit for one moment:

The director . . . pointed out certain premises, with a gesture of disgust.

"I am not taking your lordship there," he said, "for those are the *aunts'* quarters" . . .

"Eh!" exclaimed Lord Durham, "and what's that?"

"The third sex, mylord." [19]

Proust, incidentally, planned originally to put a footnote quoting this passage at the point where the first homosexual episode occurred in *Sodome et Gomorrhe*.[20]

As the "fresco" *Illusions perdues — Splendeurs et misères* provides a convenient point of refuge into literature for both Charlus and Oscar Wilde, so *Les Secrets de la princesse de Cadignan* fulfills a similar function. "How profound, how heart-rending the evil reputation of Diane, who is afraid that the man she loves may hear of it" [21] exclaims Charlus, disguising only inadequately the fact that in his mind he has taken the place of D'Arthez.

A member of the Guermantes family who does not care for Balzac is the Marquise (as she is called in "Le Balzac de Monsieur de Guermantes") de Villeparisis. She asserts that Balzac's depiction of reality is inaccurate and finds his portrayal of society unauthentic. "First of all, he didn't move in society, he wasn't admitted to it, what could he have known about it?" [22] The snobbery has been retained in *A l'ombre des jeunes filles en fleurs*, where the Narrator comments, "She found fault with Balzac, whom she was surprised to see her nephews admire, for having pretended to describe a society 'in which he was never received' and of which his descriptions were wildly improbable." [23] Madame de Villeparisis, after all, is the type of reader who reads Balzac for the observations contained in his books. It is not surprising that she dislikes Balzac for his pessimism:

Moreover, this Balzac was a nasty person. There isn't a single high sentiment in his writings, there aren't any nice people. Reading him is always disagreeable, he never sees anything but the bad side of everything. Nothing but Evil. Even if he depicts a poor curate, he has always got to be unfortunate, and everybody has to be against him.[24]

The Marquise, as Proust reflects in "Le Balzac de Monsieur de Guermantes," belongs to a class of readers who visit the blame of an author's subject matter upon the author himself.

> When a writer reads a book, the exactness of the author's social observation and his pessimistic or optimistic bias are looked upon as "given" and not to be discussed, not even to be noticed. But for the "intelligent" readers, the fact that this or that is "false" or "sad" is like a personal fault on the part of the author. Such people are astounded, and quite delighted, to find the same flaw over and over again in every volume, even with exaggerations, as if the author had not been able to rid himself of it; and thus the author ends by becoming antipathetic to these readers, like a person devoid of judgment, tending toward morbidity, one on whom they had better not waste their time.[25]

This passage defines the difference between the ordinary readers of Balzac and the true Balzacians. The majority of readers are like the Guermantes, who, in spite of their intelligence, expect from an author a certain amount of literalness and reassurance. Consequently, the deficiency of their attitude toward a writer lies in their insistence on making him over in their own image and looking upon him primarily as a recorder of observed reality and as a balm against despondency.

The author C., who figures in the framework that serves to introduce the history of Jean Santeuil — it is *his* manuscript which the Narrator in *Jean Santeuil* purports to be preserving from oblivion — also pays tribute to Balzac's art. C. is used as an intermediary between Proust and his materials; he expresses, somewhat tentatively, Proust's opinions on Balzac. Voicing an appreciation of *Le Curé de village,* he says that it

> ". . . begins if I remember with some terrible crimes committed in the heart of a city, and then very gradually the characters become quite different people. They move into a land of hills, halt for a while in a village, and finish up at a great height in a sort of idyllic, Fénelon-like countryside, where the crimes of the heroine, who sets to work reclaiming the land and clearing away the poisonous growths, are ultimately pardoned."

When pressed for further commentary on Balzac, C. continues,

"There's nothing much I can tell you about Balzac. I know him very slightly. There are people who, when anybody asks them which of Balzac's books are the ones to read, reply, 'All!' It sounds rather simple-minded, but it's true. The full quality of Balzac is to be found not in this or that book, but in the whole lot. The individual novels read separately are not very good, though the characterization is always excellent. Strange, isn't it? I've never been able to hit on the explanation. The people you ought to get to talk about Balzac are those who know him well — and by that I don't necessarily mean literary blokes . . . There is something powerful about him, earthily powerful, but powerful all the same, which appeals to a great many people, though not very much to artists because few writers seem to work at a lower level. Still even artists have a weakness for him, which is odd. It's not by art that he produces his effects. The pleasure we get from him is, in some sort, adulterated. He wins us over, like life itself, by presenting us with an accumulation of badnesses. He is the very epitome of life." [26]

C. is here a considerable step beyond the Guermantes — "people who know him well" — and therefore closer to the Proust of "Aimer Balzac," although he seems more concerned with a definition of the double attraction of Balzac to the general reader and to the artist. The need to judge Balzac by the totality of *La Comédie humaine*, rather than by the individual novel, is stressed explicitly here and will become implicit in the "Sainte-Beuve et Balzac" chapter of *Contre Sainte-Beuve*. The other idea, which Proust was to elaborate subsequently, is the relationship of Balzac to life, to the "heap of wretched things" that resembles life, and the stylistic problem which Balzac encountered but did not solve when he attempted to render life through art.

Proust's own perspective on Balzac, then, is an extension of Charlus' and C.'s point of view. In a letter to René Boylesve (toward the end of 1917) he expresses the same sentiments which Charlus voices in *Sodome et Gomorrhe*:

My admiration for the immense fresco composed of *Illusions perdues* and *Splendeurs et misères* does not prevent me from placing *Le Curé de Tours* or *La Vieille Fille* or *La Fille aux yeux d'or* on as high a plane, and from equating the art that went into these miniatures with the art that produced the fresco.[27]

The inclusion of *La Fille aux yeux d'or* deserves a comment here. Its literary value is not equal to that of *Le Curé de Tours*, since the story exploits the "sensational" elements of the plot. But the subject matter of the novelette completes, in a small way, Proust's allusions to *Sodome* in *Les Illusions perdues* and in *Splendeurs et misères: La Fille aux yeux d'or* is the story of Henry de Marsay's attempt to reach the golden-eyed girl Paquita Valdès, who is being kept prisoner, not by a male rival, but by the Marquise de San-Réal. A curious chain of transpositions, *à la* Charlus, from Balzac to Proust's life to Proust's novel! Incidentally, the novelette is in Swann's library, and after Gilberte has become a part of the high society of the Guermantes, she begins her Balzacian apprenticeship by reading that very volume.[28]

The complexity of Proust's relationship to Balzac is as fascinating to follow as are Vautrin's successive incarnations. And indeed Vautrin himself has become incarnated, to some extent, in *A la recherche du temps perdu*. Fallois analyzes this phenomenon as follows:

> If Proust in his own manner retells a scene from *Illusions perdues*, such as the meeting of Lucien and Vautrin, he is doing it not so much for the sake of the pleasure of discovering beauties in Balzac that no one knows about, not even Balzac himself, but because he recognizes in Balzac's work some of his own ideas, sanctioned by time and success, concerning the novel and concerning style. Besides, his admiration is so great, and he is so convinced that he is the only person who has grasped the meaning of that scene, that a few years later he himself will re-create it — the meeting of Charlus and Morel on the platform of the Doncières station.[29]

The important word in this passage is "re-create": Proust does not copy the scene from Balzac, nor does he exactly transpose it: he reënacts it by means of his own characters. On another occasion, Proust had made a significant criticism of Balzac: "Balzac . . . whose novels are rarely without this kind of alloy [of imagination and historical fact], being a mixture of invention and of an actuality which has been too little sublimated . . ." [30] Proust believed that Balzac's subject matter was insufficiently digested and absorbed and appears to have felt the challenge to remake certain scenes. It is precisely for this reason that Balzac serves as the springboard that propels Proust from criticism (of Sainte-Beuve) to creation (most of the *Contre Sainte-Beuve* and leading straight into *A la recherche*).

A study of the influences of Balzac on Proust leads to interesting results, as Professor Levin's essay shows. For example, Charlus owes something both to Vautrin and to the Baron Hulot; at times he even identifies himself with Diane de Cadignan. These ramifications indicate that Proust's mind was so impregnated with Balzac that he could draw on the *Comédie humaine* at will. As Professor Levin notes concerning Charlus, "In the final analysis, the source is Proust himself," and the clue to the relationship of Proust to Balzac may be summarized as one of "elective affinities":

> It seems to me that the points of contact between the two writers are numerous enough to permit us to discern a significant relationship between them; on the other hand, they are also so far apart that their affinities must necessarily be elective.[31]

Whatever the similarities and differences between the two writers, they do belong to the same lineage of novelists. Balzac outlined his own program — retrospectively — in his Preface to the *Comédie humaine*; and in doing so, he also showed the way to subsequent novelists. His most important formulation lies in his conviction that "les Choses" are to be given equal rank with the men and women. The subsequent development of the novel can be read as an effort on the part of the novelists either to absorb, or to liberate themselves from, "les Choses," and Proust belongs to the category of the writers who attempt to mediate between the two extremes by a synthesis. In placing his emphasis on the *relation* between things and in making these relations the ordering principle of his artistic vision, he is claiming his right to inclusion in the family of all great artists, writers as well as painters. And as far as Proust is concerned, the critic's task is to analyze and make verbal the "quality of vision" which he discerns in a great artist. Between Chardin's still-life canvases and Balzac's "Choses" the only difference that interests Proust is the difference in the quality with which Chardin and Balzac see and re-create objects. In Balzac's case, the component parts of the vision are not always "fused," reality has been "trop peu transformée," as the quotation showed.

Often the first thing that strikes the casual reader of Balzac's novel is a certain vulgarity of style and of content: the surfaces are rough, the images are often crude, and the artificial and sensational elements are often too glaring; moreover, the impression which the reader gets from Balzac's letters, with their evidence of petty social ambitions and their naïve preoccupations with money and social rank, is one of vulgarity of sentiments. Such seems to have been the reaction of Proust's mother, or such it is at least at the opening of the chapter "Sainte-Beuve et Balzac." Proust does not excuse this latter characteristic of Balzac:

> The vulgarity of his sentiments is so great that life was unable to educate him . . . At the age at which Rastignac goes out into the world he has made the accomplishment of the lowest ambitions the goal of life, or at least has so entangled this goal with nobler goals that it is impossible to tell them apart.[32]

Nor is the vulgarity of Balzac's language excusable. It is "so all-pervasive that it even corrupts his vocabulary and makes him use expressions which would blemish the most casual conversation."[33] Examples which Proust cites are the expression used to describe the astonishment of D'Arthez, "It sent cold shivers down his back," and the expression used to characterize the feline aspect of certain ladies in society: "They would gladly have given *their prettiest slippers* to have some misfortune happen to him." And in conclusion, Proust observes

> And every time he wants to dissimulate his vulgarity, he assumes that superiority of vulgar people which is like certain sentimental poses, the way big fat stockbrokers in carriages put their fingers carefully on their foreheads. Then Balzac says "chère," or even "cara," "addio" for "adieu," etc.[34]

Proust could have chosen his examples with still greater severity. Balzac's affectations extend even farther: his naïve references to painters and musicians, in the vein of "only Leonardo could have painted her smile," or "only Raphael would have been worthy of painting that angelic face," or "she was as lovely as the loveliest courtesan that ever posed for Titian's Venus" are ludicrous, even though they contain (as Proust observes) a grain of truth. But somehow these comparisons and epithets add nothing to the descriptions at hand, being insufficiently precise and inadequately analytical. Professor Levin, in his monograph on Balzac, remarks that Balzac "is at his worst when he conjures with names or airily mentions works of art, in the naïve hope of enhancing his artistic tone."[35]

Just as Henry James realized that Balzac's style was the source of his strength and his weakness, containing "a certain quantity of everything, from immaculate gold to flagrant dross,"[36] Proust, too, felt that in the vulgarity of Balzac's own personality, and its reflection in literary terms, there lay a certain strength. Balzac's baser aspects, he observes, have simply not been transformed. "When you come right down to it, even in those among us who out of loftiness do not want to admit vulgar motives, but condemn them and strive to purify them, even in those people such motives may exist in a sublimated form."[37] This statement can also be regarded as a complement to the writer C. in *Jean Santeuil*, who asserted that Balzac appeals to the artist precisely because his art has the unpleasant texture of life itself. Balzac's inability to transmute vulgar ambitions into ambitions of a higher order, observes Proust, accounts for a peculiar strength in him which eventually offers the reader a reality which might be closed off to a more discriminating writer. Thus Eugène de Rastignac may be a tender lover when at bottom he is ruthlessly ambitious, and still his "reality" is not destroyed. The peculiar result of this individual strength of Balzac is, in Proust's opinion, that just as Balzac's vulgarities in his correspondence and in his novels are one and the same thing, the line of demarcation between Balzac the man and Balzac the writer becomes exceedingly tenuous — an observation which is further strengthened by the well-known fact that Balzac often treated his fictional characters as real. This attitude has its counterpart in *La Comédie humaine*, where Balzac is fond of mixing the real and the fictitious in enumerations of persons.

> This half-baked reality, too chimerical for life, too down-to-earth for literature, makes us often find pleasures in Balzac's literature which are hardly different from those we derive from life.[38]

This sense of semireality is for Proust one of the real achievements of Balzac, and will enable the author of *A la recherche* to make his transpositions without having to go through too many modulations. Proust, by the very criticism which he has just enunciated, shows himself already deeply enmeshed in the strange network which links him to Balzac. One is witnessing at this juncture the disappearance of the critic and the appearance of the novelist — the point at which Proust discovers Balzac's loose threads, only to wind them again after his own fashion. Fallois, referring to Proust's transpositions, characterizes this phenomenon as

> a very astonishing moment in Proustian creation: the little boy who loves books finds his heroes in real life, perpetuates them, makes up a sequel to their story — the moment when the critic becomes metamorphosed into the novelist.[39]

Moreover, Proust points out, when Balzac dissolves the boundaries between the real and the fictitious, he is working altogether within the scope of his stated intention. For he wanted to write "anonymous history," to study certain collateral individuals outside history whom the accidents of history failed to make great. In support of this observation he cites Lucien's farewell letter to Vautrin:

> There is the posterity of Cain and the posterity of Abel, as you used to say. In the great drama of humanity Cain represents opposition. You are descended from Adam through that lineage . . . People of Cain's race are dangerous in society . . . When God wishes, then those mysterious individuals are called Moses, Attila, Charlemagne, Mohammed or Napoleon; but when He lets these gigantic instruments rust at the bottom of the ocean of one generation, they are only called Pugachev, Robespierre, Louvel and Abbé Carlos Herrera.[40]

Turning now from Balzac's scope to his style, Proust makes the following reflection: "Style is to such an extent the sign of the transformation to which the writer's mind subjects reality that in Balzac there is, properly speaking, no style at all."[41] The difference between Balzac's and Flaubert's styles, Proust explains, lies in the fact that Flaubert has transformed his reality into one and the same substance, with all the edges polished, whereas in Balzac "there coexist, undigested, not yet transformed, all the elements of a style in the making, which has not yet come into existence."[42] Balzac's style does not reflect, as does Flaubert's, but it explains, and for this reason remains rough and dissonant. Proust notes that Balzac makes his explanations with the help of the most striking images he can find, regardless of whether they harmonize with the rest, "images . . . which are striking and right, but they are out of key, they explain instead of suggesting, they have not been subordinated to an aesthetic and harmonious whole."[43] What Balzac the artist lacked was the ability to organize his images into a coherent pattern; the emotion is not evoked but named. This tendency to explain also manifests itself in sentences such as "There was a terrifying expression on his face." Proust remarks here, "Instead of contenting himself with producing the sentiment he wishes a thing to produce on us, he immediately qualifies the thing in question." [44] In this category also belong those naïve references to painters which are intended to explain details, rather than suggest analogies. Similarly, he points out later, this impulse to explain often leads to digressions that are completely uncalled for. "And when an explanation is needed, Balzac does not beat around the bush; he writes 'Here is why,' and a whole chapter follows." [45] (It is worth remarking, however, that, as Pierre Abraham notes, Proust resorted to this device occasionally in *Sodome et Gomorrhe*, but rarely used it as extravagantly or irrelevantly as his predecessor.)

After piling up dozens of well-chosen examples in support of his observations concerning the unpolished surfaces of Balzac and concerning the vulgarities of his sentiments which they often betray, Proust nevertheless asserts that Balzac is deserving of admiration:

> But these very things are a pleasure to those who love Balzac; they repeat, smiling, "the ignoble name of Amelia," "Biblical, repeated Fifine, astonished," "the Princess of Cadignan was one of the best women for getting dressed up." To love Balzac! Sainte-Beuve, who took such joy in defining what it meant to love a writer, could have done a fine article on such a subject. For one loves other novelists by submitting to them, one accepts the truth from a Tolstoi as one would from someone greater and stronger than oneself. On the other hand, one knows all of Balzac's vulgarities, for they often produce a recoil at the outset; later one has begun to love him, smiling at all those naïvetés which are so much part of him; one loves him with a tenderness diluted with just the slightest bit of irony; one loves his eccentricities, his pettiness because these things characterize him sharply.[46]

Has Proust weakened his critical position by admitting that one must "love" Balzac first? Rather, he attempts to put his finger on exactly what there is worth cherishing in Balzac: he has not the gigantic force of Tolstoi, the ability to survey life from above; instead, though he seems inextricably bound up in its complexity, and somewhat tainted by it, he draws his artistic strength from precisely this *engrenage.*

The pastiche of Balzac is a pleasurable mixture of *témoignage* and criticism. This pastiche is the first in the series of nine that were published separately in the *Figaro* and later assembled in *Pastiches et mélanges* in 1919. It is characteristic that "L'Affaire Lemoine," involving the De Beers international diamond syndicate and a swindler named Lemoine who claimed the invention of synthetic diamonds, is a made-to-order Balzacian *fait-divers*, so that one could call the nine Pastiches "Variations on a Balzacian Theme." The Balzac pastiche is one of the most delightful of them all, having caught so well the naïveté and the gossip of the Balzacian *salon*, and earmarked by Proust with all sorts of Balzacian stylistic idiosyncrasies. There are such ludicrous and outrageous epithets, as in "the cream of Parisian aristocracy (the most elegant in Europe, according to what M. de Talleyrand says, that Roger Bacon of social physics, who was bishop and prince of Benevento)," [47] a sentence which alone illustrates most of the characteristics observed by Proust in "Aimer Balzac": mixture of fiction and reality, Balzac's naïve pride at quoting others on social matters, explicative material that serves no aesthetic purpose. Similarly, the Princess of Cadignan is described as "that Carmelite of worldly success," [48] in a burlesque of Balzac's ill-chosen metaphors. In the next quotation there is also a family tree, and some free publicity for Lavater:

> The marquise — a de Blamont-Chauvry, blood-relation of the Navarreins, the Lenoncourts, the Chaulieus — proffered each new arrival that hand which Desplein, the greatest savant of our time, not excepting Claude Bernard, and pupil of Lavater's, declared to be the most calculated hand that it might have been his task to examine.[49]

A few lines below, Proust-Balzac *names* the emotion he should have evoked and adds a rhetorical reflection on genius and criminality:

> Hearing D'Arthez' [step] resound, you would have trembled.

Only a sublime genius or a great criminal could walk like that. For that matter, isn't genius a sort of crime against the routine of the past, which our time punishes more severely than crime itself, inasmuch as the savants die in the poorhouse, which is worse than the galleys.

Then there are observations of a certain validity or expressions of a certain forcefulness which are insufficiently absorbed and often jar the reader: ". . . the impenetrable calm that women of high society preserve even at the moment when they plunge a dagger into your heart"; "a cajoling grimace dissembling the most biting mockery," "that ambiguous look, the true privilege of those who had long enjoyed Madame's confidence"; "that was spoken in so perfidiously epigrammatic a tone . . ."; and finally, the masterpiece of them all: "Mme Firmiani was sweating in her slippers, one of the masterpieces of Polish industry." [50] All of Balzac's vulgarity and ingenuousness seem to have been caught in this sentence.

Besides these stylistic traits there are a number of cross-references to Balzac's other works, exactly as Balzac proudly scattered them through the volumes of *La Comédie humaine*; there is the Baron de Nucingen's pidgin French ("*Cesde iffire esd eine crant dressor,* the baron exclaimed, dazzled." [51]); and Balzac's artistic affectations:

> Diana . . . had a sublime stare. Only Raphael would have been able to paint it. And certainly, if he had succeeded in painting it, it would have served as a pendant to his famous *Fornarina*, the most striking of his canvases, the only one which places him above Andrea del Sarto in the opinion of the connoisseurs.[52]

Enumerations in which real and fictitious persons are listed are also present in Proust's pastiche: "Alter the circumstances, and they will end up like the Marshal d'Ancre, Balthasar Claës, Pugachev, Tasso, the Countess de la Motte, or Vautrin." [53] Finally there is Balzac's typical name-conjuring ("Napoleon, Montcornet, isn't there something like a mysterious resemblance between those two names?") which gives rise to one of the most hilarious portions of the entire pastiche, in which Balzac "juggles" the name of Sir Julius Werner, the head of the De Beers syndicate:

What's more, the man who was then at the head of the most stupendous diamond scandal in England was named Werner, Julius Werner, Werner! Doesn't that name strangely evoke the Middle Ages to you? Just hearing it, can't you already see Doctor Faust, bent over his crucibles, with or without Gretchen? Doesn't it imply the idea of the philosopher's stone? Werner! Julius! Werner! Change two letters and you have Werther. *Werther* is by Goethe.[54]

In Proust's observations on *La Comédie humaine* itself, there is the assertion that the unorganized style of Balzac nevertheless allows Balzac to have a very definite organization in mind, not only in the form of sequences of certain novels ("for in Balzac the novel is seldom the unit; the novel is composed as a cycle, of which the individual novel is but a link" [55]) but also in the form of the evolution of certain characters. Balzac's objective is to synthesize, to embrace a totality.[56] Here Proust falls back on his (and Charlus') favorite example of the *Illusions perdues*—*Splendeurs et misères* cycle and the rise and fall of Lucien and Vautrin. This reference brings Proust to what he considers one of Balzac's finest achievements, a judgment in which many other novelists and critics since Balzac have concurred. "Such effects would hardly be possible were it not for Balzac's admirable invention of having kept the same characters in all his novels." [57] It is easy to see why Proust admired this invention, even though he had only one magnum opus to write, whose broad outlines had been planned by the time *Du côté de chez Swann* was published. For Proust's composition is Wagnerian, rather than Balzacian. But Proust realized that the *retour des personnages* provided not only continuity but also a concrete sense of time passing. In the words of Professor Levin:

. . . Heretofore no novelist had made it an instrument for catching the facets of personality, for recording the passage of years, for registering the shifts and compromises and realignments that interrelate a series of careers. If psychology added a third dimension to the flat, old-fashioned technique of characterization, Balzac's system of cross-reference added a fourth — the dimension of time and change in which Proust was to move.[58]

Furthermore, Balzac must not simply be credited with a discovery which proved to bear fruit for Proust, but also for his intrinsic merit, which Proust in no way misjudges. For Balzac is not merely a literary painter of his society, but, as Proust was glad to demonstrate, a writer with ideas: "His books were the result of fine ideas, of ideas of fine paintings, if you wish (for Balzac often thought of one art in the form of another), but if that is true, his books were the result of a fine pictorial effect, of a grand pictorial idea." [59] Here is surely one of the most appropriate observations that one can make about Balzac. Other readers besides Proust have read, and continued to read, Balzac, without sharing Proust's excessive affection for his predecessor. Part of the reason is that Balzac's power and attraction lie in his well-conceived canvases, small or large — the intention being usually better than the execution. "Balzac has made the novel into the universal form in which modern life finds its expression . . . ," observes Curtius. "Balzac as an artist was not merely one of the most powerful figures that illustrated the nineteenth century but also among those who discovered it." [60] Henry James sees Balzac's principal distinction in his "all-desiring, all-devouring love of reality," [61] without which the modern novel would never have come into being. If Balzac had set out, more or less methodically, to survey the society of his day, making sure that all walks of life would somehow be represented — somewhat in the programmatic manner of the Rougon-Macquart series — the history of the realistic novel might have been different, but as it turned out, the idea of *La Comédie humaine* came to Balzac only when a considerable number of novels had already been written. This intuition on Balzac's part marks *La Comédie humaine* as primarily a work of imagination, rather than of demonstration (like Zola's cycle). For Proust — and for any practitioner or lover of fiction for whom the word "fiction" implies more than the photography of empirical reality, or a series of experiments upon it — Balzac's discovery makes him into the first modern novelist:

> This lifelike reality of Balzac's novels causes them to give us a kind of literary value to a thousand things in life which up till then appeared too casual to us. But precisely the law of these contingencies is redeemed in his work.[62]

These "contingencies" enrich the reader's understanding of life, for they are observations carefully set down from life; in other words — and here is Proust's chief point — these contingencies *deepen* the reader's concept of life. "Under the apparent external action of the drama throb mysterious laws of flesh and of sentiment." [63] The two aspects of a great writer to which Proust always returns are in evidence here: the writer's observation must be anchored in "things"; for it is the small detail, the contingency, that matters more than the whole; and these contingencies must be treated so as to preserve the sense of their mystery even after the intellect has gone to work on them. This was Proust's criterion for evaluating the poets; it is equally valid for Proust's analysis of Balzac's art; and finally, it is true for Proust's art itself. The contemplation of "les Choses" may at times afford a glimpse into their essences; in the process, the "mysterious laws" to which Proust referred may perhaps be revealed. Literary criticism for Proust, on the highest level, is also a search for a writer's "essence," for the "figure in the carpet"; and for this reason, Proust the literary critic never moves too far away from his hawthorn blossoms in *Du côté de chez Swann.* The transcendent truth revealed by the hawthorn blossoms, in which aesthetic contemplation transfigures life, also defines the direction in which the artist-critic is to move.

3. FLAUBERT AND "LA BEAUTÉ GRAMMATICALE"

Proust's criticism of Flaubert takes almost exclusively the form of stylistic analysis. He is little concerned with themes, or recurrences; and the allusions to Flaubert in *A la recherche du temps perdu* are few and negligible. The two Flaubertian sketches in *Les Plaisirs et les jours* entitled "Mondanité et mélomanie de Bouvard et Pécuchet" should be regarded as literary diversions on a Flaubertian theme; Bouvard and Pécuchet have been transferred to a late-nineteenth-century milieu, where they continue their researches. There is no intention on Proust's part to write a pastiche, since practically all Flaubert's stylistic idiosyncrasies have been eliminated. The principal sources to be used here are the essay in *Chroniques* ("A propos du 'style' de Flaubert")[1] and the pastiche in *Pastiches et mélanges*. There are also a few remarks about Flaubert in Proust's essay on style, which serves as an introduction to Paul Morand's *Tendres Stocks*.

"Marcel used to do pastiches of Flaubert with extraordinary ease," writes Robert de Billy.[2] The pastiche bears ample witness to Proust's *intoxication flaubertienne*. Using the subject of "L'Affaire Lemoine" as the basis of all the Pastiches, Proust was able first to look at the material with the eyes of each one of his authors, then to apply the pen of each to the material observed. In the Flaubert pastiche the realistic detail of the court room gives way to the vague reveries of the spectators, as if Emma Bovary or Frédéric Moreau were present. The peculiarities of Flaubert's style are grasped with uncanny precision; as Mouton observes, "the extraordinary exactness of imitation might remind us at times of a mosaic made up of excerpts from Flaubert himself, and one might be tempted to accuse Proust of having copied the original."[3]

Since the pastiche bears out all of Proust's observations on Flaubert's style, it may be best to consider the essay and the pastiche together. The essay was Proust's contribution to Flaubert's defense in the so-called "Flaubert Controversy,"[4] which flared up in 1919 when Louis de Robert claimed that Flaubert wrote badly. A discussion followed in the Paris press, in which Paul Souday, Albert Thibaudet, Marcel Proust, and others participated. Proust's article was occasioned by a remark of Albert Thibaudet to the effect that Flaubert was not "un écrivain de race" — a statement which, incidentally, Thibaudet retracted after Proust's defense of Flaubert's style. (As Jacques Boulenger put it: "And, because one simply does not resist M. Marcel Proust, M. Albert Thibaudet, convinced, admitted having 'expressed his ideas erroneously' . . .")[5]

In a letter to Louis de Robert written at the time of the Controversy, Proust expressed his admiration — with reservations — for Flaubert:

> I admire Flaubert greatly (at least, *L'Education sentimentale*, whose title is incomprehensible and poor French), but I don't need to be in agreement with an author's conclusions in order to admire his dialectic.[6]

This explains, to some extent, why Proust came to Flaubert's defense only reluctantly. He made sure that the reader of the essay kept that fact in mind by reminding him at the beginning, "It is not that I am particularly fond of all of Flaubert's books, nor even his style";[7] and at the end he spoke of Flaubert as a writer whom he actually did not care for very much.[8] The fact is that Proust respected Flaubert rather than cherished him, and owed a considerable debt to his style but not to his subject matter.[9] Proust recognized Flaubert's contribution to the technique of fiction, namely, the solution of the problem of stylistic polish which Balzac had left as a legacy to the novelists following him. Flaubert's own attitude toward Balzac was considerably less indulgent than Proust's; he praised Balzac's breadth of conception but deplored his inability to write well.[10] Setting out to make prose fiction into an art, Flaubert achieved remarkable results, and Proust gives him due credit:

> In Flaubert's style, for example, all portions of reality are converted into a homogeneous substance, with vast surfaces which have a monotonous glitter. No impurity has remained in it. The surfaces have become reflecting areas. All things are outlined in them, but by reflection, without altering the homogeneous substance. Everything which had been different has been converted and absorbed.[11]

This idea already contains the germs of the later essay on Flaubert, which is, so to speak, a detailed analysis of the technique behind Flaubert's powers of "fusion."

That essay begins with an explanation of Proust's reasons for taking up arms in Flaubert's behalf. He is fully aware of Flaubert's weaknesses as a stylist:

> . . . I believe that metaphor alone can give a species of eternity to style, and there is probably, in the whole of Flaubert, no single instance of a really beautiful metaphor. I would go even further and maintain that his images are, generally speaking, so weak that they scarcely rise above the level of those that his most insignificant characters might have used . . . but had it been Flaubert speaking in his own person and not through the mouths of his characters, he would not have managed much better.

As an example, Proust cites the closing paragraph of *Saint Julien l'Hospitalier*, in which Flaubert finds nothing but banal imagery (stars, sun, roses) to describe the transfiguration of Julien.

> There is nothing actually bad about it, nothing incongruous, shocking or ridiculous, as there quite often is in a descriptive passage by Balzac or Renan — it is just that, well, that a mere Frédéric Moreau, without any Flaubert to help him, might have managed just about as well. But, after all, there are other things in style besides metaphor.[12]

These two passages actually contain the nucleus of Proust's aesthetics and also a concrete application of Proust's notion of the metaphor to another writer's style. The metaphor, as Proust emphasizes in *Le Temps retrouvé*, is the device whereby the writer can transcend reality and place his work *sub specie aeternitatis*; as such, it becomes the element that brings about the alchemy that a writer operates upon his materials, the component whereby his particular vision is made harmonious and meaningful. Artists like Balzac, Flaubert, and Renan never quite attain this high objective: the Balzacian or Flaubertian image, as Proust notes, is rare and, when it does appear, it is usually no better than what the more or less mediocre heroes of Balzac and

Flaubert themselves might have written. But Proust knows that if a writer is not a creator of metaphors, he may nevertheless be a great artist: he may revolutionize the entire conception of the novel, as Balzac did, or he may revolutionize the use of grammar and syntax, as Flaubert did. It is not given to many novelists to extend the craft of fiction along several lines simultaneously.

Accordingly, Flaubert's strength does not lie in his use of metaphors. Martin Turnell speaks of them as "dispersing emotion," rather than concentrating it,[13] and Proust finds the following analogy for Flaubert's prose:

> It would be impossible for anyone to get on to the great Moving Staircase of Flaubert's pages, which go on and on, never stopping, never breaking their monotony, without color and without clearness of outline — and not to realize that they are without their like in literature.[14]

By means of the fine metaphor of the "moving staircase" Proust has caught the monotonous fascination that takes hold of Flaubert's readers. A few pages earlier, he had boldly compared Flaubert's revolution in literature with Kant's revolution in philosophy. Even if the comparison is extravagant, it enables one to judge how strongly Proust felt that Flaubert's stylistic innovations were of immense literary significance. Just as the modern philosopher cannot philosophize without Kant, the modern novelist cannot very easily write a novel without Flaubert.

The "grammatical beauty" of Flaubert's style, Proust asserts, has nothing to do with the grammatical errors that certain critics hostile to Flaubert were pleased to point out. The Flaubert controversy had originally begun with the claim that Flaubert was a poor writer because he often wrote incorrect French. This is a problem which all critics of Flaubert have had to face; Thibaudet, who devotes some space to the issue in his book on Flaubert,[15] concludes that many of Flaubert's mistakes are inexcusable but that his style remains nevertheless a great prose style. Proust's position is essentially the same, although the examples which he uses to illustrate Flaubert's solecisms are not well chosen. He calls attention to ambiguous uses of the personal pronoun in *L'Education sentimentale* (from which most of Proust's examples are chosen), but this is actually not a grievous error (except to purists) and easily clarified within the context of the sentence. To continue Proust's argument, Flaubert was much more concerned with preserving "a narrow and closed continuity of style," [16] that is to say, with keeping the various components of his vision uninterrupted. Proust chooses this example from *L'Education*:

> La colline qui suivait à droite le cours de la Seine s'abaissa, et il en surgit une autre, plus proche, sur la rive opposée.
> Des arbres la couronnaient . . .[17]

The close linking of the various elements of Flaubert's description, Proust observes, became for Flaubert the central problem as he evolved from *Madame Bovary,* in which "the elements which are not wholly 'him' have not yet been completely eliminated," to *L'Education sentimentale,* in which the revolution has been accomplished (though not consolidated):

> . . . What, up to the time of Flaubert, had been merely action, has become impression. Objects have just as much life as men, for it is the process of reasoning that, at a later stage, attributes external causes to visual phenomena. What reaches us in the form of a first impression contains no causal implication.[18]

This "impressionism" which Proust finds characteristic in Flaubert's style not only throws light on his own "impressionism" (Proust's style has been too often labeled "impressionistic," when the term is actually more applicable to the first two volumes than to the succeeding ones, and then only in a limited sense); but it places the entire movement of realism of the nineteenth century in a different perspective, moving it, so to speak, nearer Manet than Courbet. Underneath the seeming objectivity lies a strongly defined personal imagination ordering the vision. In Flaubert's style Proust detects the following techniques: new uses of tenses, of prepositions, and of adverbs, the latter two being relegated primarily to a rhythmic function.

Discussing the use of tenses, Proust begins by saying that when Flaubert wishes to prolong a state of being, he uses the imperfect, except when an action or a movement intervenes (in which the agents are usually "things"); in that case the past definite takes over, but only to be relieved shortly afterward by the imperfect. These are, of course, features which most analysts of Flaubert's style have noted; moreover, a reader of Flaubert cannot help but be struck by the monotony, the "dispersed emotion," so appropriate to the vague impression that Flaubert's landscapes leave on his characters, which a series of imperfects in Flaubert sets up — then the irruption of life, marked by the appearance of the past definite and occasionally sustained for a few moments, only to let the sentence lapse into the old languor once more. Examples of this technique can be found on practically every page of Flaubert's novels. Proust chooses to single out a more exciting variation: "But, quite often, the passage of the imperfect to the perfect [i.e., the past definite] is indicated by a present participle, which shows the way in which the action occurs, or the moment at which it occurs." [19] Proust uses the following passage for illustration:

> [A travers le brouillard,] il contemplait des clochers, [des édifices dont il ne savait pas les noms; puis il embrassa, dans un dernier coup d'oeil, l'île Saint-Louis, la Cité, Notre-Dame;] et bientôt, *Paris disparaissant*, il poussa un grand soupir.[20]

However, this is not a good example, as Proust himself adds (since he seems to be quoting from memory); for the "embrassa" preceding the participial phrase, not quoted by Proust, actually destroys the effect which Proust thought was there. Here is a better one:

> Toutes les poitrines haletaient; la chaleur de plus en plus devenait suffocante; les deux amis, craignant d'être étouffés, sortirent.[21]

Two interesting examples in *L'Education* show the participle used to mark a transition from the imperfect to the past definite, in the first instance; and from the past definite to the imperfect in the second:

Quant à la République les choses s'arrangeraient; enfin, il se trouvait l'homme le plus heureux de la terre; et, s'oubliant, il vanta les qualités de Rosanette, la compara même à sa femme.

And,

Tout à coup, Frédéric aperçut, à trois pas de distance, M. Dambreuse avec Martinon; il tourna la tête, car M. Dambreuse s'étant fait nommer représentant, il lui gardait rancune.[22]

The same device is reproduced in the pastiche:

. . . Pour entrer en conversation, les malins se plaignaient à haute voix du manque d'air, et, quelqu'un ayant dit reconnaître le ministre de l'intérieur dans un monsieur qui sortait, un réactionnaire soupira: "Pauvre France!" [23]

The participle, as it is used in the preceding examples, has the wonderful effect of suspending the action (or inaction) for a moment, letting it hover, before something new occurs.

But the key device remains the imperfect tense, that "eternal imperfect," as Proust calls it. Flaubert has a special predilection for it when he wishes to render the indirect speech of a character, with the result that he fuses, as it were, his characters with the "things" in his novels:

. . . this imperfect, a newcomer to literature, entirely changes the look of people and of things, as, when the position of a lamp has been slightly shifted, the appearance of a new house may strike one as one enters it for the first time, or of an old one when one is in the process of moving. It is this kind of melancholy, made up of the breaking of old habits and of the flimsy unreality of the setting, that Flaubert's style produces, that style which, if only by reason of this single effect, strikes one as being so new. His use of the imperfect serves to narrate not only people's words, but their whole lives. *Education Sentimentale* is the prolonged narrative of a life, in which the human characters, so to speak, do not play any active part at all.[24]

The phrase "entirely changes the look of people and of things" goes beyond the simple notion that things and persons are riveted together by Flaubert's imperfect. The way in which this welding takes place gives a certain characteristic pattern to Flaubert's novels. The imperfect is the tense by which the French primarily express prolonged states; it is a static tense. The use of the imperfect over long stretches, alternating occasionally with the vibration of the perfect and then returning to stasis once more, leaves the effect of a gentle, not insistent monotone, producing the vague "kind of melancholy" of Emma, of Frédéric, of Julien; it is Time congealing, becoming viscous. Or, as Charles Du Bos suggests, Time envelops the reader: " . . . It appears at times that the reader is in the very heart of time, which flows on. The sensation of time in *L'Education sentimentale* releases some deep contagion, a sort of vertigo . . ."[25]

The device of the "eternal imperfect" is used to advantage in the pastiche in reporting the daydreams of the spectators as they hear the Lemoine testimony. The conditional tense — in itself a kind of "suspended future," like the English "would," to indicate habitual action — serves here to alternate between the felt actuality and the wished-for, dreamed-of, paradise:

Some were dreaming of giving up their business, or of a *hôtel* in the Avenue du Bois, or of wielding influence with the Academy; or even of a yacht which in the summer might have conveyed them to cold countries . . .

For some, these millions were not sufficient; they would have gambled them away immediately on the Stock Market; and buying stocks at the lowest quotation on the day before they would go up — a friend would have tipped them off — they would see their capital increase a hundredfold in several hours . . . They would not join the Jockey Club, taking the aristocracy at its face value. Perhaps a papal order would appeal to them more. Perhaps it might be obtained without paying for it . . .

But some, musing that wealth might have come to them, were ready to swoon; for they would have placed it at the feet of a woman who had spurned them until then, who would at last have revealed to them the secret of her kiss and the sweetness of her body. They could already visualize themselves by her side, in the country . . . And they ended up by seeing nothing but two clusters of purple flowers . . .[26]

Lest this "eternal imperfect" becomes too monotonous, Flaubert occasionally varies the procedure. As the present participle was used to make transitions from the imperfect to the past definite in either direction, so by a sort of crisscross device the past definite can sometimes do the duty of the imperfect, in which case, Proust notes, the imperfect is introduced to add a touch of precision to the tableau. Proust chooses the following example of Flaubert's use of an "indefinite" past definite:

> Il voyagea, il connut la mélancolie des paquebots, etc., il eut d'autre [*sic*] amours encore.[27]

The past definite in this passage does not destroy the vagueness of the tone; all of Frédéric's actions seem mechanical, passive: there is a stasis in his mobility. Actually, the complete passage is worth quoting:

> Il voyagea.
> Il connut la mélancolie des paquebots, les froids réveils sous la tente, l'étourdissement des paysages et des ruines, l'amertume des sympathies interrompues.
> Il revint.
> Il fréquenta le monde, et il eut d'autres amours encore. Mais le souvenir continuel du premier les lui rendait insipides; et puis la véhémence du désir, la fleur même de la sensation était perdue.[28]

The word "souvenir," characteristically enough, brings about the juncture of perfect to imperfect, and lets Frédéric slide into the customary groove once more.

Besides using the conditional, as seen in the pastiche and also pointed out by Thibaudet,[29] Flaubert has another device to break the continuity of the imperfect; whereas the conditional, as has been shown, does not actually break the monotony of a passage, the unexpected use of the present tense sometimes provides a brief outlet, a momentary crack in Time, one might say. Proust points out the following example:

> They lived in the most remote part of Brittany . . . Their house was situated below, with a garden stretching to the top of the hill, from where one *can look out* on the sea.[30]

This sudden jump across Time is occasionally used by Flaubert, with startling effect, like one of those *sauts brusques* which Proust is fond of pointing out in Racine, Saint-Simon, or Baudelaire. Naturally enough, Proust used it in his pastiche:

> And they ended up by seeing nothing but two clusters of purple flowers, reaching down as far as the fast-moving water which they almost touch, in the drab light of a sunless afternoon, along a reddish wall which was crumbling.[31]

Turning from Flaubert's use of tenses to his use of conjunctions, Proust arrests his attention on the "et."

> The conjunction "and" never, in Flaubert, plays the part assigned to it by grammar. It marks a pause in the beat of the rhythm, and acts as the means of dividing a picture into its parts. It is true to say that wherever one would normally put "and," Flaubert suppresses it. This suppression provides the model, the form of many admirable sentences.[32]

Proust's observation is extravagant, even though his explanation is correct. Proust is thinking undoubtedly of the "et" that is used in enumerations when he speaks of the function that grammar assigns it. But this conjunction has had more than one function. Thibaudet distinguishes an emphatic "et," "designed to keep things moving, repeated at the beginning of sentences — which is an inevitable temptation of the 'epic' style."[33] Flaubert uses this kind of initial "et" to create a special emphasis for the sentence that is to follow; occasionally the "et" is used to augment the tension of the third element of a ternary construction. Moreover, the "et" in Flaubert's prose often has a euphonic or a rhythmic function. Proust also discerns that it fulfills a plastic need — that of dividing the portions of a tableau. Rather than saying, then, that Flaubert's "et" is unorthodox, one might say that it is multiplex. Thus Flaubert omits it in the first sentence of *Saint Julien l'Hospitalier*: "Le père et la mère de Julien habitaient un château, au milieu des bois, sur la pente d'une colline." (Proust observes here that by varying the prepositions, Flaubert enhances the beauty of the ternary sentence.) On the other hand, the unexpected use of "et" where it is not required is like "a sign that another part of the picture is beginning, that the moving wave is about to build itself up again." He quotes the following example:

> La place du Carrousel avait un aspect tranquille. L'Hôtel de Nantes s'y dressait toujours solitairement; *et* les maisons par derrière, le dome du Louvre en face, la longue galerie de bois, à droite, etc., étaient comme noyés dans la couleur grise de l'air, etc., tandis que, à l'autre bout de la place, etc.[34]

The "tandis que," Proust observes, is a device used by all great descriptive prose stylists when they want to keep the parts of a tableau unified without making the clause too long. In other words, the "tandis que" produces an effect contrary to the effect of the "et" in this sentence. This is not to say that the two conjunctions neutralize each other but that Flaubert's tableau is composed of two elements, an introductory short one representing the solidary Hôtel de Nantes, and a second long element representing the entire panorama exclusive of the Hôtel de Nantes.

> Briefly, "and" in Flaubert always begins a secondary sentence, and scarcely ever terminates an enumeration.[35]

Jacques Boulenger is perhaps more illuminating on the subject of Flaubert's use of "et" in enumerations:

> In reality, he uses "et" the way everybody does, to terminate an enumeration when it is finished, precise, complete . . . But, like everybody, he does not use "et" when he gives an imprecise, indeterminate enumeration, and this is the more frequent case.[36]

This formulation seems to solve the problem adequately and disposes of Proust's "scarcely ever."

In the pastiche the "et" is now omitted, now grafted onto the sentence. The examples are numerous. Here are two such omissions:

Two young people wondered at it, would have liked to know if it had been put there as a souvenir or perhaps for reasons of eccentricity.

Finally the presiding judge made a sign, a murmur arose, two umbrellas fell on the floor.

Now follow two uses of the "et" to connect parts of the tableau:

He was terrible on Lemoine . . . And his long sentences followed one another without a break. . . . [The hall] had dust on the wooden floor, spiders in the corners of the ceiling, a rat in each hole, and it had to be frequently aired because of the vicinity of the hot stove . . .[37]

Another singularity of Flaubert's style, as remarked by Proust, is his fondness for heavy, sometimes ugly, adverbs. Frequently they are placed at the end of a sentence, as in the last sentence of *Hérodias*, "Comme la tête de Saint Jean était très lourde, ils la portaient alternativement." But usually Flaubert places them "in the ugliest, the most unexpected, the heaviest manner, as though they are intended to serve as cement for his compact phrases, so that each tiniest hole in the fabric shall be efficiently blocked." [38] Examples of "heavy" adverbs in Flaubert are frequent, but their occurrence rarely makes the sentence ugly, as Proust claims. A sentence from *L'Education sentimentale* which is comparable in effectiveness to the end of *Hérodias* is the following:

Enfin, l'aiguille ayant dépassé les vingt-cinq minutes, elle prit son chapeau par les brides, lentement.

Here is an example of an adverb weighing the sentence down:

Il lui demanda, seulement, comment elle avait fait la connaissance d'Arnoux.[39]

Obviously the commas serve to "frame" the adverb, so that it stands like a boulder in the middle of the sentence. In the pastiche Proust made use of the heavy adverb:

> [Some were dreaming] even of a yacht which in the summer might have taken them to cold countries, not to the Pole, nevertheless, which is strange . . .[40]

The "nevertheless" (*pourtant*) is here used to make the sentence awkward, even unattractive.

In addition, Proust points out some minor features of Flaubert's style — or at least, features which he does not discuss at length. For instance, in spite of the fact that Flaubert's "eternal imperfect" required him to keep a large variety of verbs at his command — as any reader of Flaubert will readily attest — he is not afraid occasionally to let a heavy, colorless verb such as "avoir" or "être" serve him instead of a more subtle one.

> Nevertheless, we love those hard, solid blocks of material which Flaubert raises and lets fall with the intermittent thud of a steam-shovel. For if, as I found recounted in some book or other, the sailors at sea used to catch the glow of Flaubert's lamp as he worked through the night, and take their bearings from it, as if from a lighthouse beam, so too it might be said that when he "unloaded" a good round phrase, it had the regular rhythm of one of those machines used in excavating.[41]

But for Proust the finest achievement of Flaubert's style, in spite of all the effects of solidity produced by the use of ponderous adverbs and of intentionally awkward syntax, is the impression of Time which he succeeds in conveying. It is interesting that Proust does not insist on the "plasticity" of Flaubert's style, as so many admirers of Flaubert do. Proust undoubtedly would not deny that Flaubert achieves striking plastic effects — he points out a great many devices which make Flaubert's prose an excellent tool for the presentation of the "uninterrupted vision" — but as a novelist and a critic he asks himself what role this technique can play in a novel, where the tableaux which Flaubert creates must be ordered in terms of the time-scheme of the novel. Thus he begins his essay with Flaubert's "hermetic continuity" and ends on the same note. For Proust, the most beautiful passage in *L'Education sentimentale* occurs when continuity is achieved by a blank. After a detailed description of little incidents, Frédéric Moreau sees a policeman kill an insurgent. Frédéric's astonished recognition of the murderer is followed by a blank — and a new chapter opens.

And Frédéric, agape, recognized Sénécal.

VI

He traveled.

He knew the melancholy of steamboats, the cold awakenings under the tent, etc.

He returned.

He went into society, etc.

Toward the end of 1867, etc.

Proust comments:

Here there is an implied "silence" of vast duration, and suddenly, without the hint of a transition, time ceases to be a matter of mere successive quarters of an hour, and appears to us in the guise of years and decades . . . In Balzac . . . the change of tempo has an active and documentary character. Flaubert was the first novelist to free this change from all parasitic growths of anecdote and historical scavenging. He treated it in terms of music. Nobody before him had ever done that.[42]

This kind of analysis, which one would hardly expect from anyone but Proust, accounts for the fact that Proust's criticism of literature is often exciting, particularly when he ventures upon an unfamiliar path. An analysis of this kind not merely throws light on his own preoccupations, but also on something very real which is to be found in Flaubert. Martin Turnell finds that in the above passage Flaubert succeeds in completely dissolving the feelings into images.

The "blanks," which Proust rather perversely described as the most beautiful thing in the book, prolong the effect of the words, suggest long periods of time passing, vast distances traversed.[43]

Proust's observation that Flaubert is the first to set Time to music is not misapplied in this connection; could Flaubert's "blanks" not be regarded in some ways as analogous to the pauses, the "blanks" which Beethoven uses frequently in his later works with exciting results? In any case, Proust recognized that Flaubert's "hermetic continuity" was an art of relationships, of keeping fluid the rapports between the various tenses and, on occasion, between the word and the blank.

In contrast with the style of Flaubert's fiction, Proust finds the mediocrity of Flaubert's correspondence startling:

> As a rule, great writers who do not know how to write (like great painters who do not know how to paint) do little more than renounce their "virtuosity," their inborn "facility," in order to create, as a medium for their new vision, ways of expressing themselves which, little by little, adapt themselves to its requirements. Now, in their letters, where the need to submit unquestioningly to their own obscure inner ideal is absent, they become once more what, had they been less great, they would never have ceased to be.[44]

Accordingly, when a writer bridles his intelligence in order to keep it from marring his books, it has a tendency to find expression in his letters.

> But nothing of the sort is apparent in the case of Flaubert. I find it impossible to agree with Monsieur Thibaudet that Flaubert's letters "give evidence of a brain of the very front rank." But it is the letters, rather than Monsieur Thibaudet's view of them, that I find disconcerting.[45]

This severe criticism of Flaubert's correspondence looks like a retraction of a more lenient view held earlier. The following excerpt from *Jean Santeuil* makes this clear. What actually interested Proust more than the contents and qualities of Flaubert's correspondence was the distinction between the "conversational" talent of a writer and his artistic personality — the paradox of the great writer whose spoken or epistolary language is essentially "artless." The problem is virtually the same as that raised by Ruskin's notion that reading is comparable to a dialogue with the great men, an attitude with which Proust had sharply differed.

> Maybe long acquired habits of work have the effect of making talk and correspondence take their places as inferior pieces of mechanism drawn onwards in the vast movement of larger, superior organisms, so that a discipline of precision, elegance, and applied intelligence controls with the lightest of light finger-touches, and with no thought involved in the process, both talk and letter-writing. But it may also be that brainwork directed to one specialized end develops its full energy only in solitude, so that the unheard and inner dialogue in the track of which the pen follows may fail to operate in conversation, as happens inversely in the case of great talkers who lose their talent when it comes to writing. That is what happens with those great writers who, concentrating their eyes on reality, work for that only and are not obsessed like Balzac with perfecting a form, or in whom, as in Flaubert, the purely literary reality — a form which fascinates them — lies so deeply buried that it cannot issue in their conversation or their letters, with the result that those letters provide only the raw material from which they can extract beauty, though now and again one may come on a trace of their true selves in a phrase cut free from the mass of that material, much as when a singer is talking to you he may give a momentary musical cadence to something he is especially anxious to stress. Such was the case with Flaubert.[46]

This earlier judgment is probably fairer than the later one with its blunt assertion that Flaubert's letters "reveal nothing." Granted that Proust might be right in speaking of Flaubert's critical intelligence as being second rate, because of the rhetorical way in which Flaubert tends to express himself about Art, without ever getting to the bottom of his problem, the fact remains that the letters reproduce so well Flaubert's excitement and enthusiasm for what he regarded to be Art. The "other" Flaubert, who is revealed in the letters, apparently does not interest Proust. He is painfully aware of the fact that Flaubert's pronouncements are not often thought through, and that there is a certain tendency on his part, especially in the letters to

Louise Colet, to talk too readily and too facilely about "pure art," "form and content"; but, on the whole, Proust's answer to Thibaudet sins in the direction of severity.

What Proust mostly admired in Flaubert was what Flaubert himself described as his alter ego, the "bonhomme" who "wants to make you feel almost *materially* the things he reproduces." [47] Otherwise, Proust remains cool on the novels as a whole (with the exception of *L'Education*). Flaubert's intelligence, as Proust pointed out, is often not distinguishable from that of his characters — a situation which is excellently suited to the purposes of his novels but not to his correspondence. Or, looking at the disparity from another point of view (since Flaubert's novels were more important to him than his correspondence), Proust wrote to Boulenger: "It would truly be heartbreaking if Flaubert's books, on which he worked so hard, were not superior to his letters." [48]

In spite of all his reservations, Proust always insisted that Flaubert's greatness was unmistakable. Replying to Anatole France in *Tendres Stocks* to disprove his "master's" assertion that nobody has written well since the eighteenth century, Proust centered one of his strongest arguments on Flaubert's "renouvellement."

It seems that, in other centuries, there was always some degree of distance between the *object* and the great spirits who discoursed upon it. But, in, for example, the case of Flaubert, the intelligence — which was not, perhaps, his strongest point — managed to *identify itself* with, say, the shuddering movement of a steamboat, with the color of churned foam, with an islet lying out in the bay. A moment comes, in reading him, when one is no longer conscious of the writer's intelligence (even when, as with Flaubert, that intelligence is somewhat mediocre), but only of the moving ship — "running into floating bales of timber which bobbed up and down in the brisk agitation of the waves." That word "bobbed" shows us intelligence transformed, intelligence that has become part and parcel of the physical scene. Similarly, it can penetrate the tangle of the heath, the trunks of trees, the silence and the light of the underbrush. Is it not the first concern of any artist intent on style to achieve just this transformation of energy in which the thinker disappears, and the objects which he is busy depicting become real and actual to our eyes?[49]

It is this "renewal" for which modern fiction — including Proust — owes a great debt to Flaubert.

4. OTHER FRENCH PROSE WRITERS

Proust's remarks on French prose writers of the nineteenth century other than Balzac, Flaubert, and Sainte-Beuve can best be considered in three groupings: two prose-writers, Chateaubriand and Nerval, whom Proust recognizes as precursors because of their use of involuntary memory; two writers, Barbey d'Aurevilly and Stendhal, whom Proust analyzes in terms of *phrases-types* (key phrases, or recurrent images); and a few other writers whose styles are analyzed by means of the pastiche.

When Marcel in the library of the Princesse de Guermantes reflects on the literary art which he is going to practice, he focuses on the experiences of his life in which his involuntary memory gave rise to genuine aesthetic impressions. Wishing to make them the core of his work, he asks himself whether these experiences are peculiar to himself alone, or whether there are other writers who had similar problems. In this way, Marcel comes at last to discern the ancestry of the "mémoire involontaire": Chateaubriand, Nerval, and Baudelaire. In an earlier chapter Baudelaire's reminiscences were characterized by Proust as being too voluntary, too "evoked," to fit into the same category as his own. In the case of Chateaubriand, however, the mechanism is more spontaneous.

Was it not from sensations of the same sort as I received from the *madeleine* that the most beautiful part of the *Mémoires d'Outre-Tombe* was derived? "Yestereve I was walking alone at close of day . . . I was roused from my meditations by the trilling of a lark perched on the topmost bough of a birch tree. On the instant this magic sound evoked before my eyes the ancestral domain; the catastrophes I had just witnessed passed from my mind and I was transported rapidly into the past, where I saw once again that countryside where I so often heard the lark sing." And is not this one of the two or three most beautiful passages in these *Mémoires*: "A sweet and subtle fragrance of heliotrope exhaled from a small clump of scarlet runner in blossom; it was not brought to us by a breeze from our native land but by a savage wind from Newfoundland, bearing no relation to the exiled plant, devoid of any sympathy of remembrance or of voluptuous delight. In this perfume, not breathed of beauty, nor purified in its bosom, nor spread along its path, in this perfume, laden with dawn, with culture and with humankind, were all the melancholies of past regrets, of exile and of youth." [1]

In the first quotation from the *Mémoires d'Outre-Tombe* in particular, Proust likes the "method of sudden transition" which makes Chateaubriand transport his reader with him from Montboissier to the Combourg of his childhood.[2]

Besides finding in Chateaubriand the first significant precursor of the technique of the involuntary memory, Proust paid tribute to Chateaubriand's great prose style. Speaking, in the course of his essay on Flaubert, of "quotable" sentences in Chateaubriand, he exclaims, "How numerous are [the sentences] over which one could go into ecstasies!"[3] Then he takes exception to the following quotation of Chateaubriand chosen by Thibaudet, to illustrate the beauty of Chateaubriand's style.

> When, in the silence of abjectness only the echo of the chain shackling the slave and the voice of the denouncer can be heard; when everything trembles before the tyrant and when it is as dangerous to incur his favor as it is to merit his displeasure, the historian appears on the scene, entrusted with the vengeance of nations.[4]

He goes on to observe:

> As a general rule, everything in Chateaubriand which preserves or anticipates the political eloquence of the eighteenth or nineteenth centuries is not Chateaubriand at his most characteristic.[5]

Proust is in no way overwhelmed by the "ring" of Chateaubriand's rhetoric; he greatly prefers the lyrical Chateaubriand, especially when he enriches his prose by reminiscences; and above all, he admires Chateaubriand the memorialist. His interest in Chateaubriand appears to have been strong enough to determine him to write a Chateaubriand pastiche in 1908, but unfortunately this pastiche was never published.[6]

Contre Sainte-Beuve contains a brief essay in praise of the romantic prose writer, probably written between 1896 and 1904; it appears to be one of the first instances in which Proust attempts to assess what a great "poet" can teach us about art, and what he ascribes to Chateaubriand could as easily have been applied to Racine or Baudelaire or any number of his other favorites. The principal value of the essay lies in the fact that Proust is here obviously striving to consolidate his ideas about art (we are, after all, in his Ruskin period); and he affirms even here the existence of a reality transparent in the poet's words, and the conquest of time by art. But these are merely preludes to *Le Temps retrouvé*.

Proust considered Gérard de Nerval one of the three or four greatest writers of the nineteenth century[7] and a spiritual kinsman of Baudelaire, "idle like him, with certainties as to detailed execution and uncertainties as to the over-all scheme."[8] The only essay which he wrote on Nerval is in *Contre Sainte-Beuve*, and, curiously enough, does not extend our knowledge of Proust on Nerval considerably, leaving a number of tantalizing gaps.

Jacques Truelle quotes Proust as saying, "Never has a book moved me as much as Gérard de Nerval's *Sylvie*."[9] The passage to which Proust likes to allude in *Chroniques* (and Marcel in *Le Temps retrouvé*) is the one in which the narrator of *Sylvie* accidentally reads an announcement in the newspaper:

> I vaguely skimmed the newspaper which I still had in my hands, and I noticed the following two lines: "*Feast of the Provincial Wreath.* — Tomorrow the archers of Senlis are to return the wreath to the archers of Loisy." These two simple words awakened in me a completely new series of impressions — a long-forgotten reminiscence of the provinces, a distant echo of the simple holidays of my

youth. — Horn and drum resounded from afar, in the hamlets and in the woods; young girls were braiding garlands . . .[10]

This type of reminiscence — it amounts to an involuntary resurrection of the past — is certainly closer to Proust's than Baudelaire's. *Sylvie* is also a work in which Nerval's delicate imagination and tenderness are wonderfully fused into an atmosphere of dream and nostalgia — comparable to a number of similar passages in Proust. Speaking of the passage quoted above, Proust remarks,

> This phenomenon of memory has served Nerval in the guise of a transition point. Nerval was a great genius, all of whose work might have had as title the words which I have given to one of my sections, *Les Intermittences du Coeur*.[11]

Moreover, Proust feels called upon to defend charges against Nerval that these transpositions occasioned by reminiscences can be explained on the basis that Nerval was mentally deranged.

> But if one looks at the matter from the point of view of the literary critic, one cannot, strictly, use the word "madness" of a state of mind which makes possible the true perception (or, better still, readjusts and sharpens the exploratory sense) of the most important relations subsisting between ideas and images. This "madness" is, really, nothing but the moment at which Gérard de Nerval's habitual day-dreams become ineffable. His "madness" is, as it were, a prolongation of his work, from which he escapes in order to resume the task of writing. The "madness" which was the *terminus ad quem* of the book just finished, becomes the point of departure, the very matter, of the book about to be begun. The poet is no more ashamed of the mental attack now over and done with than are we embarrassed when we wake each morning faced by the knowledge that we have spent the night in sleep, or than, perhaps, we shall feel confused when we come to realize, some day, that we have made the momentary passage of death. What he does is to try to classify and describe his various dreams.[12]

These arguments are interesting, not only if regarded as a thinly veiled defense of himself, but also from the point of view of Proust's aesthetics. The writer's occupation, he is saying, is one requiring clearsightedness, one which cannot be carried out in a state of madness; and Nerval's madness occupied an intermediate position between the dreamer and the writer, serving as an escape from reverie and as an incitement to creation. Once more one finds the conviction, implied in all these observations, that the text alone must provide the answer to the artist, and its lucidity must be the decisive criterion — not the biographical data that have been accumulated about the writer.

Sylvie is actually the only work of Nerval's discussed in *Contre Sainte-Beuve*; for Proust it is "the dream of a dream," peopled with beings that are "but the shadows of a dream," impregnated by Nerval's genius for making names and places his own, and all bathed "in purple." [13] Such statements would remain too impressionistic (though beautiful in their own way) if it were not for such perceptions as the "memory-landscapes" of Nerval: "that return to a country which is rather a past which exists for him at least as much in his heart as on the map"; [14] or that fine page of analysis in which Proust describes Nerval as "a mind almost too reasonable, too positive, tormented only by a melancholy that was altogether physical. In Gérard de Nerval the nascent and not yet overt madness is but a sort of excessive subjectivity, of greater importance so to speak for being bound to a dream, to a memory, to the personal quality of sensation, than to the thing which the sensation means commonly to all, perceptible by all, namely, reality." [15]

One of Proust's favorite passages from Nerval is on the same topic. In *Tendres Stocks* he holds up against Anatole France's condemnation of all nineteenth-century literature the preface of *Les Filles du feu*, dedicated to Alexandre Dumas, as a criterion of good writing. Nerval's well-known preface deals with his states of madness. Speaking of his sonnets, Nerval writes (and Proust quotes):

They . . . would lose their magic by being explicated, if that were possible; grant me at least some skill in expressing myself; the only folly that I shall probably have left is to think of myself as a poet; it is up to the critics to cure me of it.[16]

One wishes that he had expressed himself more fully on Nerval's works, notably *Aurélie* and *Les Chimères*. The poems are only casually mentioned — *El Desdichado*, to show parallel with *Sylvie, Fantaisie* as "one of those pictures of an unreal color"; [17] and the famous opening of *El Desdichado* as an example of one of Nerval's "admirable poems in which there are perhaps the loveliest lines in the French language, but lines as obscure as Mallarmé" [18] — a statement which, though obviously not incorrect, is woefully inadequate. More puzzling is the lack of mention of *Aurélie*, a work that, had Proust known it (we can only assume that he did not), would have affected him even more deeply than *Sylvie*. For Nerval, like Proust himself, belongs to the category of writers which only Romanticism made possible: the lyrical writer — whether he be a poet or a prose writer — who was embarked on a journey to discover the bonds between the outer and the inner worlds. What Balzac and Wagner tried to achieve largely by external means, Nerval, Proust, Baudelaire, and certain other writers tried to accomplish by an inner alchemy, particularly by the transforming or transcendental power of the memory, reaching out toward a "vita nuova." Hence the strong emphasis on autobiography, as in Rousseau, Chateaubriand, Nerval, and Baudelaire, since the path could be traversed only in that way, and the concomitant effort to resurrect an authentic self with the help of memory. Proust actually stands at the culmination of this development, being able to synthesize the two currents of the inner, Nervalian, alchemy and the outer, Balzacian, architecture.

In the passage in *La Prisonnière* in which Marcel explains to Albertine that the beauties of art and literature can often be discerned in recurrent patterns, *phrases-types*, he alludes to the works of two French novelists, Barbey d'Aurevilly and Stendhal. His analysis of Barbey d'Aurevilly's recurrences is as follows:

These typical phrases [*phrases-types*], which you are beginning to recognize as I do, my little Albertine, the same in the sonata, in the septet, in the other works, would be for instance, if you like, in Barbey d'Aurevilly, a hidden reality revealed by a material trace, the physiological blush of *l'Ensorcelée*, of *Aimée de Spens*, of *la Clotte*, the hand of the *Rideau Cramoisi*, the old manners and customs, the old words, the ancient and peculiar trades behind which there is the Past, the oral history compiled by the rustics of the manor, the noble Norman cities redolent of England and charming as a Scots village, the cause of curses against which one can do nothing, the Vellini, the Shepherd, a similar sensation of anxiety in a passage, whether it be the wife seeking her husband in *Une Vieille Maîtresse*, or the husband in *l'Ensorcelée* scouring the plain and the "Ensorcelée" herself coming out from Mass.[19]

It is true that Barbey d'Aurevilly is remembered today as a critic writing during the middle decades of the nineteenth century, rather than as a novelist. Nevertheless, his novels are skillfully wrought and give evidence of his fine powers of lively narration. What Proust admired in him is the more sophisticated use of Balzacian "reality" — the more harmonious style, the authentic recreation of the Norman atmosphere. This Balzacian side of Barbey is also stressed in a letter to Jean-Louis Vaudoyer, in which Proust compares the heroine of Vaudoyer's book *La Maîtresse et l'amie* to the characters of Barbey:

I am tempted to compare that strange physiological reserve of your heroine . . . to those deep peculiarities, which are almost medically ingrained in the flesh of *all* the great characters of Barbey d'Aurevilly (I shall explain that to you more effectively in conversation, for I enjoy talking about that writer) and of the heroine of the *Curé de village*.[20]

The allusion to *Le Curé de village* can be clarified by a quotation (which has already been given in more extensive form in the chapter on Balzac) from *Jean Santeuil*, in which Proust speaks of the action of the book as being "lifted up," physically as well as morally, until at the end there results a purification of the crimes of the heroine.

The allusions in the *Prisonnière* passage are to the novel *Le Chevalier Des Touches*, whose heroine is Aimée de Spens; and to "Le Rideau cramoisi," the first novelette of *Les Diaboliques* (the only one among the works mentioned whose locale is not Norman). Proust's observations on Barbey are by no means of an unusual nature; many of the elements which Marcel finds in Barbey's novels have also been pointed out by Barbey's biographers and critics. The description of the Lande de Lessay in the opening chapter of *L'Ensorcelée*, the sustained *ambiance* of Norman life, with its Norman types, Norman patois, and Norman customs — all these details evoked a response from Proust, who was himself so devoted to the genuine native attributes of his characters, whether they be Françoise or Oriane de Guermantes, and in whose work landscapes and places — and especially Norman and Breton landscapes — play such an important part.

The second author to figure in the *phrases-types* demonstration of *La Prisonnière* is Stendhal. In Stendhal's works, Proust notes, happiness and contemplation are usually associated with altitude. He observes that in Stendhal

> . . . a certain sense of altitude [combines] with the life of the spirit: the lofty place in which Julien Sorel is imprisoned, the tower on the summit of which Fabrice is confined, the belfry in which the Abbé Blanès pores over his astrology and from which Fabrice has such a magnificent bird's-eye view.[21]

This is one of Proust's favorite discoveries, since he also mentions it prominently in his essay on style which serves as the preface to Morand's *Tendres Stocks*:

> It would give me great pleasure to demonstrate how, every time that Julien Sorel or Fabrice abandoned their vain broodings, and plunged into a life of pure animal enjoyment in which self-consciousness played no part, it was always when they were in some place raised high above the earth's surface (whether the prison where

> Fabrice was confined, or Julien in the Abbé Banés's [*sic*] observatory). The effect is as fine as that produced by those figures who, with something of Angels in an Annunciation about them, bow down, in Dostoievsky, before the very man for whose murder they know themselves to have been responsible.[22]

Examples could be added to support Proust's analysis: from *Le Rouge et le noir* alone, Julien's moments of happiness reading Rousseau while perched on the rafters of his father's sawmill, in the mountains behind Verrières, on top of the ladder in the library of the Marquis de la Môle, and so on.

The *Nouveaux Mélanges* recently published as an appendage to *Contre Sainte-Beuve* contain an interesting collection of notes on Stendhal which Proust made for his own uses.[23] These notes are too fragmentary to be utilized for discussion, and the reader is advised to examine them himself. Proust notes in particular the irony of Stendhal: irony in the eighteenth-century manner and ironic treatment of his character, with Voltairean elegance. He remarks particularly on Stendhal's "exclusive predilection for the sensations of the soul," and under this rubric he discerns (probably for the first time) the Stendhal equation involving elevation of the soul and physical height and its corollary, "emotion before nature and generally in elevated places." This love of nature, he adds, is the eighteenth-century variety of "l'amour de la belle nature," and its sensations are very simple. At the end there is a fine observation on *Le Rouge et le noir* (all of Proust's examples, incidentally, are taken from that book or from *La Chartreuse*), which is not further developed:

> In a sense, beautiful books add a coincident slice of the soul to the events. In *Le Rouge et le Noir*, every action is followed by a part of the sentence indicating what goes on unconsciously in the soul; it is the novel of motives.

Stendhal's style, however, comes in for criticism in the Preface to *Tendres Stocks*.

> When Beyle described a landscape as "an enchanting spot" or a "ravishing spot," and one of his heroines as "this adorable woman," "this charming woman," it was because he felt no need of any greater precision. He was quite capable of saying — "She wrote him a letter that went on forever." [24]

This criticism may be related to the objections which Proust had offered in the case of Balzac's and Flaubert's styles. Some of the inadequacies of Stendhal's style pointed out by Proust have their counterparts in Balzac; and yet Balzac's conception of reality was found to rise above the weaknesses of his writing. In Flaubert, Proust noted that the metaphor alone does not serve as a criterion for the excellence of the style. Even if *la beauté grammaticale* of Flaubert, which compensated for Flaubert's dearth of imagery, is not present in Stendhal, yet Stendhal's ability to make palpable a way of looking at life triumphs above other considerations. It may be, Proust points out, that this vision manages to express itself unconsciously:

> But if one considers the great unconscious, bony structure which underlay the conscious and deliberate development of his thought as being a part of style, then style Stendhal most certainly had.[25]

And at this point Proust cites the passage dealing with Stendhal's "high places." Proust is undoubtedly too severe on Stendhal's style, which not only served his purpose admirably, but also had the precision and the wry humor which Stendhal felt warranted by the situation, with the result that the reader of Stendhal is more frequently struck by the "rightness" rather than by the literary beauty of the expression. Another problem is whether the "unconscious, bony structure" of any style can be discussed without extensive demonstration and documentation. Proust's implication here is that in some cases the unconscious organization of a writer's sensibility may be more important than his conscious organization, inasmuch as a writer's unconscious mechanisms, particularly his images, guarantee his style a certain authenticity, a genuineness of experience and feeling, which might be destroyed by too much intellectuality.

After all, Proust himself placed the sensibility above the intellect, and needed the stimulus of sensations to set into motion his analytical intellect. Similarly, in Proust's analysis of Dostoevski's *phrases-types*, which will be discussed in a later chapter, he makes a reference to the recurrence of certain aspects of the "houses of murder" which Dostoevski has created, probably more or less unconsciously. For this reason, Proust's allusion to Dostoevski's "kneeling characters reminiscent of new angels" is entirely apposite after an analysis of Stendhal.

Proust is strengthened in his conviction that "Beyle was a great writer — without realizing it" by Stendhal's frivolity, or even disdain, regarding his own work.

> He ranked literature not only lower than life (though, in fact, it is life's fulfilment), but even lower than the most insipid of distractions. I must admit that the following passage from Stendhal would, were it sincerely meant, shock me profoundly: "Several people arrived, and the party did not break up until very late. The nephew had an excellent *zabaglione* sent in from the Cafe Pedroti. 'Where I am going,' said I to my friends, 'I am not likely to find a house such as this, and, to occupy myself during the long evenings, I shall set about writing a story on the subject of the charming Duchesse Sanseverina' . . ." The idea of the *Chartreuse de Parme* having been written as a compensation for the lack of a house where he could find agreeable conversation, and eat *zabaglione*, is a far call from that poem, or even from that single line which, according to Mallarmé, is the justification of the various and vain activities of the human hive.[26]

Proust refuses to take Stendhal's trifling remarks seriously — for it is hardly plausible to consider Stendhal's novels as simple *divertissements* — and recognizes Stendhal as a great novelist, even though he may have written *faute de mieux*. Stendhal himself was aware of his qualities; he had written in his *Mémoires d'égotisme*, "I am used to seeming the opposite of what I am. I consider, and always have considered, my works as lottery tickets. I only attach importance to being reprinted in 1900."[27] This observation serves admirably as an answer to Proust's misgivings about Stendhal's flippancy. In this connection, Proust liked to administer a thrust to Sainte-Beuve, who took Stendhal at his word instead of at his letter.

> As to Stendhal the novelist, the Stendhal of *La Chartreuse*, our "guide" [Sainte-Beuve] laughs out of court the idea that such a person ever existed and merely sees in all the talk about him the disastrous effects of an attempt (foredoomed to failure) to foist Stendhal on the public as a novelist, much as the fame of certain painters seems to be due merely to the speculative activities of art dealers.[28]

In the preface to *Tendres Stocks*, Proust "disposes" of a number of writers of the nineteenth century who seem to justify Anatole France's charge that "bad writing has become the rule since the end of the eighteenth century." The writers discarded immediately are Guizot, Thiers, Villemain, Cousin, and finally Taine:

> Monsieur Taine, whose prose reminds one of a colored relief map designed to arouse interest in the minds of very junior schoolboys, may still find honor with some, but his name is down, nevertheless, for banishment.[29]

In a letter to Jacques-Emile Blanche, Proust elaborates on the "colored relief map":

> I find images that are born of an impression superior to the ones which serve only to illustrate an argument . . . I don't disdain that type of image, which Taine made considerable use of, but I prefer those in which you maintain contact with truth and poetry, whether you are speaking of men or of nature.[30]

In the midst of his "pastiche period" (1908–09), Proust amused himself by writing a short pastiche of Taine as a postscript to one of his letters to Robert Dreyfus.[31] This interest in Taine may have had something to do with the project to write his Sainte-Beuve essay "in the manner of Taine," although in this instance "à la Taine" presumably stands for a general form of the critical article, not its style.

Proust's next target in the preface to *Tendres Stocks* is Renan, with whose style he had become impregnated to such an extent that he felt that he had to exorcise it by means of the pastiche. As early as 1905 Proust had certain misgivings about *La Vie de Jésus*. In a footnote commentary of his translation of *Sesame and Lilies* he charged Renan with writing a sort of *Belle Hélène* of Christianity.[32]

Proust's exact reasons for thinking of Renan as the Offenbach of Christianity are given in the Preface to *Tendres Stocks*, in which Proust still respects Renan as a moralist, but not as a stylist.

> If, out of consideration for his accurate enunciation of moral truths, we spare Monsieur Renan, we can hardly avoid admitting that he often wrote very badly. Not to mention his later works, in which the colors so constantly jar that one is tempted to believe in a deliberate effort on his part to be comic, or his earliest, to which a rash of exclamation marks gives the appearance of a sentimental effusion perpetrated by a choirboy, even the lovely *Origines du christianisme* is, for the most part, badly written. It is rare to find in a prose writer of merit so complete an inability to paint a picture.[33]

As an example, he refers to the description of Jerusalem in *La Vie de Jésus* which he calls "composed in the style of Baedeker." The somewhat tawdry enumeration of details, sprinkled with superlatives, in that chapter, as well as in other chapters of *La Vie de Jésus* (although there are often good descriptions, not reminiscent of Baedeker), justifies the remark. Furthermore, Proust objects to Renan's occasional pompousness:

> Whenever he sets himself to provide a fitting ending to a book, or a Preface, he can achieve nothing better than one of those ready-made images to the school essay writer, which express no genuine personal impression at all. "Now the apostolic ship could spread its sails." "When the dazzling glare had withdrawn before the innumerable army of the stars." "Death struck both of us with his wing." [34]

Finally, the "Offenbach" strain in Renan, that facile simplification designed to please the reader rather than to move him, is alluded to once more in a passage on Jesus.

When, in speaking of the time spent by Jesus in Jerusalem, Monsieur Renan insists on referring to him as the "young Jewish democrat," and refers to the "crudities" that were forever falling from the lips of this "man from the provinces" (how like Balzac!) one is inclined to wonder, as I did more than once, whether, for all its author's genius, *La Vie de Jésus* is not really just the *Belle Hélène* of Christianity.[35]

That the repudiation of Renan's style was both a pleasure and an effort is attested by the fact that Proust's pastiche of Renan is longer than any of the others, except the pastiche of Saint-Simon; that he wrote for Jacques Boulenger's *La Revue de la semaine* a second pastiche of Renan (in 1922) which was never published.[36] Proust admitted to Robert Dreyfus in 1908 that writing Renan pastiches was "natural" to him:

I haven't made a single correction in the Renan. The ideas came to me in droves, and I glued entire pages to the galley-proofs, and all this happened at the last moment, so that I couldn't verify some quotations from Madame de Noailles. I had set my interior metronome to Renan's rhythm, and I could have written ten volumes that way. Be thankful that I didn't do so.[37]

In the pastiche one finds Renan's long sinuous sentences, a certain intentional sweetness in the extensive description of landscapes. As one student of Renan put it, "It is well known with what sharp exactness Marcel Proust has made a pastiche, not only of his sometimes venturesome manner of reconstructing the past, but also of Renan's descriptive style, its rather soft and graceful touch and its delicate, scattered hues." [38] Then there are typical Renanesque features, such as Renan's skepticism regarding literary authorship:

The drab collection of unlikely tales bearing the title *Comédie humaine* by Balzac is perhaps not the work of one man nor of one age. However its rather formless style, its ideas characterized by old-fashioned absolutism, permits us to date the publication of the collection at two hundred years, at least, before Voltaire.[39]

Similarly, Victor Hugo's *Chansons des rues et des bois* is spoken of as "commonly attributed to Victor Hugo, although the book is probably somewhat later"; and Madame de Noailles' authorship of the poems "attributed to her" is put in question.[40] By way of further parody and criticism, Proust includes Latin quotations, exclamation points, apostrophes in the earlier Renan manner. The following quotation combines all these elements:

Patience, Humanity, patience! Rekindle tomorrow the furnace, thousands of times extinguished already, whence the diamond will one day issue forth! With a faith that will elicit the envy of the Eternal, perfect the crucible in which you will raise carbon to temperatures unknown to Lemoine and Berthelot. Repeat untiringly, "*Sto ad ostium et pulso*," without knowing if ever a voice will answer, "*Veni, veni, coronaberis*." Your history has henceforth entered on a new path from which the silly fantasies of the vain and the aberring will not succeed in deflecting you.[41]

Incidentally, Proust's remarks to Robert Dreyfus on his use of the word "aberring" (*aberrant*) in the last sentence of the quotation are both amusing and illuminating.

I find "aberring" extremely Renanesque. I don't think Renan ever used the word. If I found it in his work, my satisfaction of having invented it would be diminished, but, if I do not find it, I shall be tempted to remove it . . . because the word does not figure in Renan's "vocabulary." [42]

Here is a concrete illustration of how sympathetically Proust was "attuned" to Renan; when the pastiche can go so far as to put characteristic words into an author's mind, it becomes truly creative; for here one finds the link between the literary mimic and the creator of talking and gesturing characters. Renan, one might say, becomes at that moment one of Proust's characters.

In the Michelet pastiche Proust preserves the "humanitarian" tone of the historian and his rhetorical style:

If the heart flinches, the stone is still there, which with its clear-burning flame, seems to say, "Have courage, another blow of the pickax, and I am yours." Besides, he who hesitates is lost. Salvation lies in speed. A moving dilemma! [43]

In addition, there are examples of Michelet's historical erudition all through the pastiche, reflections of Michelet's own revolutionary prejudices, and above all, that vibrant "sense of humanity" which animated him; there are echoes of the sentimentality and naïve faith of *La Bible de l'humanité*. All these elements are to be found in the following excerpt, amusingly manipulated:

My mind still upset by this Lemoine affair, which quite rightly struck me at once as an episode in the gigantic struggle between wealth and knowledge, I used to go to the Louvre every day, where the common people instinctively stop to admire the Crown Jewels, rather than *La Gioconda*. More than once I found it hard to get near the Jewels. Need I say this investigation fascinated me, yet I did not like it? And the secret behind it all? I did not feel the pulse of life in it. This need of life has always been my strength — as well as my weakness. At the culmination of the reign of Louis XIV, when absolutism seems to have eradicated all liberty in France, for two long years — which seemed more than a century — (1680–1789), strange headaches made me think that I would be forced to interrupt my History. I did not really regain my strength until the Tennis Court Oath (June 20, 1789).[44]

In contrast with the respectful good humor of the Michelet pastiche, the Goncourt pastiche serves Proust to cast out the demon of the *style artiste*, which may have required of him an even greater effort than the exorcism of Renan; it is significant perhaps that the only pastiche contained in *A la recherche du temps perdu* is a rather long pastiche of the Goncourt Journals at the beginning of *Le Temps retrouvé*.[45] In addition to the indirect criticism of these two pastiches, there are a number of direct critical remarks in an article published in *Le Gaulois* of May 27, 1922 and entitled "Les Goncourt devant leurs cadets."

The two pastiches illustrate well enough the fact that the

Goncourt excess of *goût*, in all its manifestations, often resulted in prose that was slightly ridiculous, sometimes devoid of taste altogether. Thus Proust uses far-fetched terminology à la Goncourt, often set off in italics: "avec un rien de verve blagueuse," "crime de lèse-bijouterie," "dans le *bondieusement* de certains paysages," "le faire miniaturé de son dire," "dans le bruit des *mazagrans* qu'on passe,"[46] and many others. Among the less burlesque aspects of the pastiches, one may single out the fondness both of the Goncourt brothers and of Proust for long sentences split apart by parenthetical elements driven into them like wedges, such as the following:

> Dined with Lucien Daudet, who, with the merest trifle of lively humbugging, speaks of the fabulous diamonds seen on the shoulders of Madame X. . . , diamonds described by Lucien in strong fine language, by heaven, and everything artistically worded, the savory way he spelled out his epithets betraying a really superior artist, as being, after all, just a middle-class stone . . .[47]

Furthermore, the Goncourt milieu and the Proustian milieu frequently coincide; and this fact explains why the "unpublished" Goncourt Journal was Proust's logical choice for a pastiche when he wanted to help Marcel, now grown old, to reminisce about the persons and drawing rooms of his younger days. The contrast of the Goncourt tittle-tattle, drenched with the perfume of the *style artiste*, with the penetrating observations which Proust had been making all through the novel, serves wonderfully to point up the results obtained when craftsmanship on the one hand and art on the other operate on the same material. In the former case, the result is likely to be no more than amiable inanity. Hence Marcel's reaction after reading the pseudo-Journal is one of disappointment, he is convinced once more that underneath the ultrarefinement of the Goncourts there lies a too easily discoverable naïveté. This is also the essence of Du Bos' remarks about Les Goncourt, who characterizes the brothers as being indiscriminate as a result of being too deliberately discriminating.[48]

The inadequacy of the Goncourts as true artists is given precise expression in the article in *Le Gaulois*. There Proust writes:

> The subordination of all worldly, affectionate and familial duties to the duty of being the servant of truth might have made Monsieur de Goncourt great if he had taken the word "truth" in a deeper and broader sense, if he had created more living beings, for the description of whom the forgotten sketchbook of the memory furnishes one unexpectedly with some new feature, which broadens and complements the picture. Unfortunately, instead of doing that, he observed, took notes, kept a journal — all of which is not characteristic of the great creative artist. The journal remains a delightful and entertaining book, in spite of all the calumny that has been heaped upon it. Its style, full of new "finds," is not that of an inept craftsman of the French language. If I attempted to analyze that style, I would use up too much space. Besides, I have already treated it critically, by way of a synthesis, in my *Pastiches et mélanges* and especially in one of the volumes of *A la recherche du temps perdu* — a criticism which was, on the whole, favorable.[49]

The article contains an implicit rejection of the entire "documentary" method of the naturalistic school of fiction, especially the mania of note-taking. Against this method Proust opposes the search for a deeper truth which can be found only by combing the recesses of one's memory. Proust is thus marking off his own divergence from naturalism and emphasizing the superiority of what was not only a new development in fiction after 1890 or so, but what was actually a reaffirmation of the Balzacian tradition, which fused a love of material objects with a reliance upon the artist's experiences, feelings, and reminiscences. With respect to Balzac, the Naturalistic school is but an aberration, which occasionally made possible charming but inconsequential books, such as the *Journal*, but more frequently produced documentary or pseudo-scientific tracts which left Proust altogether indifferent. That is the reason why there is no discussion of Zola or of the novels of the Goncourt brothers in Proust's writings.

In conclusion, a brief remark about George Sand, whose

novels figure so prominently in Marcel's childhood memories and in whom he had found a "bonté" and a "distinction morale." [50] The Narrator's admiration for George Sand's country idylls is intended as an illustration of his early literary and psychological development, not as a piece of criticism, Proust explains in a letter to Lauris.[51] In this sense, *François le Champi* serves the same function as Gautier's *Le Capitaine Fracasse*, which enriches the childhood "days of reading" — in *Jean Santeuil* particularly — but whose covers must be left unopened by the maturing reader, who cannot resuscitate his childhood at will.[52]

The above discussions indicate that Proust's interests in the nineteenth century were by no means confined to his favorite predecessors in the realm of fiction. As was shown in the chapter on the poets, Proust allowed his sensibilities to range freely over the writers of the nineteenth century, noting *phrases-types* here, or a stylistic characteristic there, or paying tribute to those with whom he felt a particular kinship. In spite of the fact that many of the observations are random and, for the purposes of a unified appraisal, fragmentary, Proust has nevertheless given certain indications of what a twentieth-century literary critic might do — that is to say, a "converted" Sainte-Beuve or even an anti-Sainte-Beuve with a firm critical grasp on the literature of his own age. It is necessary now to let Proust pay off an old score to Sainte-Beuve.

5. SAINTE-BEUVE, THE "POOR GUIDE"

Proust's bête noire, Sainte-Beuve, has strayed into the discussion a number of times already. His name had a way of obtruding itself whenever Proust's favorite authors of the nineteenth century were under consideration, with Proust reiterating the idea that Sainte-Beuve, whose business it was to appreciate these writers, failed to understand them. Yet his grievances with the nineteenth-century critic are more deeply rooted, for Sainte-Beuve's entire critical method comes under attack; and we find ourselves, in the last analysis, in the presence of a deep-seated antagonism between two attitudes toward the psychology of the artist and the nature of literary art itself.

This explains why after the Ruskin period everything points toward Sainte-Beuve; we are not dealing here with a case of exorcism, as in Ruskin or in the pastiches, but with a simple case of expulsion. Sainte-Beuve is wrong, says Proust, in his method of judging literature; he misunderstands the entire process of literary creation; and even though he is in some ways a fine critic, especially of the classics, and even though he is a good stylist, he must be rejected by the serious writer. The importance for Proust's career of the casting out of Sainte-Beuve must not be underestimated. Before *Contre Sainte-Beuve* we have Proust, very much like the Narrator in his great work, "à la recherche d'une vocation"; with *Contre Sainte-Beuve*, and particularly right after it, we have "la vocation trouvée" (or *retrouvée*).

Another factor influencing Proust's need to come to grips with Sainte-Beuve (or, for that matter, with any rationalistically oriented critic of the nineteenth century, such as Taine) lies in his growing conviction around 1908 that the intelligence is inadequate when used as the sole instrument of literary analysis — and, by implication, of literary creation. He had felt for a long time that impressions were nearer artistic truth than were intellectualizations. The content of *Jean Santeuil* is, accordingly, strongly impressionistic. But the work was abandoned. What Proust needed was a conception of his work in which the impression would be preserved in a pure state, without being clouded by excessive subjectivity, and in which the intelligence would find its proper place, albeit a subsidiary one. Feeling must precede analysis, without creating discontinuities and imbalances. After all, Proust is as much an heir of the "dreaming" romantics (Nerval, for instance) as of the realists (Balzac and, to a lesser degree, Flaubert). *A la recherche* is a monumental synthesis of the two traditions. Here again *Contre Sainte-Beuve* stands midway between the aspiration (*Jean Santeuil*) and the fulfillment (*A la recherche*). But the work already looks toward the great novel to be created. The Preface of *Contre Sainte-Beuve* begins in this way:

> Every day I attach less value to the intelligence. Every day I understand better that only outside of it the writer can grasp something of our impressions, that is to say, can reach something that is himself and the only subject matter of art. What the intelligence offers us under the name of the past is not the past at all.[1]

This introduction leads directly into a discussion of the past as hidden in some object and accessible to us only through sensation — a prefiguration of the remarks introducing the *madeleine* episode in *Du côté de chez Swann.* And indeed the subsequent pages are taken up with a description of affective memory experiences, as found in *Swann* and in *Le Temps retrouvé*.

The assertion of the tenet that feeling precedes reason, and its elucidation by examples, marks the beginning of Proust's final liberation from the seduction of the intelligence. His literary taste had naturally gravitated toward the intellectual precision of the seventeenth century, and he had found in the literature of the Grand Siècle a standard of reference. From that age he had acquired the flair for succinct moral generalizations. In Baudelaire, one of his heroes, he had discerned an ideal marriage between "le rêve" and "l'esprit classique" and had insisted on Baudelaire's kinship with — even his occasional superiority over — Racine. Consequently, one of Proust's major aims in 1908 was to put the intelligence in its place, not to repudiate it. Sainte-Beuve becomes the subject of a lengthy investigation to illustrate by concrete examples the shortcomings of the "intelligent" critic confronted by great literary works. The "essay in the manner of Taine," had it been consistently carried through, would have had the effect of undermining the critical literary essay, whose structure is based on a rational sequence of perceptions arising from the critic's intelligence. As it turned out, Proust turned more and more to the *récit*, which offered the possibility of utilizing personal impressions and divagations; and before long he found himself embarked on something that resembles a novel rather than a work of criticism. The actual anti-Sainte-Beuve portions occupy the central third of the work; the surrounding portions constitute a preview of *A la recherche*. The brilliant middle chapters of the work not only take Sainte-Beuve to task but offer us an antidote to the nineteenth-century critic, namely, Proustian literary analysis.

In the chapter "Conversation avec maman," Proust (he has not yet become the Narrator, "the character who uses the first person" of *A la recherche*) broaches the subject of Sainte-Beuve's famous method and in the subsequent chapter launches into a long disquisition:

> It seems to me that I might have . . . a good deal more to say à propos of Sainte-Beuve than about Sainte-Beuve himself — things which are perhaps of importance, if by showing where in my opinion his faults as a writer and critic lie, I might perhaps reach the point where I make certain statements (which I've often thought over) on the subject of what a critic ought to be and what art is.[2]

This declaration serves as the keynote of what follows. First Bourget's and Taine's praises of Sainte-Beuve are dismissed as misleading and the entire problem of the artist's relation to his work is taken under scrutiny. Proust categorically denies that there is any such thing as a precursor in literature; each writer begins all over again. Whereas Sainte-Beuve makes no real distinction between the writer and his work, Proust asserts that there is a sharp cleavage between the social or habitual self of the writer and the creative self. The case of Stendhal illustrates Sainte-Beuve's error clearly enough (and Proust was to come back to this problem in his Preface to *Tendres Stocks*); but, as a matter of fact, he claims that the same error of judgment lies at the base of all of Sainte-Beuve's criticisms of the great ones among his literary contemporaries. For the critic did not really understand that the poet works in solitude; and that the true appreciation of literature lies in the critic's ability to listen to the poet's solitude, as it were, rather than to his conversation. "The writer's *moi* shows itself only in his books; he does not show his *moi* to society."[3] Conversation is therefore not the right method of approach; and just as reading is not a substitute for conversation, or a higher form of it, as Proust had been at pains to point out in his preface to *Sésame et les lys*, criticism or literary analysis is not a way of holding converse with an author. There is something incomplete and misleading in this method of analyzing a work of art by consulting the artist's social or everyday personality. Proust finds this inadequacy exemplified in the very nature of Sainte-Beuve's *Lundis*: the critic's thought is incomplete, it takes pleasure in this very fact, since thereby he establishes a sort of conversational contact with his readers, who are expected to complete the idea. He compares it to an arch which takes its origin in Sainte-Beuve's mind and which completes its curve and receives its coloring from the admiring reader. For Sainte-Beuve, he concludes, all literature is like that: it is a series of Monday chats, pleasing to the Monday audiences, unmindful of the judgment of posterity. This is the real crux of Proust's objection to Sainte-Beuve: the author of the *Lundis* saw literature *sub specie temporis* and literature for him was time-bound, its worth was equivalent to the worth of the person producing it. In Sainte-Beuve the attitude is aggravated by a parallel impulse to preserve his freedom, with the result that if a man wishes to please and yet remain independent, he will find himself writing contradictory articles, such as Sainte-Beuve's on Chateaubriand, or Hugo or Lamartine or Lamennais or even Béranger.

All this is a consequence of Sainte-Beuve's personality and his critical method — to misunderstand the nature of artistic creation, to judge the artist in terms of his social self, to evaluate art in terms of an epoch rather than of eternity: it all adds up to a critical method which is not only conditioned by time but also operates materially (Taine was to go so far as to say "scientifically") on the epoch under consideration. "This ill will which refuses to look into the depths of oneself. . . . is my main objection to Sainte-Beuve; it is a material criticism (even though the author speaks only of Ideas, etc.)."[4]

As concrete illustrations of the deficiencies of the author of the *Lundis*, Proust singles out the cases of Nerval, Baudelaire, and Balzac, and allots to each a separate chapter. In addition to these writers, there are random allusions to Stendhal, Flaubert, and Chateaubriand. These observations in the *Contre Sainte-Beuve*, however, by no means exhaust what Proust felt he had to say on the subject, although everything is there in essence. It is as though he felt that he had to wage an intermittent battle over the aesthetic implication of Sainte-Beuve's method as contrasted with his own. He frequently speaks of Sainte-Beuve in his correspondence and comes back to his grievances in the introductions to Blanche's *Propos de peintre* and Morand's *Tendres Stocks*, both written during the last years of his life; and in *A la recherche* there is a curious transposition of the Sainte-Beuvean attitude as incarnated by Madame de Villeparisis.

The choice of Nerval, Baudelaire, and Balzac in the *Contre Sainte-Beuve* is both significant and fascinating from the point of view of Proust's own artistic preoccupations at that moment: he purposely selected three writers, misjudged by Sainte-Beuve, whom he regarded as ancestors of his own creative techniques and aesthetic attitudes and who, incidentally, had a large share of the irrational, with which the author of the *Lundis* had little patience.

The Nerval essay deals rather with Nerval's *Sylvie* than with Sainte-Beuve's judgment of Nerval. As a matter of fact, Sainte-Beuve paid practically no attention to his poetry or prose; for the critic, Nerval was little more than "the traveling salesman from Paris to Munich" (as Proust contemptuously quotes). In another place (the Flaubert essay) Proust points out Sainte-Beuve's typical condescension toward the poet, whom he treats as "gentil Nerval" on the occasion of a Goethe translation.[5]

The case of Sainte-Beuve and Stendhal is similar. Sainte-Beuve habitually shrugged off the assertion that Stendhal was a serious novelist. After all, Proust tells his readers, Sainte-Beuve knew him as a jovial table companion, who, "delightful companion though he might be, would have been the first to laugh in one's face had one treated him as a great novelist!"[6] Sainte-Beuve did as a matter of fact regard Stendhal's novels as late as 1857 as "failures in spite of good parts in them, and, on the whole, detestable."[7]

The result of all of Sainte-Beuve's blunders is that a novice in French literature, taking the *Causeries du lundi* for a guide would learn

> that there were, at that time in France, a number of remarkable writers, such as Monsieur Royer-Collard, Monsieur le Comte de Molé, Monsieur de Tocqueville, Madame Sand, Béranger, Mérimée, and others, and that Sainte-Beuve had known personally several intelligent people who had not been without a certain charm, a certain ephemeral value, but whom it would be foolish to reckon, now, as great artists . . .[8]

To be sure, Proust is extremely harsh on Sainte-Beuve, forgetting perhaps too readily that Sainte-Beuve often made perspicacious and relevant remarks on a few first-rate authors of his day, including Chateaubriand[9] and Flaubert. Nor is he interested in paying tribute to Sainte-Beuve for his fine perceptions on the "classics." He does not give Sainte-Beuve credit for having made literary criticism into a craft, even into a genre. Proust, after all, is not concerned with matters of literary history. His position is as follows: Sainte-Beuve's final rating as a judge of the nineteenth century is not high. He aptly points out that Sainte-Beuve has a way of spoiling his praises by condescension and patronizing airs. Proust is certain that Sainte-Beuve, by adopting for himself the perspective of history rather than of art, aggravates his blunders of taste and arrives at a point where he often classifies his contemporaries "much as Madame de Boigne or the Duchesse de Broglie might have done . . ."[10]

Another way in which Proust gave vent to his disapproval of Sainte-Beuve's methods was in the pastiche of Sainte-Beuve, the third in the series written just before the *Contre Sainte-Beuve* (or, better, when Proust had Sainte-Beuve on his mind and was rereading his works). It is ramified in a typically Proustian way. Entitled "Critique du roman de M. Gustave Flaubert sur l'Affaire Lemoine par Sainte-Beuve, dans son feuilleton du Constitutionnel," it can be described as a pastiche by Proust of Sainte-Beuve reviewing a Flaubert novel on a Balzacian theme! Naturally, the pastiche of Flaubert serves as a basis for the "Sainte-Beuve" review. It includes the usual summary of the story (as in Sainte-Beuve's review of *Madame Bovary*), punctuated by the usual interpellations:

> But you who have just told us (as if indeed you had counted them!) the number of elephants and onagers in the Carthaginian army, how do you expect to be taken at your word, I ask you, when you commit blunders like that for a reality so close at hand, so easily verifiable, so succinct and in no way complicated by detail!

Then there is the humorous reaction which the pseudo-Flaubert's designation of someone in the courtroom as a "reactionary" elicits in the pseudo-Sainte-Beuve:

> It's a rather frequently used term these days. But here I should like to ask Monsieur Flaubert a question: "A reactionary? how do you recognize one from the distance? Who told you so? What do you know about it?"

And in line with a certain judgment which Sainte-Beuve pronounced on *Madame Bovary* ("the good is too conspicuously absent; not a single character stands for the good"), Proust's pastiche echoes, "The author belongs to a school which never sees anything noble or praiseworthy in humanity." [11]

The case against Sainte-Beuve on the subject of Flaubert, it must be admitted, is not as strong as Proust might have wished it to be. To be sure, the familiar Sainte-Beuve features are discernible, but the patronizing tone which one finds in Sainte-

Beuve's writings on Balzac has been modified; and there are at least two major articles on the works by Flaubert (reviews of *Madame Bovary* and *Salammbô*) which appeared during Sainte-Beuve's lifetime. Proust felt that Sainte-Beuve ought to have devoted an article to Flaubert's achievement, in addition to the reviews of the novels. Yet, whatever one might think of this suggestion, the fact remains that Sainte-Beuve's treatment of Flaubert must be regarded as generous compared with his treatment of Baudelaire. Proust did not fail to notice — and resent — Sainte-Beuve's behavior toward the poet. His indignation is here more violent than usual:

> The account of the contacts between Baudelaire and Sainte-Beuve (Sainte-Beuve whose stupidity was such that we sometimes wonder whether it was not assumed in order to conceal his moral cowardice) is one of the most heartrending, but at the same time, most comical chapters in the whole history of French literature.[12]

The bitterness of this statement is in part influenced by Fernand Vandérem's monograph *Baudelaire et Sainte-Beuve*,[13] to which Proust makes a respectful allusion in his essay on Baudelaire. One might say that Vandérem only added fuel to a long-smoldering fire. Vandérem had recounted and documented the entire history of the bizarre behavior of the critic toward the poet. In the Preface to *Tendres Stocks*,[14] Proust repeats a number of condescending and unctuous remarks which Sainte-Beuve made to Baudelaire in his letters, and allusions to the poet appearing here and there in the *Lundis*. Moreover, both Proust and Vandérem call attention to the puzzling fact that Sainte-Beuve never saw fit to devote an article to Baudelaire or any of his works. Whereas Vandérem suggests in addition an element of jealousy in Sainte-Beuve, Proust does not ascribe the critic's behavior to more than his inadequacy and to a certain cowardice in the *Fleurs du Mal* trial. In all fairness, however, the habitual *bizarrerie* of Baudelaire is not brought into the discussion.

Another concrete example of the differences between Proust

and Sainte-Beuve as critics is found in the chapter "Sainte-Beuve et Balzac." Here one notes Proust's irritation with Sainte-Beuve's charges that *La Comédie humaine* has little "reality" and that the characters are larger than life. Some of this is carried over into the pastiche:

> Or, take the *Comedie humaine*, so-called, where Monsieur de Balzac, with a conceit that becomes ridiculous, pretends to depict "scenes (pretty incredible ones, actually) of Parisian and provincial life" (Balzac, of all people, who did not know how to observe *anything*); did not his imagination permit him to create an Adeline Hulot, a Blanche de Mortsauf, a Marguerite de Solis by way of contrast to, and redemption for, creating the Hulots, the Philippe Bridaus and the Balthazar Claeses, as he calls them? [15]

The source of these assertions is primarily Sainte-Beuve's review of *La Recherche de l'absolu*, a somewhat grudging tribute to Balzac, in which the critic, in his characteristic manner, spoils many of his favorable judgments by a deferential and pontifical tone. Interestingly enough, he gives Balzac credit for having a "very deep sense of private lives," but in the next sentence he says, "He surmises the mysteries of provincial life, sometimes invents them," and a little later, "The question arises where, with the petulant turn of his imagination, did he pick it all up?" [16] These criticisms of Sainte-Beuve account for Proust's use of such terms as "incredible scenes," "didn't he imagine. . . ," "a man incapable of observing" in the pastiche.

The same sort of criticism appears in *Sodome et Gomorrhe* through the university professor Brichot, who calls *La Comédie humaine* "bien peu humaine," makes Balzac into a "copieux improvisateur" who strikes him as "un scribe insuffisamment méticuleux" and describes his novels as "rédigés en pathos, en galimatias double et triple." Criticism of Balzac is used here to criticize the personality of Brichot, too absorbed in his academic activities, too formal in matters of literary style — in brief, a man who lets petty considerations blind him to the real art of Balzac. Charlus' reply to Brichot echoes Proust's own to Sainte-

Beuve in "Sainte-Beuve et Balzac": "You say that because you know nothing of life." [17]

Sainte-Beuve did not care for Balzac's style — but, in Proust's eyes, he disliked it for the wrong reasons. He calls it

> . . . that style which so often titillates and melts, enervated, rosy and veined with all tints, that deliciously corrupt style, quite "Asiatic," as our teachers used to say, more broken up and more softened than the body of an ancient mime.[18]

Proust's position is that Balzac's reality is not sufficiently transformed into a literary equivalent and that therefore there is no style, properly speaking. In other words, Balzac's style is explicative and descriptive, not lush and elegant.

Criticism of Sainte-Beuve's opinions continues along the same vein: "Sainte-Beuve's other criticisms are no less absurd," or "Sainte-Beuve is his usual self in the case of Balzac." [19] According to Proust, Sainte-Beuve's misunderstanding is nearly complete. He fails to see the idea underlying Balzac's work, he fails to understand its design; when he ought to be discussing the "femme de trente ans" in Balzac, he talks instead about the thirty-year-old woman in general; when he ought to be concerned with Balthazar Claes in *La Recherche de l'absolu*, he drags in a comparable document from "real life" and expresses the wish that Balzac had known it and thus "steered clear of many a false conjecture." [20] Here is the old familiar — and slightly malicious — voice of the entrenched critic, taking himself too seriously.

In his essay on Flaubert, Proust acknowledges the seduction of Sainte-Beuve's style: "I have more than once debauched myself by indulging in the delicious but shoddy music of Sainte-Beuve's florid conversational style" (*langage parlé, perlé*).[21] The pastiche reproduces exactly this "shoddy music," and so well that Mouton calls it "so faithful a reproduction that it astonishes by its resemblance and truthfulness." [22] In addition to its "florid conversational style" it bristles with the characteristic traits of Sainte-Beuve's criticism. There are, first of all, the references to classical writers, presented in strange juxtapositions:

Without going back to the writers of antiquity (who are much more "naturalistic" than you will ever be, but who on a clearly-defined canvas and within a framework of reality always left the air free and the sky open for a divine ray of light to break through and settle on the pediment to light up the contrast), without going back to them, be their names Homer or Moschus, Bion or Leonidas of Tarentum . . .[23]

This fragment illustrates more than the irrelevant, rhetorical classicism presented in an obfuscating arrangement; the long parenthesis produces a conversational effect (*langage parlé*), and the elaborate, though beautiful, architectural image chosen to represent classical clarity, adds the "florid" (*langage perlé*) element — for the image is arbitrary within this particular context.

Then there are Sainte-Beuve's stylistic eccentricities, such as his peculiar insistence on using a sequence of three adjectives in diminishing rather than increasing order — that "corruption of taste . . . that drove Sainte-Beuve to upset all the normal relations between words, to alter any expression that was at all conventional."[24] Proust has reproduced stylistic discontinuities of this sort in the pastiche: ". . . when literature was but the token and you might say the flowering of urbanity and wit . . . ," ". . . the very considerable Chaix d'Est-Ange (whose published speeches have certainly not lost all their force and flavor, but their *à propos* and their chattiness). . . ," and "those men of refinement and study." At the end of the pastiche Proust adds a Sainte-Beuvean apostrophe: "Ah, posterity of Atala, posterity of Atala, you can be found everywhere today, even on the anatomist's dissection table!"[25]

Sainte-Beuve's occasional deferential tone in his criticism is made the butt of Proust's scorn.

Monsieur Flaubert . . . does not belong to the category of writers whom Martial cleverly mocked, who, past masters on a certain terrain, or at least having that reputation, take up a position there and fortify themselves, careful above all to avoid fighting the critics at close quarters, exposing only one wing at a time in the manoeuver.[26]

Certain key sentences, such as the one just quoted, always do multiple duty in the pastiches. Here is the classical allusion to Martial (quite unnecessary), Sainte-Beuve's predilection for military imagery, and the sly "or at least having that reputation," whereby Proust's Sainte-Beuve leaves Flaubert's proficiency slightly open to question. The condescending tone is found in the reference of "Sainte-Beuve" to his friendship with Flaubert's family: ". . . not to forget that the author is the son of a very fine man, whom we have all known . . . and that this excellent son — whatever objection one might raise to the tendency of certain premature friends, swayed by considerations of friendship, to speak of his talent already. . . ," and so on.[27] The unctuous and protective tone which Sainte-Beuve often used toward his younger contemporaries is wonderfully preserved here. The most devastating thrust is administered by Proust when he lets Sainte-Beuve hold up the *vérité* of third- and fourth-rate novelists as a model to Flaubert:

> But there is more truth in the smallest sketch, say, of Sénac de Meilhan, of Ramond or d'Althon Shée, than in yours, which is so painstakingly inaccurate! Don't you know it's all so wrong as to set one's teeth on edge? [28]

The sentence also illustrates Sainte-Beuve's "chatty" way of criticizing, of adopting an unwarranted exhortatory and moralizing tone toward his author.

Generally speaking, this pastiche offers one major and one minor criticism: the more important aspect is the exposition of Sainte-Beuve's inadequacy as a critic of the literature of his day; and the lesser feature is the re-creation of Sainte-Beuve's characteristic style. As a mild criticism of Sainte-Beuve's somewhat facile stylistic refinements, this pastiche falls in line with the general tendencies of all the pastiches, notably those in which certain styles attractive and too seductive for Proust are "exorcised" — especially those of Saint-Simon, Renan, Flaubert, and the Goncourts. "And still, nothing has remained so intelligent, so alive as those fine books [*Les Causeries du lundi*] . . ."[29] In *A la recherche*, when Marcel finally sees his own article in print, he rereads it and muses upon it for a while, arriving at the conclusion that the value of such articles, like the value of Sainte-Beuve's articles in the *Constitutionnel*, resides in the impression which they produce upon their readers.

> It is a synthetic Venus, of which we have but one truncated limb if we confine ourselves to the thought of the author, for it is realised in its completeness only in the minds of his readers. In them it finds its fulfilment. And as a crowd, even a select crowd, is not an artist, this final seal of approval which it sets upon the article must always retain a certain element of vulgarity. Thus Sainte-Beuve, on a Monday, could imagine Mme. de Boigne in her bed with its eight columns reading his article in the *Constitutionnel*, appreciating some charming phrase in which he had long delighted and which might never, perhaps, have flowed from his pen had he not thought it expedient to load his article with it in order to give it a longer range.[30]

The critic who is excessively conscious of his reading public — like Sainte-Beuve — makes compromises, to the detriment of the material which is being judged.

In *A la recherche du temps perdu* Madame de Villeparisis takes the place of a modern Madame de Boigne. She had been brought up in the period of the *Lundis* and talks like a faithful reader of the *Constitutionnel*; and her inability to judge the literature of her day is supplemented by another Sainte-Beuvean feature — that of making her personal acquaintance with the artist a criterion in judging his works. Her rejection of Vigny and Musset as poets because of their aristocratic aspirations has already been pointed out; Balzac was taken to task for setting himself up as the painter of a society where he was not "received"; and Hugo was condemned as a poet who received his acclaim only as the result of "making a deal" with the socialists. Incidentally, Madame de Villeparisis characterizes

Sainte-Beuve as a man "qui avait bien de l'esprit," and whom she echoes by saying of the writers of her day, ". . . In forming an estimate you must take the word of people who saw them close, and were able to judge more exactly of their real worth."[31] In other words, Madame de Villeparisis represents a living pastiche of Sainte-Beuve, or at least of a reader of his articles. This is the conclusion at which the Narrator arrives, in so many words. Indeed, a large portion of the Sainte-Beuve pastiche might have been put into Madame de Villeparisis' mouth.

Yet Proust's rejection of Sainte-Beuve's critical output is not absolute; only the method is under attack and the extent to which it falsified an author's work. The fact that both men show the highest regard for the literature of the seventeenth century indicates that the standards of their tastes were more or less similar. Perhaps this is one of the reasons why Proust feels with particular cogency that Sainte-Beuve moved in the wrong direction. In any case, the Sainte-Beuve problem continued to occupy him at a time when most of *A la recherche* was already complete.

> I do not say that every one of his *Lundis* taken separately is absolutely false. I don't doubt but what the Comte de Molé or Chancellor Pasquier were men of parts. I think they do less honor to French literature than Flaubert and Baudelaire, about whom Sainte-Beuve spoke in a way that implied that personal friendship, respect for their characters, dictated at least in part the slight praise he granted them. I don't think that to make a mistake about the value of a work of art is always very serious . . . but Sainte-Beuve was a critic, and, moreover, proclaimed at every turn that criticism manifests itself in the exact appreciation of contemporary works.
>
> It is easy enough, he says, not to be mistaken about Virgil or about Racine, but the book which has just been published, etc.
>
> One can therefore apply to him the same judgment he brought to bear on the critics who praised only the past![32]

The important criterion for judging the critic in Sainte-Beuve is to meet him on his own ground and to let him stand or fall by his own standards. If Sainte-Beuve had not set out to challenge future generations with his stated claim to judge his contemporaries accurately, his essays on Molé and Pasquier, as Proust points out, would have done him credit. But Sainte-Beuve showed himself inadequate not only on Flaubert and Baudelaire, but also on Stendhal and Balzac. In Proust's judgment, these errors are decidedly too numerous and too vast to be pardoned. For this reason Proust never tires of quoting ironically Sainte-Beuve's touchstone of the *good* critic.[33]

> The true touchstone of the critical judgment comes with contemporary works. Everybody is eager to have his say on Racine and Bossuet, and it can be done in perfect safety; from that sort of thing one gets "developments" rather than judgments — statements in which talent may exercise itself and shine to its heart's content. But the acuity of judgment, the critic's perspicacity is most effectively tested by new works, which have not yet been touched by the public. To judge on first sight, to make predictions, to anticipate — those are the things which indicate genuine critical talent. How few possess it.[34]

Keeping these assertions in mind, Proust queries: ". . . Surely no one ever failed so completely as did he in performing the functions of a guide?" [35] Or, in a more contemptuous vein: " 'Our daily bread is worth more to posterity than confections,' said Sainte-Beuve, who will always be a confectioner." [36]

However, it is not sufficient for one critic to point out the errors and pretensions of another; Proust leaves no doubt about his conviction that Sainte-Beuve's original mistake lies in his preoccupation with the man in the work of art instead of the artist in the man. ". . . The man who lives in the same body with any great genius has little connection with him; and it is that man whom his friends are acquainted with; consequently it is absurd to judge the poet by the man or by the talk of his friends, as Sainte-Beuve does. As for the man himself, he is but a human being and may perfectly well be ignorant of the demands of the poet who lives within him." [37] Proust is in the vanguard of the modern reaction against Sainte-Beuve by writers and critics who have not only found Sainte-Beuve's authority and example oppressive and who are convinced, moreover, that the biographical method has very little to say about the work of literature but a great many things of dubious relevance about the writer. Sainte-Beuve's critical technique actually led to ethical rather than aesthetic conclusions. Sainte-Beuve wrote in his essay on Chateaubriand, ". . . It is difficult for me to judge [a work of art] independently of the knowledge of its author; I would gladly put it this way: Judge the tree by its fruit. The study of literature thus leads me quite naturally to the study of ethics."[38] Proust knew that between the writer as a man and as an artist there exists a disparity, an imbalance, which a critic with Sainte-Beuve's approach would have to define and reconcile in each case. It is apropos to recall one of Proust's aphorisms here: "In a writer we try to find the man when that man was only striving to lift himself to the level of the writer." This does not mean that for Proust the work of art is everything and the artist nothing. But, as the aphorism shows, if one does succeed in discerning the author in his work, one finds him in a process of self-purification, self-transcendence. If the work of art is vision, then the author one discovers in it must be *voyant*.

By way of practical application of this idea, Proust's criticism of Jacques-Emile Blanche's articles on painters takes the form of advice to his friend to avoid Sainte-Beuve's example:

> You were at one time, in your criticisms, and the parallel is exact, the Sainte-Beuve of painting (I say parallel simply for your writings, the parallel ceases since you are foremost a painter, and Sainte-Beuve was only accessorily a poet); you showed us the unexpected human truth in Manet, in Fantin, as Sainte-Beuve did for Chateaubriand, for Vigny; you gave us the joy of delightful discoveries and the chance of being mistaken, which we always run when we talk about art or history, when we deal with the man himself, and within the man, not exactly with the essential part he expresses in his work.[39]

The error of this method, as Proust elaborates further in his preface to Blanche's book, is that the critic who uses it is explaining the true, the "eternal" Fantin or Manet, who can be found only in his work, by inquiring into the unauthentic Fantin or Manet,

> the perishable individual of flesh and blood, like [his] contemporaries, compounded of many faults in whom an imprisoned and original personality is forever at war with the fleshly envelope, and is striving to break away from it, and to find freedom in its work.[40]

The whole argument is reminiscent of what he felt the function of the true critic should be: the critic should help the reader to define the essential traits of the writer, and, if possible, help him to reconstitute the writer's particular vision of reality. Whatever else the critic attempts to do — whether he looks for the man, or the artist, or the influence or the ideas in a work of art — no matter how cleverly he accomplishes his task, he produces merely a footnote to the critic's real objective. If one may say that the artist and the man stand in a Platonic relationship, then any attempt to grasp the man amounts only to grasping his shadow; Proust's literary critic (that is to say, himself) aims at the reality in the writer, namely, his artistic essence. As a result, Sainte-Beuve, for Proust the professional shadow hunter, never arrives at what is really important in literature — and this is the real dissension between Proust and the author of the *Lundis,* more significant than Proust's critique of Sainte-Beuve's style and his mannerisms.

"I sometimes ask myself whether Sainte-Beuve's poetry isn't the best part of his work." Thus begins the final page[41] of Proust's essay on Sainte-Beuve's method. It attempts to vindicate at least a portion of Sainte-Beuve and establish a kind of dialectical relation between the critic and the poet. When Sainte-Beuve wrote his poems, Proust notes, he stopped trying to be clever, he stopped looking for witty angles from which to view his material. "It is as if the constant mendacity of his thought depended on his gift for clever expression, and when he stopped speaking in prose, he stopped lying." Sainte-Beuve the poet is as straightforward and direct as Sainte-Beuve the critic is sophisticated and elusive. The result is a directness of sentiment, such as is found in *Les Rayons jaunes* and in *Les Larmes de Racine*; but there is also a concomitant loss of resourcefulness. "There is nothing more affecting than this poverty of means in the great and dazzling critic," a sort of *dépouillement* of his entire cultural apparatus, which leaves nothing but the "studied and exquisite" quality which reminds Proust of André Chénier or Anatole France. This becomes particularly pathetic in view of the fact that Saint-Beuve was making a "learned and sometimes successful effort" to express "the purity of love, the sadness of late afternoons in big cities, the magic of memories, the emotions aroused by reading, the melancholy of incredulous old age." These are, as it were, Proust's own themes, the subjects which he particularly admired when they were given moving expression by Chateaubriand, Nerval, or Baudelaire, or by the painters. These same things were *real* in Sainte-Beuve, too, and they should have been the very center of his activity as a man of letters; instead, they exist on the periphery and are generally marred by awkwardness, with an occasional glimpse of something genuinely felt and well expressed. As a result, it is not surprising that Proust pays little attention to the claim generally advanced that Sainte-Beuve is the founder of a modern *poésie intime* in France, the discoverer of a *corde secrète* in the lyre. One might even have expected Proust to claim him as an ancestor, a sort of genre poet, *le côté Vermeer de la poésie*. But the quality is missing, and Proust was only too aware of the straining on Sainte-Beuve's part to justify his poetic modesty: "Moi, j'aime à cheminer, et je reste plus bas."

"Appearance, the *Lundis*. Reality, this handful of verses. The poems of a critic are the weight on the eternal weighing-scales in which his entire work is judged." Proust saw a double warning in Sainte-Beuve's example. The critical method is fallacious and dishonest, and it mars the poetic inspiration, which should remain genuine: the "temporal" and "intelligent" Sainte-Beuve inhibited or destroyed what might have been timeless and authentic in him. Proust, who at the moment at which he wrote this, was on the threshold between criticism and creation, thought fit to remind himself that the critic within him must not be allowed to displace the artist, even if the critical method were superior to Sainte-Beuve's. There was too much danger in being caught in the web of appearances; what was needed was an integration of the two aspects, with the critic playing a definitely secondary role. The *Contre Sainte-Beuve* bears witness to an inner aesthetic struggle, in which the artist in Proust emerged victorious over the critic.

6. FOREIGN AUTHORS

Proust's acquaintance with foreign authors, especially novelists, was unusually broad. He expressed a decided preference for English and American authors and owed a tremendous debt to Ruskin. Cattaui lists the following writers: Shakespeare, Ruskin, Emerson, Stevenson, Henry James, Hardy, George Eliot, Thackeray, Carlyle, William Morris, and John Stuart Mill.[1] Jacques Porel is somewhat more specific, and his statement might be used to amplify Cattaui's list: "He knew by heart entire passages . . . even of translations, as *The Idiot* and *War and Peace*. He was inexhaustible on the subject of Meredith. . . His enthusiasm for Dickens (*Bleak House* was one of his favorite books) and Ruskin needs no further comment." [2] Ruskin was probably the only author whom Proust read, at least to some extent, in the original; for the rest he relied on translations. He appears to have been interested in Poe; [3] what French writer who was even vaguely associated with the symbolists could have avoided him? Besides his fondness for writers in the English language, Proust had a special admiration for the Russian novelists, to whom he probably owes as great a debt as to George Eliot and Thomas Hardy. With German prose he seems to have been only moderately well acquainted; only a few German writers, notably Goethe, Schopenhauer, and Nietzsche, are mentioned in his correspondence. As a matter of fact, he once complained of the sterility of the German literature of his day.[4] Yet one wonders whether this complaint was based on any direct knowledge.

He had, however, a special interest in Goethe's prose fiction, notably *Wilhelm Meister* and *The Elective Affinities*, to which he devoted a short essay, now collected in *Nouveaux Mélanges*.[5] In this essay Proust isolates a number of recurrent patterns in Goethe's two novels and attempts to see their relation to Goethe's creative personality. "Locale has an extreme importance in Goethe": there are points of vantage from which the landscape becomes more clearly visible; there are also rooms which art- and nature-lovers fill with paintings and collections from natural history. All these things, he concludes, have their importance with respect to Goethe's intellectual life. Furthermore, Goethe is generally not satisfied with maxims to explain his characters' actions; he uses the device of the interpolated diary extract to show us the habitual preoccupations of a character's mind and sometimes allow us to glimpse much more of the character than the narrative implies.

The importance of art as well as the tools of art — acting, architecture, music, pedagogy — is also significant. Proust calls specific attention to the comedies and improvisations in *Wilhelm Meister* and to the gardening and building activities in *The Elective Affinities*. "And it is shown how many lives are uselessly sacrificed to these arts, the point of view adopted being a false one." In addition, there is Goethe's sense of ceremony which often invests his novels with a certain frigidity, as Proust correctly notes. (This, it must be admitted, is particularly true of *The Elective Affinities*.) "It seems also that the need to symbolize by ceremonies what the invisible, the essential is for us — allegorical ceremonies which seem so cold and unimportant to us — held a great importance in Goethe's eyes." Natural history seems to have constituted a negative pole for Goethe's mind, something that "drives away inspiration and is antipathetic to our true development."

It should be obvious from these remarks how tentative Proust's criticism of Goethe really is: there are many fine and correct perceptions, but they lack focus. The words "seems" and "appears" occur too frequently, as though to indicate that Proust were not quite sure of himself. Possibly he felt somewhat hesitant to make critical generalizations about a writer of whose work he knew only a small segment. In particular, statements such as the one on natural history are meaningful only in the general context of Goethe's attitude toward nature and must therefore be related to the appropriate phase or phases of Goethe's thought. As for Proust's observations on the importance of sites and landscapes and architecture in these works, he might easily have ventured one step further to show that these images often have a symbolic quality (especially in Goethe's later prose), and frequently with ironic overtones. In *The Elective Affinities*, there is a parallel of external and internal gardening — how to arrange one's property and how to arrange one's propriety; the contrast here is decidedly ironic. Furthermore, there is a contrast between imitation and art and between lack of personal spontaneity (most of the characters in the novel) and naturalness (Ottilie). These and other patterns could be isolated, and Proust surely was on their track but did not venture quite far enough. On the other hand, the essay does wind up with a fine observation about the theatricality of the novels — which is, after all, another way of stating the problem of art versus imitation.

The world in these novels is arranged quite like a marionette theater; you have a strong feeling that Goethe pulls the strings for a mysterious purpose. Moreover, such is the charm of his characters. In the rooms, there are little children's play-theaters. In the studies, there are pictures or art implements. Inside the story, there is another story told by one of the characters and broken by the actual story. Some characters have, intentionally, no well-defined personality, being simply "two theater lovers" (*Wilhelm Meister*) or "two persons for whom morality does not exist" (the count and the baroness in *The Elective Affinities*). Characters appear at the beginning of the narrative, but only to reappear at the end or at one or two points during the course of the drama. Often persons you encounter are there for an end which only they themselves are aware of, so that your meeting with them takes on something very mysterious. And finally certain incidents are forecasts of what is to happen. Certain characters symbolize a side of nature which seems to interest Goethe: the useless display of factitious activity in women (Philine [in *Wilhelm Meister*], Luciane in *The Elective Affinities*). And the author delegates and portions out his role of judge and guide to different characters who have a sort of moral specialty (Mittler in *The Elective Affinities* and the powers of the Tower in *Wilhelm Meister*).

A few conclusions might be drawn from these critical remarks. Since these notes are probably prior to 1904, we can see further confirmation of the author's preoccupations at that time: interest in structural patterns within a book, concern for the sense of "mystery," which must be preserved at all costs. It is interesting that Proust should have encountered Goethe's *Bildungsroman* at this particular juncture of his quest. Somehow one has the feeling that some years later he would have had more to say about the novel in which a young man attempts to realize his "form" (to translate *Bildung* literally), a problem not too far removed from Marcel's "vocation." The major difference between the Goethean concept of *Bildung* and the Proustian vocation is that Goethe tends to move in the direction of abstraction, whereas Proust does not. This, too, would have been a fascinating topic for critical reflection.

In 1921 the *Nouvelle Revue française* asked Proust to write an essay on the occasion of the Dostoevski centennial; but Proust declined, being far too eager to get *A la recherche* completed. "I admire that great Russian passionately, but I know him only imperfectly. I should have to read him and reread him, and my work would have to be interrupted for months."[6] However, it is reasonable to assume that if he had written the essay, it would have contained all the observations — and probably more — which are to be found in Marcel's penetrating dissertation to Albertine on Dostoevski's *phrases-types*, at the end of *La Prisonnière*. After an introductory reflection on Vinteuil's ability to make the listener grasp an "unknown quality of a unique world," Marcel turns to literature, asserting that writers, like composers and painters, "have never created more than a single work, or rather have never done more than refract through various mediums an identical beauty which they bring into the world." [7] (Proust has here restated his analogy of the author with the optician; moreover, the statement parallels James Joyce's notion that a novelist writes only one novel in his lifetime.) This unity manifests itself in literature by means of recurrences peculiar to any particular author — whether in the form of persons or things or stylistic devices — which are repeated and varied throughout his work. In Dostoevski these devices are numerous. First of all, his women are equally mysterious:

> . . . the Dostoievski woman (as distinctive as a Rembrandt woman) with her mysterious face, whose engaging beauty changes abruptly, as though her apparent good nature had been but make-believe, to a terrible insolence (although at heart it seems that she is more good than bad), is she not always the same, whether it be Nastasia Philipovna writing love letters to Aglaé and telling her that she hates her, or in a visit which is wholly identical with this — as also with that in which Nastasia Philipovna insults Vania's family — Grouchenka, as charming in Katherina Ivanovna's house as the other had supposed her to be terrible, then suddenly revealing her malevolence by insulting Katherina Ivanovna (although Grouchenka is good at heart); Grouchenka, Nastasia, figures as original, as mysterious not merely as Carpaccio's courtesans but as Rembrandt's Bathsheba. Notice that he certainly knew only that particular kind of face — radiant, deceitful, with its sudden slackening of pride — making the woman appear other than what she is.[8]

Proust could have extended the list of "mysterious" women considerably; nevertheless, the statement "is she not always the same?" is open to discussion. Even though Dostoevski's women are remarkably similar from one volume to the next, the variety is somewhat greater than Proust indicates (for example, Sonia in *Crime and Punishment*, Marya Timofyevna in *The Possessed*); yet it is true that they are usually mysterious in their motivations and in their behavior. The degree of contradiction within each woman seems to be proportional to the intensity of emotional stress on her and to the acuity of her intelligence: the chain stretches from the humble imbecile Marya Timofyevna to the proud intellectual Nastasia Philipovna.

The same aura of mystery Marcel finds hovering about Dostoevski's dwelling-places — the somberness, the heights, and the vastness of houses in which murders are committed — in *Crime and Punishment* or in *The Idiot* and in *Karamazov*. Proust might easily have appended a disquisition on staircases in Dostoevski's houses here:

> That novel and terrible beauty of a house, that novel beauty blended with a woman's face, that is the unique thing which Dostoievski has given to the world, and the comparisons that literary critics may make between him and Gogol, or between him and Paul de Kock, are of no interest, being external to this secret beauty.[9]

This art is akin to that of the painters, and Dostoevski's houses are another example of his affinity with Vermeer, Elstir, and Madame de Sévigné, as well as with many others. Marcel adds that Dostoevski introduces his characters in the same way, making their actions seem as deceptive as the effects of Elstir, "where the sea appears to be in the sky."[10] And then the reader learns that such and such a character who at first appears to be malicious is actually good, and vice versa. This method is as basic to Proust's psychology as it is to Dostoevski's, with the difference that the element of time plays a more important role in Proust. In Dostoevski contradictions coexist in stronger concentration, made plausible, however, by the explosive situations into which the persons are thrust; a character may easily fly from one extreme to the other (Rogozhin in *The Idiot,* for instance, and the various buffoons who can lapse from excessive pride to abject humility).

Elaborating on the particular characteristics of Dostoevski's world — those that give all its components the unmistakable imprint of his artistic vision — Marcel points out the endless procession of buffoons, men like Lebedev, Fyodor Karamazov,

Ivolgin, "a humanity more fantastic than that which peoples Rembrandt's *Night Watch*,"[11] figures reminiscent of ancient comedy, but revealing profound truths of the human soul. Their internal torments, their external awkwardness, complicated by their almost brutal sincerity, create complexities that defy facile classifications. Moreover, vanity and pride often complicate, or split, such persons even further, as Marcel shows:

> Have you ever noticed the part that vanity and pride play in his characters? One would say that, to him, love and the most passionate hatred, goodness and treachery, timidity and insolence are merely two states of a single nature, their vanity, their pride preventing Aglaé, Nastasia, the Captain whose beard Mitia pulls, Krassotkin, Aliosha's enemy-friend, from shewing themselves in their true colors.[12]

This observation can be set alongside a statement in the *Nouveaux Mélanges*:

> All of Dostoevsky's novels might be called *Crime and Punishment* . . . But it is probable that he divides in two persons what in reality was a single one. There is certainly a crime in his life and a punishment (which perhaps has no connection with the crime) but he preferred to distribute them over two areas, placing the impressions of the punishment upon himself if necessary (*The House of Death*) and the crime upon others.[13]

Proust here hints at a perception that was to be worked out by Freud in his "Dostoevsky and Parricide." It is surely too much to say, however, that Dostoevski tended to place the punishment upon himself — unless we identify Raskolnikov, Mitya, and Stavrogin with their author; and this is permissible only so long as we remember that Dostoevski's characters are enlarged aspects of himself; and Proust's suggestion that crime and punishment tend to be distributed over two areas is too generalized and not complex enough to shed light on Dostoevski's exceedingly intricate manipulation of the "double." In any case, Proust is aware of the role which Siberia played in Dostoevski's inner development: "It is probable that his forced labor constituted for Dostoevski the favorable stroke of destiny which opened his inner life." [14] Again, it would have been more correct to say "deepened" his inner life, or "redirected" it, because there is evidence of a considerable complexity of his inner existence in his earlier work, notably in *The Double* and *The Eternal Husband,* which Proust appears to have been unfamiliar with.

The notes in *Nouveaux Mélanges* conclude with the observation that Dostoevski's originality lies in his composition (rather than in his psychology). It raises so important and so valid a point about Dostoevski that one wishes that Proust had expanded it into the long essay that the N.R.F. commissioned. In *La Prisonnière* we at least have an indication of what he had in mind, and it is one of Proust's finest pieces of literary analysis, the great design of *The Brothers Karamazov*:

> But is it not a sculpturesque and simple theme, worthy of the most classical art, a frieze interrupted and resumed on which the tale of vengeance and expiation is unfolded, the crime of old Karamazoff getting the poor idiot with child, the mysterious, animal, unexplained impulse by which the mother, herself unconsciously the instrument of an avenging destiny, obeying also obscurely her maternal instinct, feeling perhaps a combination of physical resentment and gratitude towards her seducer, comes to bear her child on old Karamazoff's ground. This is the first episode, mysterious, grand, august as a Creation of Woman among the sculptures at Orvieto. And as counterpart, the second episode more than twenty years later, the murder of old Karamazoff, the disgrace brought upon the Karamazoff family by this son of the idiot, Smerdiakoff, followed shortly afterwards by another action, as mysteriously sculpturesque and unexplained, of a beauty as obscure and natural as that of the childbirth in old Karamazoff's garden, Smerdiakoff hanging himself, his crime accomplished.[15]

Proust's observation points to the real greatness of Dostoevski the artist. This greatness lies not only in his ability to create the world in his own image and to crowd it with people and objects that give it its own particular authenticity, but to charge it with meaning, to inject into it the very pattern of human existence, akin to the power and mystery that underlie Aeschylean and Sophoclean tragedy. Proust could have chosen no better example in Dostoevski than *The Brothers Karamazov*, for here Dostoevski's world is in its most nearly complete form: the mystery of sin and expiation, of crime and punishment, the conflict between God and the Devil, between faith and reason, between love and violence — all these antitheses confront each other, become embroiled, and diverge again as expressions of the soul, the mind and the body, respectively substantiated by Alyosha, Ivan, and Dimitri. And these patterns, in one way or another, though not with the same force of finality, bind together all the other great novels of Dostoevski as well.

Proust's pronouncements on Tolstoi are brief, unfortunately, in view of the admiration he expressed for the great Russian. This admiration can be measured by the fact that he accorded Tolstoi a place above his special favorite, Balzac. In *Nouveaux Mélanges* he wrote (probably around 1910):

> Nowadays they elevate Balzac above Tolstoi. That's madness. Balzac's output is antipathetic, snarling, full of ridicule, and mankind is judged in it by an *homme de lettres* who is anxious to write a great book; in Tolstoi it is judged by a serene god. Balzac succeeds in giving the impression of size; in Tolstoi everything is naturally larger.[16]

No one will find anything to quarrel with in this statement; it is surprising, however, to see so harsh an estimate of Balzac from Proust's pen. He elaborates the statement with specific references to scenes which give a feeling of grandeur, especially spatial grandeur, in *Anna Karenina* — harvesting scenes, hunting and skating episodes; they are "like large reserved surfaces which space the rest and give an impression of greater vastness"; and then he points out how a reader begins to develop a fondness for Tolstoi's world and all its particularities, and emphasizes, by means of a number of allusions to *War and Peace*, that this great novel is not so much an enormous piece of careful observation, but a carefully planned work, in which each part is a fragment of a truth about the world as Tolstoi perceived it in his innermost being:

> That work is not one of observation but of intellectual construction. Each feature supposedly drawn from observation is simply the covering, the proof, the example of a law isolated by the novelist, be it a rational or an irrational law. And the impression of power and of life comes precisely from the fact that it is not observed, but that since every gesture, every word, every action is but the token of a law, you feel yourself moving in the midst of a multitude of laws.[17]

Here we have a clear case of *War and Peace* seen through Proust's own refracting prism: observation is notational literature, naturalism, and as such inadequate unless the notebook of the novelist's sensibility and memory is consulted. Tolstoi thus deserves to be regarded as one of Proust's masters, as this observation indicates, and merits greater consideration than has been accorded him whenever the formation of Proust's concept of the novel is assessed. (The formula is perhaps Balzac plus Eliot plus Tolstoi plus Dostoevski, rather than Balzac plus modifications.) Proust, incidentally, admits that sometimes Tolstoi's truth seems obscure to us; why for example did Kitty have a sly expression on her face when she spoke of religion, or why did Anna take joy in humiliating Vronsky's pride? But these are questions which Proust makes no attempt to answer.

In a passage from "Contre l'obscurité" he had bracketed *War and Peace* with *The Mill on the Floss*. Speaking of the problem of the universal and the particular which the literary artist has to solve, he asserted:

> . . . Another law of life . . . is to realize the universal or the eternal, but to realize it only in individuals. In works of art as in life, the more general men are, the more markedly individual they must be (see *War and Peace, The Mill on the Floss*) and one can say this about them, as about each one of us, that when they are most clearly themselves, they incarnate the universal soul in the widest sense.[18]

This is a commonplace observation about the novelist's art, and yet it needs to be stated from time to time: it is no more than a simple creed which requires the novelist to worship at the shrine of life *first.* In this way, and only in this way, all the great creations of fiction (and of drama) fall into their proper place as both records of human behavior and as symbols. And how appropriate to think at this particular point of *War and Peace,* in which the characters struggle so long and so hard to be "most clearly themselves" and in which Tolstoi, by this very method, produces in the reader such an enormous impression of the vastness of life!

Albertine has an annoying way of interrupting Marcel's dissertation on novelists whenever the latter strays off the subject of Dostoevski. In this way what might have become a fascinating discussion or criticism of Tolstoi falls by the wayside. Marcel is permitted to say only:

> Besides, if I have said to you that it is, from one novel to another, the same scene, it is in the compass of a single novel that the same scenes, the same characters reappear if the novel is at all long. I could illustrate this to you easily in *War and Peace*, and a certain scene in a carriage . . .[19]

This tantalizing statement has finally been clarified by the publication of *Nouveaux Mélanges*, in which Proust lists the recurrences in Tolstoi and suggests that Tolstoi was able to construct his novels from relatively few materials, by ingenious transpositions:

> Nevertheless, in that creation [*War and Peace*] which seems to be inexhaustible, it seems that Tolstoi repeated himself and had only few themes at his disposal, which are disguised and renewed but remain the same in the other novel. The stars, the sky which Levin observes like a fixed point are indeed somewhat the same as the comet seen by Pierre, the great blue sky seen by Prince Andrey. Moreover, Levin, first rejected in favor of Vronsky, then loved by Kitty, makes you think of Natasha leaving Prince Andrey for Pierre's brother, then coming back to him. And as for Kitty passing by in a carriage

and Natasha going past the armies in a carriage, might this not mean that the same reminiscence served Tolstoi for a model? [20]

Nor is there any general comment on *War and Peace*, except for a brief observation in a letter to Cocteau, "I believe one can 'sprawl' in a book like *War and Peace* (although I prefer concentration, even when the work is long)," [21] a curious statement when correlated with his own *A la recherche*, in which "sprawling" often becomes a necessity, albeit a pleasure.

In *La Prisonnière*, Marcel notes an affinity between Dostoevski and Tolstoi; the latter, he says, imitated the former to a great extent. "In Dostoievski there is, concentrated and fretful, a great deal of what was to blossom later on in Tolstoi. There is, in Dostoievski, that proleptic gloom of the primitives which their disciples will brighten and dispel." [22] This statement is hardly true. First of all, Dostoevski and Tolstoi were contemporaries; *War and Peace* and *Crime and Punishment* began to appear in 1865 and 1866, respectively; *The Brothers Karamazov*, Dostoevski's masterpiece, appeared after *Anna Karenina*. If Proust is talking in a broader sense of a comparison between Dostoevski the "primitive" and Tolstoi the "refiner" — since the two men were familiar with each other's work — there may be some small justification for Marcel's statement; yet the difference in emphasis, in temperament, is so great between the two men that one can hardly consider Tolstoi an *épanouissement* of Dostoevski. Admirers and followers of Dostoevski have attempted to adapt his great insight and technique to their own uses; the result of this apprenticeship has certainly not been the "brightening and dispelling" of Dostoevski's gloom — but rather its (legitimate) extension to the technique of contemporary fiction.

I have just been reading something very beautiful which unfortunately slightly resembles what I am doing (only it is a thousand times better): *The Well-Beloved* by Thomas Hardy. It doesn't even lack that slight touch of the grotesque which is an essential part of all great works . . . It is curious that in all the different *genres*, from George

Eliot to Hardy, from Stevenson to Emerson, there is no literature which has as much hold on me as English and American literature. Germany, Italy, very often France, leave me indifferent. But two pages of *Mill on the Floss* reduce me to tears. I know that Ruskin loathed that novel, but I reconcile all these hostile gods in the Pantheon of my admiration.[23]

Thus Proust expressed his predilection for English and American literature to Robert de Billy in 1909. In some respects, the pronouncement is strange; in other ways, it is altogether understandable. Proust is often closer in spirit to the English novel of manners and has, on occasion, a more indulgent, more relaxed attitude toward his characters than other French novelists, such as Balzac, Stendhal, and Flaubert. One might summarize it by saying that he knows how to coordinate sentiment and analysis. Moreover, he has the same tendency as the English novelists to build his fictional edifice on moral groundwork; this tendency is by no means characteristic of him, nor is it his purpose to edify the reader, but it is nevertheless real; or else he would not have troubled to show at such length the Guermantes' world as empty, the rites of Sodom and Gomorrha as monstrous. To be sure, in Proust ethical values are superseded by the mystical-aesthetic vision of the artist, but insofar as the artist moves in the world of people and things, he is subject to moral restrictions.

From the standpoint of criticism, however, the statement of Proust leaves something to be desired. Granted, of course, that the entire comment was occasioned by his reading of Hardy's *The Well-Beloved*, which had a special interest for him, and that the reference to George Eliot also reveals a felt kinship, still one wishes Proust's praise of English literature had been more comprehensive, or more selective. For *The Well-Beloved* is one of Hardy's weakest works, and no amount of adulation can raise it beyond the level of the mediocre. Even if the "light touch of the grotesque" is there, Hardy makes very little of it, and it quickly becomes submerged in awkward characterizations and the contrived sequence of events. Proust's unduly modest reference ("only it is a thousand times better") to the work's similarity with his own has to do with the fact that in *The Well-Beloved* the hero, a sculptor, is in love with successive incarnations of a Platonic ideal of woman. At a point in the story, Jocelyn holds his ideal "prisoner" for a while — but there the resemblance ends. However, the Platonic attitude toward love is reflected in the early portions of *A la recherche*, as Thomas Hardy himself was quick to point out in his Journal. In July, 1926, quoting the passage about the "purely subjective nature" of love from *A l'ombre*, he writes: "It appears that the theory exhibited in *The Well-Beloved* in 1892 has been since developed by Proust still further." [24] These ideas are more fully analyzed and extended in later portions of *A la recherche*, with the difference, however, that Marcel is infinitely more conscious of the subtleties which can be discerned in the process of love.[25] The "particular forms," which Marcel discovers as differentiating each successive love affair, are so absent from Hardy's work — the whole "form" of Jocelyn's three loves being cast from the beginning, and invariable thereafter — that Proust's treatment of the same theme is comparable to Hardy's only by way of contrast. It is clear that behind Proust's admiration for *The Well-Beloved* lies a considerable measure of personal interest, and very little more.

Proust found other things in *The Well-Beloved*, these latter observations being of greater significance as examples of literary analysis. The theme of stone-cutting ("that stonemason's geometry") runs through many of Hardy's works as a *phrase-type*:

> Do you remember the stonemasons in *Jude the Obscure*, in *The Well-Beloved*, the blocks of stone which the father hews out of the island coming in boats to be piled up in the son's studio where they are turned into statues; in *A Pair of Blue Eyes* the parallelism of the tombs, and also the parallel line of the vessel, and the railway coaches containing the lovers and the dead woman; the parallelism between *The Well-Beloved*, where the man is in love with three women, and *A Pair of Blue Eyes*, where the woman is in love with three men, and in short all those novels which can be laid one upon another like the vertically piled houses upon the rocky soil of the island.[26]

Much of this "parallelism" tends to be contrived for melodramatic effect. In *A Pair of Blue Eyes* the parallelism of the tombs (and in another instance, of kissing scenes and lost earrings) is artificial almost to a point of embarrassment.[27] Whether this symmetry was felt rather than contrived by Hardy is another question; but if it is too intentional, it loses its force as *phrase-type*; or even as vision "refracted" in a uniform manner. In any case, the recurrence of stonemasonry is a more genuine aspect of Hardy's "vision." Still, in *The Well-Beloved* Hardy says absolutely nothing — perhaps on purpose — about the sort of sculptures Jocelyn created, and thus the beauty which Proust finds in the whole progression from rugged nature to polished art is considerably diminished. Besides, *The Well-Beloved* is characterized by a mediocrity of style and a monotony of content which can hardly have escaped Proust's discerning eye.

Proust's affinity to George Eliot is surely closer than to Hardy and was detected as early as 1923 by Edmond Jaloux.[28] The resemblance of the opening of *Du côté de chez Swann* with the opening chapter of *The Mill on the Floss* has been pointed out by André Maurois [29] and treated at greater length by L. A. Bisson, who says: "George Eliot dwells on the unsought re-awakening, not the conscious remembering, of the experience of childhood . . ." [30] and calls attention to the fact that, especially in the earlier portions of *A la recherche,* there are many resemblances between Proust and Eliot. However, since Proust's critical comment on that book is lacking, all that could be done would be to trace the parallels between *The Mill on the Floss* and *A la recherche* in order to establish his affinity to Eliot, and that is outside the scope of this study. Proust was ready to pay generous tribute to Eliot, either in the form of childhood reminiscences, as in *Jean Santeuil,*[31] or by references to characters and works, such as allusions to *Adam Bede, Scenes from Clerical Life,* and *Middlemarch* in the essays on Ruskin;[32] in that essay Proust praises Eliot's portraits of the gentle clergyman, whom Proust compares with Carlyle's "amiable" prophets.

In the absence of an extended essay on George Eliot, we must content ourselves with the set of notes that Proust jotted down on the subject of *Adam Bede* and *Silas Marner*. These have been printed in *Nouveaux Mélanges*.[33] They give us a glimpse of Proust's deep affection for George Eliot, which is based on a similarity of orientation: "What strikes me in *Adam Bede* is the attentive, detailed, respectful, poetic and sympathetic painting of the most hard-working and humble life." This is the Vermeer, the Chardin aspect that Proust liked above all to find in his favorite authors. And indeed with George Eliot it is a conscious procedure. (At the beginning of Book II the author relinquishes her function of storyteller for a moment to comment on "this rare, precious quality of truthfulness . . . in many Dutch paintings, which lofty-minded people despise. I find a source of delicious sympathy in these faithful pictures of a monotonous homely existence . . .") Proust, as is usual with him, finds a heightening of the mystery of existence in the humble portrayal of humble life, "the sentiment of the mysterious grandeur of human life and of the life of nature, sublime mysteries in which we participate knowing as little as the flower that grows (in *Silas Marner*)" and "above the concatenation of our vices and misfortunes a sort of superior order of powerful providence which makes our evil the incomprehensible instrument of our good (in *Silas Marner*)." In a subsequent series of notes Proust lists a number of characteristics of Eliot's view of the world of things, with illustrative examples. They include: novelty of the images deriving from a "tender and new way of looking at things, a way which discovers in them unnoticed sentiments and is then able to paint them as symbols of the analogous sentiments (hearts melting like small brooks, somewhat heavy jokes directed against men of the world)"; the sentiment of the usefulness of suffering, of moral progress; conservatism (social and political); a sincere sentiment for humble occupations; a lively feeling for the development of friendly relations among men; an interest in the progressive steps whereby the human will yields; and the sense of increased suffering in a being without spiritual life, cut off from moral solidarity with others. "One of the conclusions one may draw from these works (a conclusion not indicated in the works themselves)," Proust writes at the end of these notes, "is that the evil that we do is indeed evil (we do evil to ourselves and to others). On the other hand, the evil which is done to us is often the condition of a greater good which it was God's wish to do to us."

Probably a long essay on the affinities between Proust and George Eliot needs to be written. It would be interesting, for example, to trace the development of George Eliot from translator (D. F. Strauss and Feuerbach) to novelist, from the early novels to the mature work; and to compare this progress with Proust's own. As one of her critics observes, the characteristic form of George Eliot's novels is "the product of a vision of life the source of which lay far back in her childhood." [34] During her entire career George Eliot sought to express her perception of the world she knew in a design that would provide the greatest degree of exactitude: how to resolve the moral dilemmas of certain individuals in a society which constitutes the source of an individual's moral strength but against which the individual has committed an infraction. George Eliot had, like Proust, an acute sense of social structure; and within this framework she "produced such rich, deep, masterly pictures of the multiform life of man," as Henry James put it.[35] The two writers also share a common admiration of George Sand; the English writer praised George Sand in 1849 for her ability "to delineate human passion and its results . . . some of the moral instincts and their tendencies — with such truthfulness, such nicety of discrimination, such tragic power, and withal such loving, gentle humor that one might live a century with nothing but one's own dull faculties and not know as much as six pages will suggest." [36] Curiously enough, this description of George Sand's qualities as a writer is more appropriately applied to the novels that George Eliot wrote several years later. As Proust grew older, he grew weary of George Sand and wound up by bracketing her with Théophile Gautier as one of the literary infatuations of his childhood. There is no indication that he ever tired of George Eliot; on the contrary, he must have grown closer to her as the years went by.

The man of letters who detested *The Mill on the Floss* but whom Proust was ready to reconcile with George Eliot in his "Pantheon" offers a fine example of Proust's critical intelligence at work. Proust is without a doubt more heavily indebted to Ruskin than to any other foreign author. The debt is the more important since Proust's apprenticeship to Ruskin falls between *Les Plaisirs et les jours* and the Sainte-Beuve period, that is to say, between approximately 1899 and 1905. Proust became interested in Ruskin about that time, and seems to have laid *Jean Santeuil* aside in 1899 in order to begin his work on the translation of the *Bible of Amiens*. At the beginning he appears to have felt an intense admiration for the English art critic, but this admiration became more and more mingled with skepticism, until he was ready to leave Ruskin behind. Thus he wrote to Montesquiou in 1912: "As a matter of fact, my fondness for Ruskin was tempered by an extreme skepticism, the extent of which I have myself defined, without losing veneration for my subject." [37] However, the respect for Ruskin never diminished; it is implicit in the two Ruskin translations, which date from the period when Ruskin's influence over Proust had already waned considerably (*La Bible d'Amiens*, 1904, and *Sésame et les lys*, 1906). To attest Proust's continued affection for Ruskin, one needs to look only at the passages in *Swann* in which the Narrator dreams of Venice and alludes to Giotto, and in *La Fugitive*, when the Narrator actually visits Venice and Padua; the spirit of Ruskin is alive in those pages. The recently published Ruskin pastiche entitled "La Bénédiction du sanglier" adds an amusing dimension to the Proust-Ruskin relationship.[38] This extravaganza, which is written as though it were a pastiche of Proust's translation of a Ruskin work on Giotto frescoes (depicting "L'Affaire Lemoine"!) is a Proustian burlesque of himself as a translator and falls under the heading of sheer *divertissement*.

The problem of Ruskin's influence on Proust's style and ideas is of considerable importance to anyone who wishes to form a comprehensive idea of Proust's development as a writer and a thinker. The publication in 1942 of a number of Proust's letters to Marie Riefstahl (*née* Nordlinger)[39] provides a running commentary on his interest in Ruskin and on his problems as a translator of Ruskin. A monograph and numerous articles[40] attempt to assess Ruskin's influence on Proust's growth.

Most important of all, Proust enriched both his translations with copious commentary, full of fascinating criticisms, revealing at the same time the preoccupations that were to come to fruition in *A la recherche.* Moreover, the two long prefaces to the translations provide a comprehensive summary of his appreciation and criticism of Ruskin (in *La Bible d'Amiens,* reprinted in *Pastiches et mélanges*), as well as evidence that Ruskin had by that time been left behind and that Proust had found his own way (in the preface to *Sésame et les lys,* entitled "Journées de lecture," also reprinted in *Pastiches et mélanges*). Finally, four more essays on Ruskin or on Ruskinian themes should be added to this list: "Les Eglises sauvées, Les Clochers de Caen, La Cathédrale de Lisieux"; "Pèlerinages ruskiniens en France"; "La Mort des Cathédrales";[41] and a review of the French translation of Ruskin's *The Stones of Venice.*[42]

His first admiration is for Ruskin's style. It is not so much the length of Ruskin's sentences or their sinuous character that Proust appreciates, but rather the unity of Ruskin's work.

> . . . The charm of Ruskin's work lies precisely in the fact that there are links between the ideas of the same book, and between the different books that Ruskin conceals and that he scarcely lets show through for a moment; besides, he perhaps wove them in afterwards, but without artificiality, since they are always drawn from the substance of his thinking, which remains ever the same. The multiple yet constant preoccupations of this thought are what assures these books a unity more real than the unity of composition, which, it must be admitted, is generally lacking.[43]

In this respect Ruskin can be classed with what Proust liked to call the "self-contemplating" artists of the nineteenth century, such as Wagner and Balzac, who retroactively gave their work a unity and a beauty which it had not originally possessed but which had been latent in it. In Ruskin, Proust admires the skilfully manipulated images or symbols which Ruskin has found in the course of a lecture. As an example, Proust points out the final sentence of the first lecture, entitled "Of Kings' Treasuries," of *Sesame and Lilies*, in which Proust notes the adroit interweaving of images:

> That is the way he works. He moves from one idea to the next without any apparent order. But in reality the train of the imagination leading him forward follows its profound affinities which, in spite of himself, impose a superior logic on his writings. So that in the long run he finds that he has followed some sort of secret plan, that, unveiled at the end, retrospectively imposes on the whole a sort of order and causes it to appear wonderfully working up to that final apotheosis.[44]

The reader of this sentence cannot help but think of Proust's own final volume, even the final sentence, of *A la recherche*. However, if Proust admires the over-all pattern of Ruskin's thought as it expresses itself in his books, he has certain reservations about the more detailed procedures of Ruskin the stylist. For instance, he finds in Ruskin's sentences a balance imposed from without — that is, imposed by Ruskin's will, not by an inner compulsion on his part (" . . . the pleasure . . . which Ruskin takes in giving to his phrases a balance which has the appearance of imposing *on* his thought, rather than deriving from it, a symmetrical pattern").[45] An even more serious flaw in Ruskin's style is his tendency to play eruditely with words; Proust points out the uselessness of this practice in one of his notes to *La Bible d'Amiens*,[46] explaining that Ruskin (as he stated in *Sesame and Lilies*) believed that an educated man should know the etymologies and the genealogies of words. In a footnote to *Sésame et les lys* Proust refers to Ruskin's veneration for words and their secret meanings:

> He is astonished by the secret virtue that lies in a word, he marvels at it; while pronouncing that word in the most casual conversation,

he notices it, makes others notice it, repeats it, utters an exclamation. Thus he endows the most humble things with a dignity, a charm, an interest, a vitality which makes people who know him prefer his conversation to almost all other conversations. But from the viewpoint of art, it is easy to see what the danger would be for a writer less gifted than he; the words may be lovely in themselves, but we do not simply want to bask in their beauty. There is no particular reason for a composer to use an E rather than a G; similarly, while we are writing we should consider words not only as works of art whose deep meaning we must comprehend and whose glorious past we must respect, but also as simple notes which will take on value (with respect to us) only by virtue of the position we assign to them and in relation to the sense or the sentiment with which we hold them together.[47]

Veneration for words is, for Proust, but another aspect of John Ruskin's idolatry, which is his principal weakness, the shortcoming for which Proust reproached him most. "It is the favorite sin of artists, and there are few who have not succumbed to it." [48] Proust knew the temptation of the idolatry of things; his own alter ego, Swann, is guilty of that intellectual sin; and the idolatry of books is one of the dangers of reading against which he inveighs in "Journées de lecture."

The same "idolatry" was defined by Ruskin himself in his *Lectures on Art*. ". . . The serving with the best of our hearts and minds, some dear or sad fantasy which we have made for ourselves, while we disobey the present call of the Master . . ." [49] Whereas Ruskin's statement relates rather to an idolatry that neglects one's moral responsibility, Proust transposes the statement to the aesthetic plane and uses it against Ruskin himself:

. . . I am inclined to believe that it is just this kind of idolatry that we find at the botton of Ruskin's work, at the root of his talent. Doubtless, he never let it grow to the extent of completely covering — even in the interests of adornment — immobilizing, paralyzing, and finally killing, his intellectual and moral sincerity. In every line of his books, at every moment of his life, we are conscious of feeling how deeply sincere he needed to be if he were to grapple successfully with the temptations of idolatry, proclaim its vanity, and force beauty to bow her head to the claims of duty, even when that duty was unaesthetic.[50]

This struggle between idolatry and sincerity, according to Proust, went on during Ruskin's entire lifetime; and Ruskin, by a self-imposed compromise with his conscience, gradually succumbed to insincerity.

At the very moment that he was preaching sincerity, he lacked it. It was not what he said that was insincere, but the manner of his saying. The doctrines he professed were moral, not aesthetic, yet he chose them for their beauty. And because he did not wish to present them formally as things of beauty, but as statements of truth, he was forced to lie to himself about the reasons that had led him to adopt them. And once the start was made, he found himself involved in a compromise with conscience so continuous, that immoral doctrines sincerely professed would, perhaps, have been less dangerous to his spiritual integrity than moral doctrines enunciated with less than sincerity, because they had been dictated by aesthetic considerations which he refused to admit. Nor was the sin occasional. It went on all the time — in the way he explained a fact or appraised a work of art; even in the choice he made of words, so that, in the end, as a result of his never-ceasing indulgence, the whole attitude of his mind became falsified.[51]

This is the real point of dissension between Proust and Ruskin, one of particular importance to the Proust who was trying to find himself. The problem which is raised here is enormous, inasmuch as it involves the entire relationship between art and morality. This explains perhaps why Proust decided to be so blunt in his condemnation of Ruskin's presumed "sincerity." He is primarily rejecting the implication in Ruskin's writings that morality and art are closely interwoven, and that morality (fortified by the Scriptures) takes the precedence. He then gives illustrations of how this belief involved Ruskin in frequent absurdities of judgment, reminiscent occasionally of the sentimental providentialism of the early Romantics.

When . . . [in the *Bible of Amiens*], Ruskin ends a short digression on Egypt with the words: "She was the Tutoress of Moses and the Hostess of Christ . . ." — the phrase about being the "Tutoress of Moses" can pass muster. Tutoring demands certain virtues. But the fact that she was "The Hostess of Christ," though the words may add something to the beauty of the passage, can scarcely be considered relevant in an appraisal of the Egyptian genius.[52]

In view of examples of this type, the argument gains a certain amount of force. Yet it is doubtful whether the charge of insincerity is to be taken at its face value. Proust certainly did not mean to equate it with hypocrisy. As usual, he tries to detect in writers the inner motivations of their creative personalities, and he finds that in Ruskin a certain insincerity was at work, more or less unconsciously, which found its expression in terms of a certain idolatry or a misplaced reverence.

Proust is aware of his harshness: "I have here, in my effort to push intellectual sincerity to its furthest, its cruellest limits, to wrestle with my most cherished aesthetic impressions." He realizes, and admits, that the criticism he has just made does not detract from the beauty of Ruskin's works and from his excellence as a literary artist.

What I have denounced is not a weakness peculiar to Ruskin. I have tried, taking him, if I may so put it, as an unusually favorable "subject," to underline an infirmity that is part and parcel of the human mind.[53]

This "infirmity that is part and parcel of the human mind" was one temptation of which Proust was well aware and against which the artist in him constantly struggled. He was willing to admit that this sin of idolatry was alluring.[54] Nevertheless, he adds, if he had not tried to discover the nature of Ruskin's alluring falsehood, he would have been guilty of a comparable sin. Ruskin hid his idolatry behind a cloak of excessive respect for the written word, a reverence that is too often uncritical.

Once the reader has understood the nature of this "idolatry," he will be in a position to grasp the excessive importance which Ruskin, in his studies of art, attaches to the literal significance of the works with which he is dealing, and also his abuse of such words as "irreverent" and "insolent" . . .[55]

Proust is here, in a sense, adumbrating his criticism of "fetishism" in reading in "Journées de lecture," which was published in *La Renaissance latine* of June 15, 1905, and later became the preface of Proust's translation of *Sesame and Lilies.* In his preface to *La Bible d'Amiens,* however, Proust chose to assume the prerogatives of the critic and consequently felt obligated to warn against the dangers of idolatry. It is in this vein that he concludes the discussion of Ruskin's unconscious insincerity:

> It is not that I undervalue . . . [the] virtue of respect: there can never be love where there is not respect. But it must never, when love has ceased, be used as a substitute for it and employed with the object of making it possible for us to believe uncritically, or to express admiration merely on the word of another.[56]

The translations of Ruskin, as was stated before, coincided with — one may even say hastened — a *prise de conscience* by Proust and contributed to the formation of the mature novelist. The letters to Marie Nordlinger give evidence of Proust's first enthusiasm for Ruskin: the avid reading of all of Ruskin's works, the discussions about Ruskin and the art he admired; then the revelation of Venice and Padua with the aid of Ruskin and the *pèlerinages ruskiniens* in France. Proust admits that his first contact with Ruskin was primarily uncritical:

> There was, at first, in my love for Ruskin's books some alloy of self-interest; what was in my mind was the intellectual benefit I should derive from them. But as soon as I started to read him, I began to feel the power and the charm that emerged from his pages. Deliberately, I set myself not to resist it, to read more or less uncritically, because I felt that if, in days to come, the delight of Ruskin's thought should color for me everything that it had touched. . .
>
> And that is precisely what happened in my case. I suddenly saw the universe as something of infinite value. My admiration for Ruskin gave such high importance to the objects he had made me love, that they seemed charged with a greater value even than life itself.[57]

As it became clearer and clearer to him that he was in danger of making Ruskin his idol, that he was being truant to the literary ideal that was slowly crystallizing in his mind, he re-evaluated Ruskin, discovered his shortcomings. And at that moment Proust was ready to go beyond his master. It may be argued that the Ruskin translations would never have been completed if it had not been for the suggestion by his mother that Proust's father, who died in 1903, would have wished him to complete the task. As a result, the translations — at least in their later stages — required a certain self-discipline of Proust, a certain artificial, conjured enthusiasm; he was surely anxious to get back to his own work. The following excerpts from letters to Leon Bélugou, written in 1906, indicate admirably Proust's state of mind:

. . . And just recently, while reading one of Ruskin's travel books and feeling my heart beating with the desire to see the same places once more, I said to myself: "If I no longer liked him, would he still be making the world beautiful for me, until I am consumed with longing and desolation whenever I look at a railroad timetable?" Yes, my affection for Ruskin has lasted. Only sometimes nothing makes me as chilly as reading him.

Alas, dear Sir, to pass that enthusiasm on to you, I would have had to keep it. Already while I was translating the *Bible of Amiens*, I admitted in a tedious preface (it was tedious for that very reason) that I had lost that enthusiasm. In any case, I never had any enthusiasm for *Sesame*, which is in my opinion Ruskin's worst book. But often enough "I recognized a trace of my love that had not quite died out," * in the others, sometimes even in that one, that if I just fanned myself on with a bit of insincerity, I managed to blaze up altogether. But my original love was more involuntary.[58]

In a letter to Lauris, written in 1908, Proust is even harsher, though one detects that he has gained a little distance from Ruskin and can now mediate between Ruskin's merits and defects: "Ruskin's works [are] often stupid, fanatical, exasperat-

* Quotation from *Andromaque*, Act I: "de mes feux mal éteints je reconnais la trace."

ing, false and irritating, but they are always praiseworthy and always great."[59] In spite of the fact that Proust undertook the translations of Ruskin somewhat reluctantly, it was fortunate that he did persuade himself to finish the task. In 1899 he had written to Marie Nordlinger, his helper, "I have been working for a long time on a long-winded work, but without finishing anything."[60] This is one of the few indications we have of Proust's activity on *Jean Santeuil*, about which he was unusually secretive. Undoubtedly Proust was dissatisfied with its form, or lack of form, and regarded the various sketches that now make up the published version of *Jean Santeuil* as tentative. The skeleton was still missing, although the impressions were numerous and the style in the process of maturing. He was perhaps glad to be diverted from creation to re-creation (for that is what Proust's rendering of Ruskin's texts turned out to be). To be sure, he often winced at the discipline required of him, but the process of close scrutiny and digestion of Ruskin's texts elicited valuable commentary and criticism from him. As L. A. Bisson summarizes it penetratingly in his article on Ruskin and Proust,

> In Proust, it is clear [the translations] had little importance, long before the end little interest, in themselves. But they served as *a tentative application of his "formula" as an artist*, an exercise and a discipline in the way in which, by this time, he knew that his mind worked.[61]

To conclude, then, Ruskin was for Proust a good guide— a fact which Proust never denied in spite of all his criticisms of Ruskin — as contrasted with Sainte-Beuve, who was his idea of a bad guide. For in the long run, Proust insisted in "Journées de lecture" and again in *Le Temps retrouvé*, books exist in order to enable the reader to read *himself;* they are like so many optical instruments trained upon the reader's undiscovered self.

> The admiration that we feel for a thought, on the other hand, brings beauty to flower at each step we take, because at each step it

> wakes in us a desire for it. Inferior minds believe, as a rule, that to surrender oneself entirely to the books one loves, means that our power of judgment must give up some part of its independence. "Why bother about what Ruskin felt: feel for yourself." This sort of opinion rests upon a psychological error, as all will agree who, having accepted a mental discipline, become aware that their powers of thought and feeling are infinitely increased, and their critical sense never paralyzed. What it comes to is that we are then in a state of Grace, as a result of which our faculties, and, among them, our ability to criticize, are enhanced. Thus, a voluntary servitude of such a kind is really the beginning of liberty. There is no better way of becoming conscious of what one feels oneself than to try to re-create in one's own mind the feelings of a master. For the deep-searching effort brings our thought, as well as his, into the light of day.[62]

This, in Proust's own words, is the recapitulation of his relationship and debt to Ruskin; it can likewise be extended to any of Proust's other literary paragons. In order to arrive at a clarification of what an author *felt*, in order to re-create this in himself, Proust found it necessary to exercise and sharpen his critical talents.

IV

PROUST AND HIS CONTEMPORARIES

> Un écrivain n'est pas qu'un poéte. Même les plus grands de notre siècle, dans notre monde imparfait où les chefs-d'oeuvre de l'art ne sont que les épaves naufragées de grandes intelligences, ont relié d'une trame d'intelligence les joyaux de sentiment où ils n'apparaissent que çà et là.
>
> PROUST, *Contre Sainte-Beuve.*

To round out the picture of Proust as a literary critic, something remains to be said about Proust as a critic of the writers of his own day. There is no doubt that he kept up with his contemporaries — many of his friends attest the fact — despite his feverish activity on the novel. It is impossible, however, to get anything like a clear view of his opinion on the value of new works of literature that were coming out during the first two decades of the twentieth century. Hence, the present chapter must perforce remain fragmentary.

First of all, the materials are still lacking whereby Proust's opinions on the contemporary scene can be adequately surveyed; Proust's letters to Montesquiou, Anna de Noailles, and Gide have appeared in print.[1] In the case of Anatole France and Jean Cocteau, only a few letters are available. If ever the bulk of Proust's extensive correspondence — extensive because of

Proust's isolation due to health and his vocation — is made public, the picture may become somewhat clearer.

Actually, the most compelling reason why Proust's criticisms of his contemporaries must be regarded as intermittent and to a certain extent unreliable for the purposes of serious evaluation lies in his own peculiarity as a person and as a correspondent. There is some truth in the statement frequently heard that Proust's letters portray more faithfully Proust's correspondents than himself. This chameleon quality merely serves to show us one side of the man, the "proustified" Proust, desirous to please, unsparing of flattery. The more vain the correspondent, the more abundant the flattery. It is obvious that literary criticism cannot flourish in that kind of soil. Proust generally confines himself to expressing his admiration, usually in excessive praises (letters to Montesquiou and to Madame de Noailles). However, as has been shown in the preceding chapters, the literary critic in him operates from the vantage point of the artist, as the artist's alter (or prior) ego. As a result, in the letters to contemporary writers, one has the feeling that the man and the artist are frequently in a state of uneasy balance. The critic wishes to rebuke the correspondent, but, undergoing a process of "proustification," voices his criticisms in language too apologetic, too *gentil*. As a result, much of the criticism from letter sources must be gleaned between the lines. As a rule, however, when Proust is writing to another correspondent about the work of a contemporary, the observations are straightforward and, as will be seen, very often severely critical. In such moments he is the same literary critic whose perceptions have been singled out and analyzed in the preceding chapters and whose sensibility produced some of the keenest insights into nineteenth-century literature.

Roughly speaking, Proust's comments on his contemporaries will here be divided into three general groups: comments about the work of those men whom he considered his "masters," that is to say, men somewhat older than himself who created the literary atmosphere of 1885–1900, to which Proust was so greatly indebted in his formative years. These men are Anatole France, Henri de Régnier, Maurice Maeterlinck, Maurice Barrès, and Robert de Montesquiou. The second and third groups are primarily composed of Proust's friends: writers of his own generation, Anna de Noailles, André Gide, Paul Morand, and Francis Jammes; and one of his younger friends, Jean Cocteau.

Proust's correspondence with Anatole France, of which only one complete letter and one fragment have been made public so far, reveals nothing of great critical value, since the judgments which Proust makes are steeped in excessive *gentillesse*. This is unfortunate in view of the fact that Anatole France was, at least in part, a model for Bergotte. Proust's admiration for France was no doubt sincere, in spite of the hyperbolic form of expression in which it is couched, such as

> . . . It is certain that your genius keeps growing without fail. And what was at one time . . . the whim of your leisure hours has already begun to be the entertainment and the education of the ages. The articles in the *Echo*, the Bergeret volumes have become the *Ring of Amethyst*, the truest human comedy, the most complete encyclopedia of manners, and the memoirs of a fair and harmonious Saint-Simon.[2]

It is worth noting here that as early as 1899 Proust's highest praise is formulated in terms of Balzac and Saint-Simon; indeed, Proust is here implying that Anatole France in his *Histoire contemporaine* is doing the same thing that Proust will claim for his hero at the end of *A la recherche* — to write the "memoirs of Saint-Simon of another epoch."

The tone of the fragment of a letter to Anatole France is similar: "What happy evenings there are in store for me with Crainquebille, Doyen Morley, General Décuir, Putois and Riquet, now brought together freshly born from the marvelous sea spume of your genius . . . ," and so on.[3] In spite of the fact that Proust appears to have lost contact with Anatole France, whom he knew intimately in the 1890's through the salon of Madame Arman de Caillavet, and in spite of the fact that France took a dim view of Proust's novel, Proust never lost his respect for his "cher maître." The transformation of the later Bergotte into a more Proust-like writer may be taken as a tacit revision of the ideal of the writer who in some respects resembles France. Where Anatole France failed to live up to his promise, Proust succeeded. Anatole France's weariness with contemporary literature, and his own failure to develop, are made manifest in the article in the *Revue de Paris* which prompted Proust's lengthy rejoinder in the introduction to Paul Morand's *Tendres Stocks*. In that essay, as has been indicated above, Proust takes issue with France's attack on stylistic singularity, and replies at length to France's assertion that "there have been no good writers since the end of the eighteenth century." Proust is on familiar and safe ground here — "I should like to ask [France] how he can believe in stylistic unity when the sensibilities are so singular" — and then turns the argument against France himself: "Is it not true that in *The Crime of Sylvester Bonnard* the dual impression of savagery and gentleness which cats convey circulates within an admirable sentence?" [4] In the long run, Anatole France's arguments (or grievances?) are completely demolished, but without malice. It is characteristic of Proust to have preserved a warm admiration for his masters even at a time when he knew he had surpassed them.

Attempting to delineate the differences between Anatole France and Henri de Régnier, Proust wrote at the end of *Contre Sainte-Beuve*:

> For France life is the dream of a dream, for Régnier things have the countenance of our dreams. The meticulous and penetrating Régnier is more anxious never to forget to verify this similarity between ideas and things; and to demonstrate this coincidence, he spreads his ideas over his work, his sentence becomes lengthened, more precise, twists about like a somber and painstaking columbine; whereas France's is radiant, full-blown and glossy like a rose of France.[5]

This tortuous, drawn-out quality of the sentences is preserved in the Régnier pastiche, one of the Lemoine series. Here Proust preserves Régnier's haughty elegance throughout ("The diamond scarcely pleases me. I do not find any beauty in it.") He remembers and recreates a number of Régnier's other stylistic characteristics: the somewhat arbitrary impressionism of "an odor of wicker, pumice, cineraria, and marquetry"; the precision of the technical vocabulary ("doves came to perch in the curves of the archivolt or on the splaying of the pedestal"); the looseness in Régnier's use of pronouns, which nevertheless achieves a certain elegance ("La majesté des cérémonies dont [les] sonneries [des cloches] annonçaient l'heure, compensait mal le contretemps d'être réveillé à celle où il convient de dormir, si l'on veut ensuite pouvoir profiter des autres."[6] Finally, the concluding passage of the pastiche illustrates Régnier's balanced, rhythmical sentence structure and reveals his proclivity for an occasionally "strained" symbolism, which is made the more hilarious by Proust's mimicry of Régnier's predilection for dealing with indelicate subjects in noble terms, his tendency, so to speak, to soar over filth:

> Lemoine was catching a cold. From his nose which he kept forgetting to blow, a little snot had fallen upon his neck-band and suit. Its viscous, tepid drop, sliding over the cloth of the former, had stuck to the cloth of the latter and held in suspension over the void the silvery and liquid fringe which was about to drip off. The sun's rays blended the sticky mucus and the diluted liquid. Only a single juicy mass, convulsive, transparent, and hardened, could be distinguished; in the ephemeral brilliance with which it decorated Lemoine's suit, it seemed to have caught the magic of a momentary diamond, still hot, so to speak, from the furnace; and, remaining corrosive and living for another moment, its unstable congealment seemed, by virtue of its deceptive and yet fascinating beauty, to mock and at the same time to symbolize the diamond.[7]

In a very short essay on Régnier which makes several allusions to that author's novel *La Double Maîtresse* Proust defends Régnier against the charge of snobbery and attributes his affectations rather to the influence of Flaubert and Leconte de Lisle — their admiration for unusual and colorful details. The above passage from the pastiche is a *reductio ad absurdum* of this very affectation. Proust adds that this same predilection undoubtedly made Régnier find particular pleasure in the language of the seventeenth century, which he to some extent made his own.[8]

A Maeterlinck pastiche was apparently written but never published.[9] A letter to Georges de Lauris (March, 1909) furnishes a comment on it, as well as on the Régnier one, and alludes to the unpublished exercise on Chateaubriand's style:

> Yet there is nothing which could displease Régnier. He must know he confuses his pronouns because this neo-Saint-Simon syntax is deliberate and as for repeating the same things several times, he must know that too. I can't have the Chateaubriand published, nor the Maeterlinck, because they need just a little polishing up and I am unable to make the slightest effort.[10]

Proust considered Maeterlinck a great stylist, worthy of being placed alongside of other innovators, such as Rousseau, Hugo, and Flaubert. In a footnote to *Sésame et les lys* there is an elaborate bow to Maeterlinck; quoting a passage about the white lily from Maeterlinck's *Fleurs démodées,* Proust praises the sentences as the finest since the Gospels, "the most truly beautiful sentences, touched by a reality full of life and marked by the profoundest appreciation." [11] On the subject of Maeterlinck's "garden" Proust likes to wax eloquent with praise, even going so far as to refer to Maeterlinck as the "Virgil of Flanders":

> Maurice Maeterlinck's garden, dominated by the "innocent, unvarying and fresh" images of a cypress and a parasol pine, so beautiful, says he in one of the loveliest pages of French prose of the last sixty years, that he "imagines no paradise or afterlife, no matter how splendid, in which those trees do not have their place" — that garden in which the Flemish Virgil, near his straw hives painted pink, yellow, and soft blue, reminding us at the moment we enter the

garden what his favorite studies are, has gathered so much incomparable poetry; can one indeed say that he is not looking for anything but poetry in that garden? [12]

On another occasion he comments on Maeterlinck's reflections on death; writing to Georges de Lauris in 1912, he observes, ". . . All the beauty with which Maeterlinck surrounds it is only a way of distracting us from what we really feel in the face of death." [13] The criticism implied in this statement is slightly out of joint with the praise accorded to Maeterlinck in the review of Anna de Noailles' *Les Eblouissements*:

. . . For that evolutionist of the absolute — if one can call him that — science, philosophy and ethics lie along the same level; and the horizon of happiness and truth is not a mirage which results from the laws governing the optics and the perspective of our intellect, but rather it is the end point of a real ideal, which we are actually approaching.[14]

One may conclude from this that Proust changed his mind about the "reality" of Maeterlinck's ideal and its accessibility. Proust's soberest estimate of Maeterlinck is perhaps the one in *Sésame et les lys*, in which he attempts to see the relationship between Maeterlinck's literary and philosophical sides:

The excellent writer in Maeterlinck has been supplemented by a fine philosopher. Even if the writer, as I believe, has thus become still greater, his friend the philosopher has not been there for nothing. One has the feeling that the writer in Maeterlinck has grown in stature, but not because the thinker in Maeterlinck has developed.[15]

Without putting Maeterlinck's sentimentality and fuzzy philosophy into the proper perspective, Proust is nevertheless emphasizing the importance of thought in a developing writer — the role that reflection plays in forcing an author to give expression to his intellectual discoveries. In Proust too the thinker surmounted gradually the derivative and tired *Les Plaisirs* until he attained the originality and certitude of *A la recherche*. In Maeterlinck, however, no such regeneration took place.

Proust repeatedly expressed an admiration for Maurice Barrès,[16] though not without some serious reservations ("having long had an immense admiration for the talent of Barrès, coupled with a deep antipathy for what I believed to be his *mauvais coeur*" [17]). The latter phrase surely is an allusion to Barrès' violent anti-Dreyfusism. Moreover, Proust disapproved of his political ambitions. In the only letter of the Proust-Barrès correspondence (dated August, 1911), which has been published in Barrès' *Cahiers*, one finds him politely but firmly criticizing the older writers political aspirations; in *Le Temps retrouvé* he voices the conviction that the artist's commitments were outside of politics and that patriotism for the artist consists of being a *good* artist.

> At the very beginning of the war M. Barrès declared that the artist (in this case it was Titian) should first of all serve the glory of his country. But he can serve it only by being an artist or, in other words, on condition that when he is studying the laws of Art, making his experiments and his discoveries, as delicate as those of Science, he think of nothing — not even his country — except the truth that is before him.[18]

Since Proust himself has been charged with being too "detached," this statement of the artist's responsibility to his country may well serve as a reply to his critics.

Germaine Brée, in an article on Proust and Barrès,[19] points out that the following excerpt, taken from Proust's letter to Barrès, contains a criticism of the latter's traditionalism and an indirect criticism of his ambitions of political leadership:

> . . . I was saying the following to myself: With relation to Chateaubriand and others, Maurice Barrès has spoken of the desire of certain great artists to lead their countries, to be political leaders. It seemed to me then (I am not going into the reasons which I had in mind) that this was a contradictory and impossible thing — at least it is now — and out of date. Perhaps you had that desire too, in that old-fashioned way just described, and did not fulfill it. Only I ought to have said to myself that there are masterpieces of action as well as

masterpieces of art and that the only ones worthy of their predecessors that a man can produce are created not by imitating past greatness but by obeying unwittingly an original genius that does something which looks quite different on the surface, namely this: it perpetuates old masterpieces in a newly composed form, without which such works would have been pastiches, not masterpieces.[20]

Proust echoes here one of his favorite notions: "classical" distinction in literature is the result of an original quest and an original discovery, not of a skillful imitation of old patterns. He discerned a tension between the great literary talent and the political aspirations of Barrès, and was therefore fond of pointing out the excellence of Barrès' style. Speaking of an address delivered by the latter in Metz and of a preface which he wrote for a book about Metz, *La Ville enchantée*,[21] he remarks

. . . In your writings there are certain changes of tone which exist only in music. In order to get an idea of that wonderful joy which bursts out with the sound of cymbals when you speak of Metz one has to go back to the almost barbaric type of diatonicism or to the intoxicating dissonances of certain liturgies. And at the same time, I found it singular and glorious to think that there is an involuntary symmetry — the only perfect kind that exists, the same one that is found in the life of one of nature's growths — between the fruits which you bear on the branches of actions and the ones which you bear on the branches of art.[22]

The Faguet pastiche seems to have been primarily a *jeu* for Proust, since it can hardly be said to fall within the category of homage (Saint-Simon, Balzac, Flaubert, Michelet, Régnier) or of exorcism (Renan, Goncourt). Proust's unwillingness to treat Faguet with fashionable scorn is shown in a letter to his mother, dated September 24, 1904, in which he writes:

It has become "smart" among young people to tear Faguet to pieces, as they used to do with Sarcey. And it is quite stupid to attribute his heaviness to ignorance of the French language. Rather, that heaviness is intentional, and Faguet knows very well what he is doing. If there is anything defensible about him, it is his form.[23]

The pastiche is reminiscent of one of Faguet's *Propos de théâtre* (Faguet is supposed to be reviewing *L'Affaire Lemoine*, a drama by Henri Bernstein), with all its gravity, with its rather irritating insistence on adopting the spectator's viewpoint, and with its chatty witticisms.[24] Jean Mouton suggests with considerable plausibility that Proust was getting some preliminary practice in the reproduction of the language of university professor Brichot in *A la recherche.*[25]

The letters to Robert de Montesquiou fail to reveal genuine critical evaluation of Montesquiou's writing. All of Proust's references to Montesquiou's work are encumbered by excessive flattery. In the earlier letters, the most frequent mode of address used by the younger man is "Mon cher Maître," as he had done in the case of Anatole France. In one instance Proust extravagantly compares Montesquiou to the great poets of the classical age, who had the gift of thinking in verse,[26] in another he writes, "You know that your honored existence is indispensable to French letters, to all the minds which you fecundate by the pen and by the spoken word. . . ,"[27] and in still another he draws a parallel between Montesquiou's verse and that of Sully Prudhomme: "Perhaps I might cause you displeasure . . . by saying that I like it for its pensive brevity which made me think of an intellectual elegiac whom you despise perhaps but who has written some engaging lines."[28] The ten-page essay on Montesquiou included in the *Nouveaux Mélanges*[29] appears to be a draft, never published, in praise of Montesquiou the man and the poet. Its opening is a string of quotations from the Count's poems with connecting prose by Proust. The rest, though more discursive and interesting, is vitiated by *préciosité.*

Whatever Proust's estimate of the poems may have been, one can be certain that he admired Robert de Montesquiou the art lover and critic. These sentiments are attested by a little known article dating from the year 1905 and entitled "Un Professeur de beauté." Speaking of Montesquiou's acute perceptions in the realm of the fine arts, Proust outlines a sort of ideal critic. For that reason, the following passage deserves to be quoted — not for any light it sheds on Montesquiou. It is strikingly similar to the prefaces and notes to *La Bible d'Amiens* and *Sésame et les lys*; here, too, is the effort to crystallize a number of notions about art and criticism:

> A vision which so carefully notes the characteristic and precise detail undoubtedly demanded — and found — an infinitely varied vocabulary, capable of furnishing at any moment the technical word, the correct, which is often the unusual, expression. In reality, when today we reread attentively certain plays which appear most classical to us, we discover on close scrutiny what precision of detail, which sometimes gets in the way of our ignorance, has gone into the making of their beauty, though from a distance this beauty had appeared so vague and general. . . . Our author demands the same kind of effort. To be sure, sometimes a seldom used expression also holds us up. The author's erudition causes each object to evoke memories in him which we have not as carefully ordered in our own memories. . . . In M. de Montesquiou . . . the unusual expression is always an excellent one, selected from the best literary *milieux* of the sixteenth, seventeenth, or eighteenth centuries. . . .[30]

The only article which Proust devoted to an appreciation of the work of a contemporary was his review of Anna de Noailles' *Les Eblouissements* (*Le Figaro*, June 15, 1907, reprinted in *Chroniques*). It is easy to see the evidences of friendship, even adulation, throughout the article; Proust's admiration for the Countess, as his letters amply prove, was apparently unbounded. The tone of *préciosité* and flattery spoils the value of the review, but this factor does not obscure the presence of a number of genuine *aperçus*. In a sense, Proust is here fulfilling the minimum function which he felt was required of the critic — to help the reader to *see* — but is not pursuing the path of his ideal critic, who helps the reader to reconstruct a writer's spiritual life. Within the framework of this kind of criticism he succeeds admirably, in spite of the hyperboles, by managing to point up the genuine merits of a somewhat monochrome set of poems by a poetess of great charm and frequently of exquisite inspiration.

The principal value of this highlighting type of criticism lies in Proust's ability to view certain images of a poem in a new light. The poem *Les Eaux de Damas* is praised as "perhaps the masterpiece of impressionism in literature," particularly for its image of the Waters of Damascus, an image which Proust finds "so sudden and so finished, which comes into being with immediacy and completeness." [31]

> Comme une jeune esclave
> Qui monte, qui descend, qui parfume et qui lave!

Moreover, he appreciates the genuinely felt impression of the poem "Jour d'été":

> One has to read the whole poem on the splendor, intoxication and sweep of those summer mornings on which one throws back one's head to allow one's eyes to follow a bird propelled into the sky, in order to feel the whole dizziness that comes from sensing the mystery of the last two lines:
>
> Tandis que détaché d'une invisible fronde,
> Un doux oiseau jaillit jusqu'au sommet du monde.[32]

Charles Du Bos characterizes this quality of Anna de Noailles' verse, which Proust conveys to us in terms of "feeling" and "mystery," by pointing out that in the poetess' works "the love of Nature comes *first*, whereas in the other great French poets it comes second and almost always tends to be an accompaniment to human love, more often still a consolation or a cure for it." [33] For Proust, Madame de Noailles' use of French place names adds a particular touch of beauty to a poem, or to her volume of poems, for example in "Les Charmettes" or "La Savoie"; or the use of metaphors "which recompose our first impression and give it back to us in all its initial deceptiveness" and bring about in our minds "the resurrection of what we have felt (the only interesting reality)," [34] an observation foreshadowing the later Proust. Finally, he notes the beauty of the "irregular" images in "La Beauté du printemps,"

> Entendez les oiseaux de mon brûlant gosier

and compares it to a similar image in Baudelaire's "Femmes damnées,"

> Et les urnes d'amour dont vos grands coeurs sont pleins,

commenting "Only the great poet dares to fill the heart with urns and the throat with birds." [35]

Proust's admiration for Madame de Noailles' style often knows no limits; he regarded her as a poetic genius, whose "vision" transfigured all her experience into terms of beauty. He praises the novel *Le Visage émerveillé* for its poetic content, which he finds "perpetual, and integrating, like a marvelous quality of your eye, which makes you see everything in beauty, in truth, in newness, in genius." [36] His comments on *La Nouvelle Espérance* are even more explicit along the same lines, manifesting, like all of Proust's writings of the "Ruskin" period, his preoccupation with problems of style and the secret of its excellence, and preparing the way for the subsequent years in which *A la recherche* slowly began to take shape in his mind.

> ". . . I see life in blue, yellow, and violet" seems to me to be the central phrase, the "source of light" [*le centre d'éclairage*] for the entire book. I mean that the most extraordinary, the most beautiful thing about this book (probably the thing that strikes you least because it is the part that emanates most directly from you without the intervention of your reasoning faculty and your will) lies in the fact that it is not composed of parts; it is made of uniform stuff, steeped — and steeped completely — in one and the same atmosphere, where one color calls up another and complements it . . . This inspired manipulation of color makes you the greatest of impressionists, and your bold strokes, smoothed out by your over-all harmony, is incredible (the "blue wind," the "rose lane," the forest enclosing the sun, etc., come to my mind here) . . . But is not that multichrome color unity itself the material symbol of that extraordinary quality that your book possesses and which only marvelous books possess; it is so astonishing and at the same time so inconceivable that this quality should be the primordial quality, the one which assures permanence and reveals genius.[37]

However, Proust was well aware of the pitfalls that beset Madame de Noailles' work and occasionally passed on his criticisms to the author herself. For instance, in the novel *Domination* he detected something — the frequent use of the historical present — which he regarded as "*barrésiste*" and advised the poetess to rid herself of the tendency if that tendency was derivative: "If it is [*barrésiste*], then you ought not to devote yourself to it; if on the other hand it is within you and dictated by your inner self, you ought not to resist it." [38] Madame de Noailles comments in a footnote that, as usual, Proust was right; "How often he proved to be a lucid counselor!" In another case, Proust wrote to Anna de Noailles concerning the "Poèmes de l'azur,"

> Though I admired the poems in *La Revue des Deux Mondes* . . . I found something rather subjective in their inspiration and sometimes too discontinuous in their expression, admirable though it is.[39]

Here Madame de Noailles comments, "One can see here that Marcel Proust's infallible critical sense is struggling with the elements in his friendship which tend to repress and silence his candid judgment." As a matter of fact, Madame de Noailles appears to have admired Proust as much as Proust admired her. "Marcel Proust," she puts it, "is the only human being who has ever made me change a line or suppress a strophe . . ." [40] Reciprocally, Proust found himself obliged to eliminate a passage from his novel — from *Jean Santeuil*? — ("almost a whole volume," as he put it) because of the supreme excellence of Anna de Noailles' treatment of the French countryside.

> . . . In my opinion, Madame de Noailles has, at least for the next fifty years, taken away from every other writer the possibility of addressing cities, etc., in direct discourse. Whatever anyone may do along those lines, in that form, no matter how sincere, how experienced, how anterior to her it may be — and unless by making a long and deep descent into one's heart of hearts, or rather into the heart's brain, one finds a different and completely individual expression —

everything will seem an imitation of her: her radiance will drown out all our light. I say "our" quite pretentiously, because I myself have had to throw into the fire almost a whole volume about Brittany which I had written before I had ever read anything of hers and in which things like

Quimperlé! . . .
Pont-Aven! . . .

seemed to come from *L'Ombre des jours* or from *La Domination.* My sacrifice was necessary but it was a bloody one nevertheless. Perhaps it will not be definitive — literary sacrifices rarely are.[41]

Proust here gives evidence of his literary discipline in action — the same literary discipline, surely, that led him to abandon *Jean Santeuil* — because he felt that it was necessary to descend into his "heart's brain" still deeper in order to create something truly individual.

Proust's critical reflections on Gide's works are sparse; the Gide-Proust correspondence centers mainly around Gide's apologies for misjudging *Swann* and the eventual publication of the novel by the N.R.F. Proust takes great pleasure in pointing out the Balzacian aspects of Lafcadio:

As far as the creation of Cadio is concerned, nobody since Balzac's *Splendeurs et misères* has been so perversely objective. Still, I believe certain personal vulgarity helped Balzac to invent Lucien de Rubempré. There is in Lucien's talk a certain coarse-grained quality whose naturalness delights us, but you run into the same thing frequently in Balzac, even in his letters. Whereas your task, in order to create Cadio. . . ! I could say a great many things to you about this novel, which is more fascinating than a Stevenson novel — about its episodes which converge, since they are constructed like a rose-window.[42]

In the same letter, Proust takes exception to the profusion of material detail. The observation is significant, inasmuch as it constitutes a criticism of the naturalistic technique.

. . . Maybe it's fatigue, or laziness, or boredom — but when I write I can't put down anything which did not either produce an impression of poetic enchantment on me or did not enable me to grasp some general truth. My characters never take off their tie, nor do they lay by a new stock of ties (as at the opening of Isabelle).[43]

In a subsequent letter, Proust denies that Lafcadio is Dostoevskian, although he admits having been tempted by the notion while reading *Les Caves du Vatican*:

. . . Since *Crime and Punishment* and the *Brothers Karamazov*, we can no longer see a criminal who does not try to escape justice without believing that there is a resemblance to Dostoevski. That's silly. If that were so, Tolstoi would not have been able to paint his *War and Peace* in dispersed sequence because Stendhal did it before him. And what's more, isn't Cadio as different from a Dostoevskian character as anyone can be? I am even convinced that Dostoevski would not have been able to understand the seductiveness and the immorality of such a character. (I should like to know if all of Cadio's "uncles" are "aunts" [*i.e.*, pederasts]. How interesting!)

From this Balzacian interpolation he continues,

The question mark, the first ray of sunlight and hope on which your book ends, is perhaps not altogether satisfying, from a purely geometrical point of view of composition. One expected all the holes to be more tightly stopped up, one expected to have a hermetically sealed book. But it interests me more the way it is, since it touches upon one of the laws which interest me most, and which I always try to bring out when I am writing, namely the differences in pressure, the variations in the moral atmosphere affecting one and the same individual. For that reason the idea of ending on the tonic gives me great pleasure.[44]

One notes here — the letter dates from early April, 1914 — Proust's absorbing interest in problems of "psychology in time" that prompted him to make large-scale additions to the original design of *A la recherche* between the appearance of *Swann* in 1913 and that of *Jeunes Filles* in 1919. Where Gide's "geometry" is deficient, Proust attempts to make his own composition continuous and "closed."

In a subsequent letter he expresses his admiration for *Les*

Nourritures terrestres, "which have already nourished a generation and on which many others will live."[45] Expanding this idea to include every great writer who draws sustenance from his predecessors and provides nourishment for those to come, he once more is insisting on the essential kinship of all great creative minds and on the process of fertilization that takes place when one writer allows himself to fall under the spell of another. "You will live because you allowed yourself to be nourished and now you have produced nourishment."[46] Finally, Proust calls attention to certain similarities of expression in *Les Plaisirs et les jours* and *Les Nourritures terrestres*:

> You might find here and there [in *Les Plaisirs et les jours*] a phrase (such as the one to the effect that the foliage of a tree is a green grotto) which has some analogy to *Les Nourritures terrestres*, but alas! only to one sentence in it.[47]

The same letter contains an uncomplimentary reference to Claudel's *Protée*, which Proust compares unfavorably with *Les Nourritures terrestres* by calling it "a *Belle Hélène* which is more pretentious, more academic, and at least as fragile as that one. But what do Claudel's artificial intentions to write free verse, or whatever you call it, amount to next to the '*accent*' of the *Nourritures*?"[48] Proust's judgment is exceedingly harsh, but one remembers Proust's lack of sympathy with free verse, as expressed in "*Contre l'Obscurité*." It is rather strange that Proust's notions of what poetry should be are more conventional than his ideas about prose. To be sure, he looked upon all artistic creation as continuous, a sort of succession of classical works, each of which gives evidence of its debt to the past as well as its departure from the present and its fruitfulness for the development of future styles. The history of literature in this way becomes a succession of organic changes which modify the exterior immediately after changes have occurred on the inside. Form is bound up secretly — Proust would say mysteriously — with the laws governing the matter which it contains. Since the relation between form and matter is subject to its own kind of logic, there must be only one way in which the two elements can remain in balance. For this reason he regarded Claudel's publication of three versions of his Violaine drama pointless (*i.e.*, *La Jeune Fille Violaine* I and II and the later version, *L'Annonce faite à Marie*). "The poet must know how to make the choice and the sacrifice . . ."[49]

The same charge is leveled at Péguy, with somewhat greater insistence, in a letter to Jacques Boulenger dated 1921: "I abhor poor Péguy's writing and have never felt otherwise about it." And then Proust recalls his opinion of Péguy after reading one of the *Cahiers de la Quinzaine*: "I find [Péguy] devoid of talent . . . [It is] the most insipid junkheap of totally useless prose that I know."[50] There exists, however, a soberer statement by Proust on Péguy's shortcomings.

> . . . One might, during his life-time, have reproached Peguy with always trying to say one thing in six different ways, whereas there is only one way of saying one thing. But the glory of his heroic death has wiped away all blemishes.[51]

If there is only one right way in art, Proust insists here, then the artist must discipline himself to exclude the "à peu près." Claudel did not do so in the case of *L'Annonce faite à Marie* and *La Ville*, but in a sense Proust's objections ought not to be regarded as fundamental, since they relate rather to a problem of conduct than of creation; on the other hand, the aspersions he cast on Péguy's verse are more serious, and actually not completely fair, inasmuch as they do not come to grips with the problem. In Péguy's verse the plodding and repetitious qualities are intentional, and Proust either was unwilling or simply failed to see this. The reader of Péguy's verse knows well enough that Proust's criticism contains a certain amount of truth — it is extremely easy for Péguy's work to become tedious. It is strange, however, that Proust did not feel the effectiveness and beauty of the plodding, ruminating quality of Péguy's style in certain poems such as "Présentation de la Beauce à Notre Dame" and writes as though he had only Péguy's later verse before him, where the repetitions become exceedingly irritating. Nevertheless, it is clear from Proust's severe condemnation of Péguy that on the point of artistic self-discipline Proust remained adamant. "Truth, even literary truth," he wrote to Léon Daudet in 1917, "is not the result of an accident . . . I believe that [literary] truth is in every case discovered like a physical *law*. You find it or you don't. To prattle *around* the necessary word and *around* the *unique* relationship between two psychological facts is like saying that those facts just don't exist." [52] This is the essence also of the advice he gave Paul Morand at the end of *Tendres Stocks*, cautioning his friend against the use of artificial metaphors.[53] Cattaui sums up the divergence of Proust and Péguy succinctly:

> If Proust did not care for Péguy's style, it probably had something to do with the fact that whereas some tend to confuse Proust's intricacies and complexities with Péguy's slowness and stumbling, the former always searched for the right and inevitable word, striving to concentrate his thought, the latter, with a simplicity which for me is very moving, drew a sort of lyrical effect from his groping, his awkwardness and even his repetitiousness.[54]

Somehow Proust never quite understood the favorable reception which Péguy — his poetry as well as his prose — received in certain quarters. In a letter to Louis de Robert, he contrasts him unfavorably with Francis Jammes.

> As for certain works of prose, Monsieur Péguy's for instance, in which there reigns a state of mind which is diametrically opposed to artistic inspiration and crystallization, plus a kind of indolence in the course of which one word makes you imagine another and in which one does not have the courage to sacrifice one's gropings, I can't sufficently express my stupefaction in seeing that in intelligent circles, as at the *Nouvelle Revue française*, one finds those works admirable.[55]

On the other hand, Francis Jammes "gropes" in a way in which his gropings become a virtue because the expressions which Jammes uses are lucid and profound, even if the over-all pattern is missing. Proust's remarks on Jammes — and perhaps, by extension, on any other artist gifted with insights and an ability to verbalize these insights, but one who still struggles to impose an order on all those miscellaneous expressions—are in themselves lucid and profound:

> . . . For me the most valuable things in Jammes are not his best works. People consider those works his best in which his faults are least apparent. But many people without genius are endowed with the qualities that he lacks and that would improve his books. The absence of certain qualities which so many people possess is not really a very serious matter. Even if he did not know how to give his feelings a certain arrangement, if he did not know how to write a book, or even a short story, or even a paragraph, or even a sentence, he would still be left with this asset: the very cell, the atom, that is to say that his use of epithet and image is of a depth and a rightness attained by nobody else. Deep down in ourselves we feel that things are like that, but we do not have the strength to get to the very bottom of it, where truth resides, the true universe, our authentic impression. And thus we put quasi-expressions magnificently in order. But as far as Jammes is concerned, he leaves expressions, each one of which is a revelation, in a state of disorder. That is the reason why, when people say that he is continually stammering, I find that only he speaks clearly. Undoubtedly I should prefer it if all those bits of truth went to make up a splendid whole, which would be a revelation of the real world. But I prefer the simple indication to the big constructions in which 10,000 failures, based on intellect and rhetoric give people (though not me) the impression of success.[56]

This letter dates from early 1913. Proust's insight into the difference between a writer's authenticity and his ability to organize is highly revealing. Not only does he offer a distinction between the artist and the artisan here, but he underscores the bitter truth that in literary appreciation there are no rules but only something which, for lack of a better word, we usually call intuition. By 1913 Proust had, after a long apprenticeship, found a way of becoming an artist in his own eyes.

Contre Sainte-Beuve and the *Nouveaux Mélanges* contain brief comments on two more of Proust's contemporaries, Romain Rolland and Jules Renard. Very few readers of Proust will be surprised at his dislike for the former's vapid idealism. "Unfortunately when Jean Christophe . . . stops speaking, M. Romain Rolland continues to heap up banality upon banality, and when he tries to find a more precise image, we get a work of searching and not of finding, a work in which he shows himself inferior to any writer of today." [57] In Renard's case, the comments are on the *Histoires naturelles*. Proust praises Renard's efforts to grasp the "hidden truth of a sensation" but finds a tendency to seal things off prematurely by drollery and *préciosité*. But, he adds, *préciosité* may sometimes be true, as in the case of Renard's butterfly — "that love letter folded in half looking for the address of a flower":

> In the butterfly, "to look for the address of a flower" is not simply *préciosité*, that is to say, when you no longer have any truth to continue, to continue the image which makes a play on the words and makes an ending which no longer stands in relation with anything but verbal appearance. There, in the butterfly, "to look for the address of a flower" has its truthfulness in the gropings of the butterfly which flies to each flower and asks, and seems to be mistaken, since it flies on to another one.[58]

The only writer considerably younger than himself on whose work Proust commented critically is Jean Cocteau. The friendship between Proust and Cocteau dates from about 1911, and there undoubtedly exists a correspondence, of which three letters have been published.[59] One of the three deals with Proust's remarks on Cocteau's long poem, *Le Cap de Bonne Espérance*, and another contains Proust's criticism of Cocteau's little tract on music entitled *Le Coq et l'Arlequin*; this letter is a valuable addition to the information we possess about Proust's musical tastes.

Le Cap de Bonne Espérance was written during World War I and published in 1917. It is chaotic and somewhat too insistently "modern," with its thick machine imagery and its geographical allusions, but it contains many fine passages, and

Proust invariably seized on them in his letter to Cocteau: ". . . In that poem you too have found the secret of raising yourself above the ground and of casting off weight." [60] At the mention of the word "pesanteur," he offers a criticism of the harshness of the image "la chiourme de pesanteur" and of certain other details of the poem:

> For instance . . . "la chiourme de pesanteur" strikes me as being too insistent an expression, after those essentially right ones like "Minerve en cuirasse de cuir" . . . In a book which is so short, even though it is so lofty, as yours, a frequently repeated image is perhaps not so suitable (I am thinking precisely of a passage near the one I just spoke about: "ses Guadalquivir, ses Gulf Stream, ses Lacs Tchad, ses Zuydersée"). But actually I think I am wrong about this and that that is variety in that hydrographic map of the sky. An idea should be drawn out so long as it can yield different things. You are right, after all.[61]

The apologetic tone of the last sentences ought not to mislead anyone into thinking that Proust is actually retracting his statements about "concentration within a broad framework." The reader of *A la recherche* knows that Proust aims for, and achieves, this concentration, and that he establishes continuity by using a technique of recurrences and leitmotivs. His remarks on the importance and rightness of metaphors is simply a footnote to the general conviction expressed at the end of *A la recherche* and in the Flaubert essay that only metaphors insure the permanence of a style.

In conclusion it ought to be stated that even though these critiques of his contemporaries are only sparse and often marred by the desire to please, Proust in his best moments reflects the same preoccupations and the same aesthetic attitudes that we find in his criticisms of the nineteenth century. In the final analysis, all of his critical observations converge on his mature reflections on the art of writing, as found at the end of *A la recherche.*

V

CONCLUSION

> Les beaux livres sont écrits dans une sorte de langue étrangère. Sous chaque mot chacun de nous met son sens ou du moins son image qui est souvent un contre-sens. Mais dans les beaux livres, tous les contre-sens qu'on fait sont beaux.
>
> PROUST, *Contre Sainte-Beuve.*

Criticism for Proust was a means to an end. The germ and the fruit of this idea are contained in the quotation from *La Bible d'Amiens* at the end of Part III of this study:

> There is no better way of becoming conscious of what one feels oneself than to try to re-create in one's own mind the feelings of a master. For the deep-searching effort brings our thought, as well as his, into the light of day.

He found it to his advantage to use an author's text in the same way in which he intended his own novel to be read — as a sort of optical device whereby the reader can read himself. This process of making a text one's own necessarily implies an intermediate analytical and critical stage, in which the Proustian reader attempts to seize the essence behind an author's "vision." For the author's vision is not necessarily one which he can analyze consciously; the very texture of his writings is the result of a more or less mysterious process, in which the artist's inner organization imposes a secret and profound order upon his materials. In his critical studies Proust attempted to attune his ear to these secret rhythms. Writing to Gide about *Les Nourritures terrestres*, he observed:

> . . . Probably you will always be unaware of the most secret beauty of that book, for you know its content thoroughly, but you cannot hear its rhythm. And the novelty of that book — a lasting quality, of course, since the new in art never lies in the realm of time — which takes hold of one even more effectively if one has put the work aside for a few years, this novelty is to be found above all in its rhythm.[1]

In order to capture this rhythm or accent Proust often casts his literary judgments in the form of analyses (discernments) rather than criticisms (judgments). Both are, for Proust, ways of discovering himself by means of discovering others.

In the above quotation, Proust uses the word "master" deliberately, rather than the more narrow "writer." All great artists have an aesthetic lesson to teach him. This statement requires no elucidation for the reader of Proust. *A la recherche* offers portraits of four representatives of the arts, Marcel's own patron saints: Bergotte, Berma, Elstir, and Vinteuil. Each one of these is studied in terms of his particular perfection, the theme of his art running as a leitmotiv throughout the novel, stimulating reflection and revealing some hitherto hidden aspect of the mystery of art. Speaking of Vinteuil and Elstir, Pierre-Quint observed that "existing on an almost divine plane, upon the heights where the Muses used to live, and resembling the Muses in having taken on human shape, they constitute the total image of artistic activity."[2] Bergotte's art serves at first as a literary ideal to the young Marcel preoccupied with literature; in Bergotte's works he discovers the first "key images" and the joy attending upon such revelations.[3] As Marcel matures he gradually leaves Bergotte behind, without losing his respect for the master, and gradually discovers his own literary vocation. The search for literary excellence finds successive incarnations in the Bergotte whom the reader meets in the first volumes, then the dying Bergotte, and finally the Marcel who discovers his own literary vocation and his aesthetics. Thus, in a broader sense, the early Bergotte parallels the refined but derivative Proust of *Les Plaisirs et les jours*; the dying Bergotte is what Proust would have been if he had not learned that style and vision are dual aspects of the same creative act. For, the dying Bergotte, grasping the secret of Vermeer's art, learns that the mystery of art may reside in a patch of yellow wall, just as it might be contained in the taste of a soaked *madeleine*, in a hedge of hawthorns, or in the shifting patterns of the Martinville steeples.

> . . . He fixed his eyes, like a child upon a yellow butterfly which it is trying to catch, upon the precious little patch of wall. "That is how I ought to have written," he said. "My last books are too dry, I ought to have gone over them with several coats of paint, made my language exquisite in itself, like this little patch of yellow wall." [4]

And the final incarnation of the writer is Marcel himself in *Le Temps retrouvé*, now to all intents and purposes identical with the Proust of *A la recherche*, grasping the significance of memory and art as ways of conquering Time, and converting this triumph into a vision of reality through the medium of artistic expression.

Elstir and Vinteuil, and to a lesser extent Berma, offer Marcel insights into the nature of art, which contribute to the clarification of his own aesthetics, for all the arts point to the same reality. As Curtius expresses it in his essay on Proust, ". . . The several arts are but different ways to the soul's kingdom, which is in a state of unchanging repose." [5] For Proust, they are the signposts along the path to eternity. And for this reason he constantly looked to the other arts for illumination along the way. Vermeer and Elstir taught him the secret of Space, Wagner and Vinteuil the secret of Time. Balzac showed him how the recurrence of characters can be used to tie a long novel together; Flaubert knew how to set Time to music, grammatically; Dostoevski knew how to split characters without disintegrating them. Tolstoi had the secret of being able to organize vast canvases by means of an intellectual pattern; George Eliot felt the poetry of humble existences; Ruskin taught him to beware of the idolatry of art; and Sainte-Beuve served as a warning against bondage to history and time and to the intellect. But even more important than the specific illuminations gained from all these masters is Proust's realization that all the creators of the world's literature are images of one and the same poet,

> that great poet who at bottom has been one single poet ever since the beginning of the world, whose intermittent life, which is as long as the life of mankind itself, had in this earthly life its tormented and cruel hours, which we call the life of Baudelaire; its hardworking and serene hours, which we call the life of Hugo; its vagabond and innocent hours which we call the life of Nerval and perhaps of Francis Jammes; its waywardness and debasement to ambitious purposes having nothing to do with truth, which we call the life of Chateaubriand and of Balzac; its waywardness and soaring above truth which we call the second half of Tolstoi's life, as well as Racine's, Pascal's, Ruskin's and perhaps Maeterlinck's.[6]

The same thing could have been said of the painters and composers. The different arts, for Proust, are never categorized; he passes easily from literature to music to art, as happens when in his analysis of *Les Petites Vieilles* by Baudelaire he recalls the late works of Beethoven, and, significantly enough, in his explanation of the *phrases-types*, which are actually the outgrowth of Marcel's discovery of the "little phrase" in Vinteuil's music. The result is that Marcel's (and Proust's) method of scrutiny is essentially the same for all the arts; it always yields a glimpse of a more essential reality behind the actual language which the artist uses; and the result is always an enrichment of experience which stamps itself indelibly on Marcel's soul. It is this revelation of art that matters to the artist; as Proust observes in his essay on Baudelaire:

> . . . the objective precision of a writer's judgments on an art other than his own are without importance. What matters, what sets him

dreaming, is the fact of his admiration, even when it may be given to what is unworthy.[7]

As Marcel was to discover, the *phrases-types* of the various writers, painters, and composers always point toward the hawthorn blossoms, the steeples of Martinville, the *madeleine* and the other privileged moments in which a transcendent reality was revealed to him for a brief moment. Thus, when the artist begins to create, he draws on all his accumulated aesthetic experience, he sloughs off his temporal self and exchanges "his soul for the universal soul." [8] The contemplation of art leads Proust, inevitably, in the direction of mystical absorption.

The focusing of the artist's mind depends completely on the inner concerns of his psyche, even insofar as these concerns determine the form and style which can shape and express his inwardness. Proust, consequently, built his critical remarks about an author around certain facets of that writer that were of particular interest to him — the centrality of Gomorrha in Baudelaire, the sense of time in Flaubert, the recurrence of characters in Balzac, the idealization of the beloved in Hardy, the mystery of the women in Dostoevski, and so on. Each of these aspects of the various authors has its counterpart in *A la recherche du temps perdu*. Proust shows himself to be aware of the novelty of his critical method and its importance as a revaluation or in some cases even a resurrection of literary beauty: "I knew that it is not only over different works, in the long course of centuries, but over different parts of the same work that criticism plays, thrusting back into the shadow what for too long has been thought brilliant, and making emerge what has appeared to be doomed to permanent obscurity." [9]

To quote Professor Levin's words, Proust's "long apprenticeship in the arts had taught him that the greatest masters are hard to recognize, that true originality must build up its own tradition." [10] This apprenticeship of necessity implies criticism, whether silent or expressed. Thus, criticism and analysis were a method of self-discovery for Proust. This explains why Proust practiced criticism from his youth up to the time when he began to write *A la recherche*; and it explains why one of the earlier conceptions of the work to be created took the form of a critical essay-*récit* about Sainte-Beuve. The later essays on Flaubert and Baudelaire, and the prefaces to *Propos de peintre* and *Tendres Stocks*, are replicas in one way or another of Proust's mature ideas on aesthetics, as set forth in *Le Temps retrouvé*. Indeed, it has been shown that Proust's own crisis occurred during the writing of the *Contre Sainte-Beuve*. "Sloth or doubt or impotence take refuge in an author's hesitation concerning the form his art is to take," he wrote in his notebook. "Is one to write a novel? a philosophical study? am I a novelist?"[11] Proust's artistic triumph lies in his having been able, by the end of the Sainte-Beuve experiment, to answer the last question in the affirmative. And thus the literary career of Proust after *Jean Santeuil* can be described as an enormous cycle that begins with the posing of a number of aesthetic problems, which only criticism could begin to solve; Ruskin and Sainte-Beuve are the catalysts here. Then follows Proust's definitive discovery of his artistic vocation and its fulfillment in *A la recherche*. And this work closes on a note of artistic certitude, which comprises the solution to the problem as originally posed.

To be sure, as we look back to *Jean Santeuil*, we can see that the germ of Proust's idealistic aesthetics was already there. In that novel Jean Santeuil muses at length about the relation of art to life, and about the nature of artistic creation. Proust's most cherished ideas are already sketched out there. The value of literature does not lie in a (naturalistic) use of materials but in the way in which the writer "operates" on his materials. The ironic relationship of life to art is compared — with Platonic overtones — to the difference between shadow and prey; and those who seek reality by embracing life and leaving behind the realm of art are substituting the illusion of material possession for the reality of spiritual possession, "les choses n'étant possédables que par l'esprit."[12] The artist's rendering of the reality as he perceives it takes the form of impressions, and the way in which these impressions are organized in the artist's consciousness remains mysterious to him, so that he can never explain to others how the amalgamation took place.[13] Proust's great achievement as a literary critic lies in the fact that he attempted to elucidate the mystery, without dispelling it — because for him art, like religion, needs its mysteries. And the contact established with this mysterious essence — the spiritual "homeland" — of another writer, and leading to self-discovery, is an experience of great joy, a kind of ecstasy comparable to the elation accompanying the *unio mystica*. The artist who has just discovered himself, notes Proust,

> dies instantaneously in the particular and begins immediately to float and to live in the general. He lives only by means of the general: it animates and nurtures him . . . But so long as he is alive, his life is one long ecstasy and happiness.[14]

We understand now Proust's repeated emphasis on the mystery of things and of art, even though at times the word appeared unnecessary and perhaps obscure. For him the whole web of human experience is suffused with this essence, which only memory and art can liberate. The process of this liberation is the highest metaphysical and aesthetic achievement of which the human soul is capable. The conquest of this reality is the highest ethical aspiration of the artist and brings with it the promise of an absolute felicity.

But the final distillation of Proust's aesthetic creed comes at the end of *A la recherche*. The principal points of the essay-within-the-novel center around the writer's, particularly the novelist's, art, the relationship of art to reality, and the problem of style. In Proust's scheme of things these three aspects are closely interlinked, culminating in a triumphant and apocalyptic vision of art: "art is the most real of all things, the sternest school in life and truly the Last Judgment."[15] It is as if art had become a mode of salvation for him, demanding its own *askesis*, whereby the artist might successfully purify himself of what was material and temporal in him. It is strange — and in no way accidental — how often Proust uses the vocabulary of theology to parallel his own aesthetic journey. This characteristic is by no means the same as the "religion of art" of the *fin de siècle*, though that was perhaps Proust's point of origin. The religion of art is transcended and becomes, instead, a religion *through* art, an *itinerarium mentis in Artem*.

Because the involuntary memory and the contemplation of "things" had afforded Marcel an insight into the "hidden essence" of things, across the vastness of Time, Proust felt convinced that the writer's sole *raison d'être* was to penetrate more deeply into this reality. The quest, he knew, was difficult:

> To read the subjective book of these strange signs . . . no one could help me with any rule, for the reading of that book is a creative act in which no one can stand in our stead, or even collaborate with us. And therefore how many there are who shrink from writing it; how many tasks are undertaken in order to avoid that one! Each happening, the Dreyfus case, the war, supplied fresh excuses to the writers for not deciphering that book — they wished to assure the triumph of right, rebuild the moral unity of the nation, and they had no time to think of literature.[16]

This truancy from literature for which Proust is here reproaching many of his contemporaries, notably Barrès, is further aggravated by their espousal of a realism without depth, a kind of journalism, against which Proust's own great work is so eloquent an argument. Reality is to be measured by the degree of penetration attained by the writer, not by the objects selected.

> The literature that is satisfied merely to "describe things," to furnish a miserable listing of their lines and surfaces, is, notwithstanding its pretensions to realism, the farthest removed from reality, the one that most impoverishes and saddens us, even though it speak of nought but glory and greatness, for it sharply cuts off all communication of our present self with the past, the essence of which the objects preserve, and with the future, in which they stimulate us to enjoy the past again.[17]

Realism, he concludes, is not a matter of reproducing observed things photographically and cinematographically, nor need the writer fill up notebooks with facts and with sketches: the synthesis of his accumulated observation is made subconsciously, not by a calculated arrangement of notes. ". . . The writer finds that he, too, has been making a sketchbook without knowing it . . . it is the feeling for the general which in the future writer automatically selects what is general and can therefore enter into a work of art." [18]

It would be wrong to regard these ideas merely as a reaction to naturalism and the "literature of notation" and to assign Proust the critic a place beside antinaturalists like Bourget and de Vogüé; Proust is rather expressing a conviction intended to be applicable to all great artists of all time. It is for this reason that he considers all great art classical — a statement which does away with the textbook classifications into movements and schools. Whether he is justified in overthrowing these cherished academic distinctions is somewhat beside the point here; the important thing is that for him all true art is, by definition, classical, and that true art is constantly being renewed, with the result that the history of all art is a succession of classical artists and works. Since this notion equates the terms "classical" and "timeless," the concept of literary movements is merely useful to designate the timely (historical) side of literary creation. Thus, the term "school" has only a relative significance, as Proust explained in a letter to Rosny:

> "Schools" . . . are only a material symbol of the time it takes for a great artist to be understood and placed among his peers, for the repudiated *Olympia* to hang next to Ingres; for Baudelaire, the judgment against him reversed, to fraternize with Racine . . .
>
> As soon as the innovator is understood, the school for which there is no longer any need is disbanded. Besides, no matter how long the school lasts, the innovator's taste is always much broader. Hugo vaunted Romanticism as his school, but appreciated perfectly Boileau and Regnard. Wagner never regarded Italian music with the severity of the Wagnerians.[19]

A literary school might thus be defined as a propaganda organization designed to make its new ideas acceptable to the public. The proper place for such ideas is to be found within the framework of intellectual history. Proust assumes all along something that literary history has amply borne out, something of which he himself was only too aware: that new writers, by virtue of their novelty, find acceptance difficult. Since every classicism is a renewal not only of vision but also of the way in which this vision finds expression — "the continuity of styles is not compromised but guaranteed by a perpetual renewal of style" [20] — he observes that every renewal of this sort requires a new effort. In his Preface to Jacques-Emile Blanche's *Propos de peintre* he spoke of those new artists who prove themselves worthy successors of the past "because they begin their lives by being situated in the future," producing works "at which one must try to look down the perspective of the years that they anticipate, bringing that modification of the sensibilities for the development of which it is time, precisely, that is needed." [21] A statement summarizing Proust's attitude is found at the conclusion of the Preface to *Tendres Stocks*, this conclusion being intended as a final answer to Anatole France's complaint that good writers had disappeared since the end of the eighteenth century.

The truth . . . is that from time to time a new and original writer appears . . . The new writer is, as a rule, rather exhausting to read and difficult to understand, because he is forever finding new relationships between things. One follows him half-way through a sentence, but then one's endurance gives out. One feels the reason to be merely this, that the new writer has a more agile mind than one's own. It is with original writers as it is with original painters. When Renoir began to paint, no one recognized the objects which he set himself to represent. It is easy, today, to speak of him as having an eighteenth-century spirit. But, in saying that, people omit the time factor, and forget that, even in the middle of the nineteenth century, it took a long time for Renoir to be accepted as a great painter. If they are to succeed, they have — the original painter and the original writer — to proceed much in the manner of oculists. The treatment administered through their paintings or their literature is not always pleasant. When it is finished, they say to us: "*Now* look!" and suddenly the world, which, far from having been created once and for all, is created afresh each time that a new artist comes on the scene, is shown to us in perfect clarity — but looking very different from the one we knew before.[22]

Since Proust's belief is that the vitality of literature depends on a continuous renewal of style, his idea of style is necessarily broad. This is one of the great virtues of his criticism: his sense of style seems almost infallible, as his pastiches and his numerous stylistic analyses have adequately shown. Rejecting all that is artificial, rhetorical, and decorative, Proust exalts the style in which the authentic impression, the natural progress of the mind are reflected:

As to style, I have endeavored to reject everything dictated by pure intellect, everything that is rhetoric, embellishment and, more or less, any deliberate or mannered figures of speech . . . to express my deep and authentic impressions and to respect the natural progress of my thought.[23]

Thus he explains in his Preface to *Tendres Stocks* that it is better to use no images at all if the "inevitable" image fails to suggest itself to the writer:

. . . An image that is merely approximate is a failure. Water (in given conditions) boils at a temperature of 100 degrees. At 98 or 99 the phenomenon does not occur. In such cases it is better to do without any images at all. Set somebody in front of a piano for six months on end, someone who knows nothing of Wagner or of Beethoven; let him try every possible chance combination of notes on the keyboard; this fumbling will never produce the Spring theme from *Die Walküre* or the pre-Mendelssohnian (or, rather, infinitely super-Mendelssohnian) phrase from the 15th Quartet.[24]

A writer's conscious effort to be original belongs in the same category and, in Proust's eyes, is equally reprehensible. Writing for the symposium on style in the *Renaissance politique, littéraire, artistique* on July 22, 1922, he remarks:

I in no way "give my support" (to use the very phrasing of your inquiry) to writers "preoccupied with originality of form." A writer should be exclusively preoccupied with his impressions, or with ideas to be translated into words.[25]

On the other hand, he welcomes a writer's originality in using the French language. As the style is renewed, the language too undergoes a renewal; for Proust, what is finest in the French language is due to the efforts of its great writers:

This idea that there is a French language that exists outside of the writers who use it and that must be protected is fantastic. Each writer is bound to create his own language as each violinist must create his own "tone." . . . I prefer — and it is, perhaps, a weakness — those who write well. But they start to write well only on condition that they are original, that they themselves create their own language. Correctness, perfection of style do exist, but not this side of originality, but through and beyond it . . . The only way to defend the language is to attack it! Because its unity is created only by the neutralizing of opposites, by an apparent immobility which hides perpetual, vertiginous activity. For one "holds one's own" and cuts a fine figure in comparison with writers of the past only inasmuch as one has tried to write quite differently. And when one wants to defend the French language, one actually writes quite the opposite of classical French. For example: the revolutionaries Rousseau, Hugo, Flaubert, Maeterlinck "hold their own" beside Bossuet.[26]

This preoccupation with language in all its aspects — the written language of his predecessors which he made his own in the pastiches with such astonishing virtuosity, as well as the spoken language of others which he imitated in the drawing rooms and later in *A la recherche* — can be noted as early as *Jean Santeuil*. There Proust offers his readers an object lesson on style by having Professor Beulier criticize Jean Santeuil's dissertation; the passage reads like an extension of "Contre l'obscurité" into fiction:

". . . No doubt you, like everybody else, have experienced the noble pleasure which certain scents can produce. It would be very much more interesting if you tried to indicate what the smells were. See how flabby and vague your phrases are. You say — *there one could breathe in heady odours from lilac and from heliotrope, rich with a wealth of obscure suggestions.* In the first place, leave *suggestions* alone, if all you can tell us about them is that they are *obscure.* If you can't throw any light upon them, you'd better say nothing at all. And don't mix up the scent of the lilac with the scent of the heliotrope. You must know that one catches the fresh smell of the lilac only after rain, whereas the heliotrope does not give the fullness of its scent — which is very subtle — except when the sun is on it. . ." [27]

It is unfortunate that Proust did not decide to retain this passage in *A la recherche*, because it would have fitted so well into the pattern of Marcel's "invisible vocation." It also illustrates how Proust began with Symbolism and left it behind in order to achieve a new kind of "classical" precision.

But the beauty of the great authors does not depend alone on their ability to renew the language. Language and style depend on something more comprehensive — on what Proust calls "vision." As early as 1904, at the beginning of his liberation from Ruskin, he had defined the absolute beauty of certain things as "a kind of blending, a kind of transparent unity." [28] This passage already contains the nucleus of Proust's mature formulation of literary style, more fully outlined in an interview with E.-J. Bois of the *Temps*, on the eve of the publication of *Du côté de chez Swann*:

> Style is in no way an embellishment, as certain persons seem to think; it is not even a matter of technique; it is — analogous to the way painters use color — a quality of vision, the revelation of a special universe which each one of us sees, which the others do not see. The pleasure which an artist offers us is to acquaint us with one more universe.[29]

In his last period Proust saw the writer's problem as one of overcoming the contingencies of objects by establishing the necessary relationships between them. In *Le Temps retrouvé* the idea is elaborated as follows:

An hour is not merely an hour. It is a vase filled with perfumes, sounds, plans and climates. What we call reality is a certain relationship between these sensations and the memories which surround us at the same time (a relationship that is destroyed by a bare cinematographic presentation, which gets further away from the truth the more closely it claims to adhere to it) the only true relationship, which the writer must recapture so that he may forever link together in his phrase its two distinct elements. One may list in an interminable description the objects that figured in the place described, but truth will begin only when the writer takes two different objects, establishes their relationship — analogous in the world of art to the sole relationship in the world of science, the law of cause and effect — and encloses them in the necessary rings of a beautiful style, or even when, like life itself, comparing similar qualities in two sensations, he makes their essential nature stand out clearly by joining them in a metaphor, in order to remove them from the contingencies of time.[30]

The whole language of these pronouncements on the secret beauty of literary style is conceived in terms of the art of the genre painter: the emphasis on objects, their relationships, the importance of light, the over-all harmony. One thinks of Chardin, of Vermeer, of Rembrandt here, and of Proust's recurrent allusions to their art; and, following Proust's analyses, we recognize the *phrases-types* as symbols of the "unité transparente" and their applicability in painting as well as in music and literature. The metaphor is the device which gives permanence to objects and frees them from the temporal and spatial contingency. When Proust defines style in the essay contained in *Le Temps retrouvé*, he once more speaks of the painter's art and the writer's art simultaneously:

. . . For style is for the writer, as for the painter, a question, not of technique but of vision. It is the revelation — impossible by direct and conscious means — of the qualitative differences in the way the world appears to us, differences which, but for art, would remain the eternal secret of each of us. Only by art can we get outside ourselves, know what another sees of his universe, which is not the same as ours and the different views of which would otherwise have remained as unknown to us as those there may be on the moon. Thanks to art, instead of seeing only one world, our own, we see it under multiple forms, and as many as there are original artists, just so many worlds have we at our disposal, differing more widely from one another than those that roll through infinite space, and years after the glowing center from which they emanated has been extinguished, be it called Rembrandt or Vermeer, they continue to send us their own rays of light.[31]

"We have as many worlds at our disposal as there are original artists." The artist is a world-builder: like Elstir, he refashions the Creation by giving its components new names — that is to say, metaphors [32] — and the reader's purpose is to discern the qualitative differences among these worlds; the critic's function is to help him achieve this purpose. The critic's first task is to see — "to see distinctly where other people see only indistinctly." [33] This recalls the definition of the critic's primary function given in the preface to *La Bible d'Amiens* — to aid the reader in discerning the artist's unique characteristics. But, it will be remembered, Proust felt that the critic could go beyond this simple function of guide and become a sharer, so to speak, of the artist's vision, "to reconstruct the peculiar life of the spirit which belongs to every writer who is obsessed by his own special view of reality." [34] All Proust's mature ideas on art, as summarized in *Le Temps retrouvé*, are already implied there: literature growing out of a writer's contact with reality; the writer as a visionary; and the necessity which forces the writer to create (". . . we are not at all free in the presence of the work of art to be created" [35]).

To what extent did Proust himself fulfill this twofold function of the critic? In many cases, he contents himself with merely acting as a guide. This is especially true of the pastiches, in which his primary purpose was to fix the *traits singuliers* of certain literary styles. And yet even here Proust often probes more deeply; when he makes Renan use a word which, to his knowledge, does *not* appear in Renan's writings but which seems to him "extrêmement Renan," is he not probing into

Renan's inner nature, into the "special view of reality" which, according to Proust's analysis, obsessed Renan? In a similar manner, the Flaubert pastiche attempts to recapture Flaubert's particular intelligence, not only his style; and the Saint-Simon pastiche recreates not only the Duke's excited violence but also his "Dostoevskian" aspect. In other words, Proust tends to move closer and closer to the second, the higher, function of the critic; his sensibility is not satisfied with a description of the characteristics of a writer, but strives to penetrate into the writer's inner organization.

The critic's function of guide to a certain author is analogous to the writer's apprenticeship to that author. The critic explains the author's style, whereas the writer adopts it, draws from it what he can assimilate, then purges himself of the style. Like Stevenson, Proust delighted in playing the sedulous ape to authors of the past:

> . . . the best advice I can give to my fellow-writers is that they would be well-advised to indulge in the cleansing, exorcising, pastime of parody, when we come to the end of a book, we find that not only do we want to go on living with its characters, with Madame de Beauséant, with Frédéric Moreau, etc., but that our inner voice, which has grown accustomed, through the long hours of perusal, to follow the Balzacian or Flaubertian rhythm, insists on talking just like those authors. The one means of escape from the toils lies in letting the influence have its way for a while, in keeping one's foot on the pedal and permitting the resonance to continue: in other words, in embarking upon a deliberate act of parody, with the object, once we have got the stuff out of our system, of becoming ourselves again, instead of spending the rest of our working lives producing *unconscious* parodies. But deliberate parody must be spontaneous. When I set about producing my own, rather detestable, parody of Flaubert, I did not stop to ask myself whether the "tune" ringing in my ears owed its peculiar quality to a recurrent series of imperfects or of present participles. If I had bothered about that, I should never have got the thing on paper at all.[36]

This observation has a curious similarity to Malraux' analysis of the importance of the pastiche in his *Psychologie de l'art.*

For Malraux, "every artist's career begins with the pastiche"; it is the artist's first attempt at a participation in the world of art. ". . . The pastiche is a gesture of fraternity."[37] Proust, to be sure, emphasizes the cleansing effect of the pastiche, which permits him to get the persistent throb of an author's rhythm out of his system; but in a certain sense, the pastiche, for Proust too, is a kind of initiation rite which must be accomplished before artistic maturity and mastery are possible.

From the pastiche to the analysis there is only a small step; what the pastiche writer often does unconsciously he may also do consciously afterwards in the form of a critical essay, at which point he approaches the critic *voyant*.

> The human mind can never be satisfied unless it can manage to achieve a clear analysis of what, at the moment of composition, it produced unconsciously, or can re-create in vital terms what, till then, it has been merely analyzing.[38]

In the writer — that is to say, in Proust himself — reading leads to analysis, which in turn leads to re-creation. The critic, as has been observed, acts as the artist's lesser double. His scope of effectiveness lies rather in the realm of the intelligence, whereas Proust relied by preference on intuition and sensibility. Nevertheless, the image of the highest type of critic which he offers us is also attuned to the intuitive basis of artistic creation.

Proust is most interesting and most successful as a literary critic when he goes beyond the basic function of the critic. As has been shown, he is never altogether content to be a mere guide. In the preface to *La Bible d'Amiens* he begins by saying that he is trying only to satisfy this basic function of the critic. Nevertheless, toward the end of the essay on Ruskin, he begins to ask himself how the insincerity in Ruskin's writings can be accounted for; this question gives rise to the "Post-Scriptum," in which he tries to penetrate into the problem of "reconstituting Ruskin's spiritual life." Proust knew — and this perception is also his answer to Sainte-Beuve — that through the work of art he could glimpse the inner structure of the artist:

. . . In fact, is not a work of art something like a sphygmogram, which records our pulse automatically, of our soul's inner rhythm, and all the more vital for the fact that we do not perceive it ourselves?[39]

This very conviction enables Proust to venture on dangerous territory — as the critic whom Proust has in mind always must — to show us the particular vision which a great artist offers the reader. The procedure is used with remarkable skill in the Flaubert and Baudelaire essays and in "Sainte-Beuve et Balzac"; it is essentially the same as the *phrases-types* analysis of Barbey d'Aurevilly, Stendhal, Hardy, and Dostoevski; in other words, it is Proust's method *par excellence* for arriving at the essence of an artist's contact with reality and the metaphors which his vision dictates to him. If Proust seems sometimes too daring or too sweeping with his *phrases-types*, it should be kept in mind that his critical method is always inextricably bound up with his artistic intuition. In this respect, too, his literary criticism moves along the same path as his literary art. Fallois is entirely correct in saying of Proust's method of criticism that it "destroys the customary boundary lines between art and criticism."[40]

It has been shown in the preceding pages that Proust had a way of "using" literary criticism to deepen a character. Here literary criticism plays a role subordinate to character portrayal — Proust knew that the intellectual side of an individual revealed many traits not directly revealed in his actions. Thus, when Bloch's or Charlus' or Madame de Villeparisis' literary opinions are presented in some detail, Proust is not criticizing the writer in question but revealing the personality of the critic. To be sure, such opinions may on occasion coincide with Marcel's (and Proust's) own, but the emphasis is always on the character in the novel. Marcel himself occupies a somewhat complex position in the novel; as an intermediary between Proust and his material, he represents Proust the child infatuated with George Sand as well as the early, groping Proust, then the maturing critic, then the writer of an article for *Le Figaro*, then the matured literary critic, and finally the artist who is going to write the novel that Proust has just finished. Thus, Marcel represents the transitory as well as the permanent literary opinions of Proust; only in the latter portions of *A la recherche* does the dividing line between Marcel's and Proust's literary opinions become tenuous. The area in which it occurs may be said to be the revelation of the Vinteuil Septet and the *phrases-types* passage, both in *La Prisonnière*. And in the opening pages of volume II of *Le Temps retrouvé* the congruence is all but complete.

The importance of Proust's personal interests in his choice of topics for critical commentary has already been pointed out. Similarly, the somewhat disorderly arrangement of the critical essays can be accounted for by the corollary that Proust let his memory, his associations, and his interests guide him in the arrangement of his material. The subjective, Proustian element of these essays is forever betraying itself; and the essays themselves often read like Proustian sentences, magnified several times, with their interlocking and parenthetical components. For behind Proust the critic stands, like a guardian angel, Proust the artist, dictating to the critic what is important, what is interesting, and what is relevant to the artist. Or, to put it somewhat differently, Proust is both pilgrim and guide in the ascent of his own mountain of Purgatory; and after the arduous discipline, the guide can finally abdicate his office, leaving the pilgrim purified, self-reliant, and able to work out his own salvation. The salvation, to be sure, was a literary one. Yet there are few writers in the world's history to whom literature has meant so much and whose devotion to art has been so religious. Few books have been so uniquely impregnated with literature, so dependent on the literary consciousness for their inner rhythm. And so it is right, after all, to call *A la recherche du temps perdu* a cathedral: not only because of its structure and its impressiveness but also because its very center is occupied by a most splendid altar dedicated to the glorification of literature.

BIBLIOGRAPHY

A. *Works by Proust*

A la recherche du temps perdu, Texte en partie inédit établi sur les manuscrits autographes variantes . . . par Pierre Clarac et André Ferré, Paris, Bibliothèque de la Pléiade, 1954. 3 vols. 1. *Du côté de chez Swann — A l'ombre des jeunes filles en fleurs*; 2. *Le Côté de Guermantes — Sodome et Gomorrhe*; 3. *La Prisonnière — La Fugitive — Le Temps retrouvé*). This is the definitive edition of Proust's novel, superseding all earlier editions of the work. It should be noted that the new title of the sixth volume is no longer *Albertine disparue* but *La Fugitive*. A full explanation of the establishment of the text is found in volume I, pp. xxi–xxxv.

English translation used: *Remembrance of Things Past*, tr. C. K. Scott-Moncrieff and Frederick A. Blossom (New York, Random House, 1932). 2 vols.

"Etudes" (ii. Avant la nuit; iii, Souvenir), *La Revue blanche* 26:381–388 (December, 1893).

Les Plaisirs et les jours (Paris, Gallimard, 1924).

English translation: *Pleasures and Regrets*, tr. Louise Varèse (New York, Crown Publishers, 1948).

"Un Professeur de Beauté," *Les Arts de la vie* 4:67–79 (July–December, 1905). Reprinted in L. Guichard, "Un Article inconnu . . . ," pp. 163–172 (see below).

"John Ruskin. *Les Pierres de Venise*," *Chronique des arts et de la curiosité*, May 5, 1906, pp. 146–147.

Pastiches et mélanges (Paris, Gallimard, 1919). Several of the "Mélanges" have been translated into English in *Marcel Proust: A Selection from his Miscellaneous Writings*, chosen and translated by Gerard Hopkins (London, Allan Wingate, 1948).

Chroniques (Paris, Gallimard, 1927). Excerpts have been translated by Gerard Hopkins in *Marcel Proust: A Selection from his Miscellaneous Writings.*

"Un des premiers états de Swann," *La Table Ronde*, April, 1945, pp. 3–31.

Le Balzac de Monsieur de Guermantes (Neuchâtel, Ides et Calendes, 1950).

"Quelques pensées inédites de Marcel Proust," *Le Figaro littéraire* 5:1 (November 18, 1950).

Jean Santeuil (Paris, Gallimard, 1951), 3 vols. This has been translated, under the same title, by Gerard Hopkins (New York, Simon and Schuster, 1956).

"Le Bénédiction du sanglier," *La Nouvelle Nouvelle Revue française* 1:763–767 (October, 1953).

Contre Sainte-Beuve, suivi de Nouveaux Mélanges (Paris, Gallimard, 1954). This includes all of *Le Balzac de Monsieur de Guermantes.*

Prefaces

Blanche, Jacques-Emile, *Propos de peintre* (Paris, Emile-Paul, 1919), volume I: *De David à Degas.*

Morand, Paul, *Tendres Stocks* (Paris Nouvelle Revue Française, 1923).

Both of these prefaces have been translated by Gerard Hopkins in *Marcel Proust: A Selection from His Miscellaneous Writings.* The preface to *Tendres Stocks* also exists in a translation by C. K. Scott-Moncrieff; see Paul Morand, *Green Shoots,* tr. H. I. Woolf (New York, Thomas Seltzer, 1924), pp. 15–42.

Translations

Ruskin, John, *La Bible d'Amiens* (Paris, Mercure de France, 1926).

———— *Sésame et les lys* (Paris, Mercure de France, n.d.).

Contributions to symposia

"Etes-vous partisan ou non des cabinets de lecture? . . . ," *L'Intransigeant* 41:2 (August 28, 1920).

"Enquête sur le romantisme et le classicisme," *La Renaissance politique, littéraire, artistique* 9:13–14 (January 8, 1921). (An English translation of Proust's reply can be found in *Letters of Marcel Proust,* pp. 360–361, see below.)

"Les Goncourt devant leurs cadets," *Le Gaulois* 57:4 (May 27, 1922).

"Sommes-nous en présence d'un renouvellement du style? . . . ," *La Renaissance politique, littéraire, artistique* 9:6–7 (July 22, 1922).

"Et si le monde allait finir . . . que feriez-vous?" *L'Intransigeant* 43:2 (August 14, 1922).

Correspondence

Correspondance avec sa mère 1887–1905 (Paris, Plon, 1953).

Correspondance générale (Paris, Plon, 1930–36). 6 vols.

Lettres à André Gide (Paris, Ides et Calendes, 1949).

Lettres à la NRF (Paris, Gallimard, 1932). (Volume VI of the *Cahiers Marcel Proust.*)

Lettres à Mme C[atusse] (Paris, J. B. Janin, 1946).

Lettres à une amie (Manchester, Editions du Calame, 1942).
Quelques échanges et témoignages (*avec René Boylesve*) (Paris, Le Divan, 1931).
"Lettres à Paul Morand 1916–1917," *La Table Ronde*, November, 1949, pp. 1651–1662.
"Letters to Natalie Clifford Barney," *The Dublin Magazine* 6:5–13 (January–March, 1931).
English translation of a selection from the foregoing (and from other collections, see below): *Letters of Marcel Proust*, tr. Mina Curtiss. Introduction by Harry Levin (New York, Random House, 1949).

B. *Works dealing with Proust*

(All titles marked * contain unpublished material by Proust.)

*Abatangel, Louis, *Marcel Proust et la musique* (Paris, Imprimerie des Orphelins Apprentis d'Auteuil, 1939).
Abraham, Pierre, *Proust: Recherches sur la création intellectuelle* (Paris, Rieder, 1930).
Alden, Douglas W., *Marcel Proust and his French Critics* (Los Angeles, Lymanhouse, 1940).
———— "Proust and the Flaubert Controversy," *Romanic Review* 28:230–240 (1937).
Ames, Van Meter, *Proust and Santayana: The Aesthetic Way of Life* (Chicago and New York, Willet, Clark and Company, 1937).
Auerbach, Erich, "Marcel Proust: der Roman von der verlorenen Zeit," *Die neueren Sprachen* 35:16–22 (1927).
———— *Mimesis: dargestellte Wirklichkeit in der abendländischen Literatur* (Bern, A. Francke, 1946).
*Barrès, Maurice, *Mes cahiers* (Paris, Plon, 1935), vol. IX (1911–12).
Beckett, Samuel, *Proust* (London, Chatto & Windus, 1931).
Bédé, Jean-Albert, "Chateaubriand et Marcel Proust," *Modern Language Notes* 49:353–360 (1934).
Béguin, Albert, *L'Ame romantique et le rêve* (Paris, José Corti, 1946).
Bell, Clive, *Proust* (New York, Harcourt, Brace and Company, 1929).
Bénoist-Méchin, J., *La Musique et l'immortalité dans l'oeuvre de Marcel Proust* (Paris, Kra, 1926).
*Bibesco, Princess, *Au Bal avec Marcel Proust* (Paris, Gallimard, 1928). (Volume IV of the *Cahiers Marcel Proust.*)
*———— *Le Voyageur voilé* (Geneva, La Palatine, 1947). English translation: *The Veiled Wanderer*, tr. Roland Gant (London, Falcon Press, 1949).

*Billy, Robert de, *Marcel Proust: Lettres et conversations* (Paris, Edition des Portiques, 1930).

*Bisson, L. A., "Deux inédits de Marcel Proust," *French Studies* 2:341–347 (1948).

——————"Marcel Proust in 1947," *French Studies* 1:191–217 (1947).

—————— "Proust and Hardy: Incidence or Coincidence," *Studies in French Lauguage and History Presented to R. L. Graeme Ritchie* (Cambridge, Cambridge University Press, 1949), pp. 24–34.

—————— "Proust and Ruskin: Reconsidered in the Light of *Lettres à une amie*," Modern Language Review, 39:28–37 (1944).

—————— "Proust, Bergson and George Eliot," *Modern Language Review* 40:104–114 (1945).

Blackert, Hermann, *Der Aufbau der Kunstwirklichkeit bei Marcel Proust, angezeigt an der Einführung der Personen in "A la Recherche du temps perdu"* (Berlin, Junker & Dünnhaupt, 1935).

Blanche, Jacques-Emile, *Mes modèles* (Paris, Stock, 1928).

Blanchot, Maurice, *Faux pas* (Paris, Gallimard, 1943).

Blondel, C. A. A., *La Psychographie de Marcel Proust* (Paris, Vrin, 1932).

Brée, Germaine, *Du Temps perdu au temps retrouvé* (Paris, Société d'Edition "Les Belles Lettres," 1950).

—————— "Marcel Proust et Maurice Barrès," *Romanic Review* 40:93–105 (April, 1949).

—————— "New Trends in Proust Criticism," *Symposium* 5:62–71 (May, 1951).

—————— "Une Etude du style de Proust dans *Les Plaisirs et les jours*," *French Review* 15:401–409 (1942).

Bret, Jacques, *Marcel Proust: Etude critique* (Geneva, Les Editions du Mont-Blanc, 1946).

**Bulletin de la Société des Amis de Marcel Proust et des Amis de Combray*, no. 2 (1951–52), Illiers, 1952.

Bulletin Marcel Proust: I. Défense de Marcel Proust (Paris, Le Rouge et le Noir, 1930).

Cabeen, D. C., "Saint-Simon and Proust," *Publications of the Modern Language Association* 46:608–618 (1931).

*Cattaui, Georges, *L'Amitié de Proust* (Paris, Gallimard, 1935). (Volume VIII of the *Cahiers Marcel Proust.*)

——————*Marcel Proust* (Paris, Julliard, 1952).

——————"Proust and English Letters," *London Mercury* 26:426–432 (1932).

Celly, Raoul, *Répertoire des thèmes de Marcel Proust* (Paris, Gallimard, 1935). (Volume VII of the *Cahiers Marcel Proust.*)

Chernowitz, Maurice E., *Proust and Painting* (New York, International University Press, 1945).

*Clermont-Tonnerre, Elisabeth de, *Robert de Montesquiou et Marcel Proust* (Paris, Flammarion, 1925).

Coleman, Elliott, *The Golden Angel: Papers on Proust* (New York, Coley Taylor, Inc., 1954).

*Crémieux, Benjamin, *Du Côté de Marcel Proust* (Paris, Lemarget, 1929).

——— *Vingtième Siècle*, 1ère série (Paris, Gallimard, 1924).

Curtius, Ernst-Robert, *Französischer Geist im neuen Europa* (Stuttgart, Deutsche Verlags-Anstalt, 1925). French translation of the Proust essay by Armand Pierhal (Paris, Editions de la Revue Nouvelle, 1928).

Dandieu, Arnaud, *Marcel Proust, sa révélation psychologique* (Paris, Firmin-Didot, 1930).

Daudet, Charles, *Répertoire des personnages de "A la Recherche du temps perdu"* (Paris, Gallimard, 1928). (Volume II of the *Cahiers Marcel Proust*.)

Daudet, Léon, *Salons et journaux* (Paris, Grasset, 1932).

*Daudet, Lucien, *Autour de soixante lettres de Marcel Proust*. (Paris, Gallimard, 1929). (Volume V of the *Cahiers Marcel Proust*.)

*Dreyfus, Robert, *Marcel Proust à dix-sept ans* (Paris, Kra, 1926).

*——— *Souvenirs sur Marcel Proust* (Paris, Grasset, 1926).

Du Bos, Charles, *Approximations I* (Paris, Plon, 1922), pp. 58–116.

Etiemble, René, "Le Style de Marcel Proust," *Les Temps Modernes* 2:1489–1496 (1947).

Fernandez, Ramon, *Messages*, Ière série (Paris, Editions de la Nouvelle Revue Française, 1926).

——— "Notes sur l'esthétique de Proust," *Nouvelle Revue Française* 31:272–280 (1928).

Ferré, André, *La Géographie de Marcel Proust* (Paris, Editions du Sagittaire, 1939).

——— "Marcel Proust critique pédagogique," *Revue pédagogique* 95:333–355 (1929).

Feuillerat, Albert, *Comment Marcel Proust a composé son roman* (New Haven, Yale University Press, 1934).

Fiser, Eméric, *L'Esthétique de Marcel Proust* (Paris, Rieder, 1933).

——— *La Théorie du symbole littéraire et Marcel Proust* (Paris, Librairie José Corti, 1941).

Fowlie, Wallace, *Clowns and Angels* (New York, Sheed & Ward, 1943).

Gabory, Georges, *Essai sur Marcel Proust* (Paris, Le Livre, 1926).

Galand, René, "Proust et Baudelaire," *Publications of the Modern Language Association* 65:1011–1035 (December, 1950).

Garver, Milton, "A Bibliographical Note on Marcel Proust," *Modern Language Notes* 47:176–179 (1932).

*——— "An Unpublished Letter of Marcel Proust," *Modern Language Notes* 47:319–321 (1932).

Gide, André, *Incidences* (Paris, Gallimard, 1924).

Green, F. C., *The Mind of Proust* (Cambridge, Cambridge University Press, 1949).

*Gregh, Fernand, *L'Age d'airain* (Paris, Grasset, 1951).

——— "Sur le pastiche," *Candide* 1:3 (June 26, 1924).

*Guichard, Léon, "Un Article inconnu de Proust: Marcel Proust et Robert de Montesquiou," *Revue d'histoire littéraire de la France* 49:161–175 (April–June, 1949).

Hier, Florence, *La Musique dans l'oeuvre de Marcel Proust* (New York, Columbia University Press, 1933).

Hindus, Milton, *The Proustian Vision* (New York, Columbia University Press, 1954).

**Hommage à Marcel Proust* (Paris, Gallimard, 1927). (Volume I of the *Cahiers Marcel Proust.*)

Hommage à Marcel Proust, special number of *Le Rouge et le Noir,* April, 1928.

**Hommage à Marcel Proust,* special number of *Le Disque vert,* Paris-Brussels, December, 1952.

*Jaloux, Edmond, *Avec Marcel Proust* (Paris and Geneva, La Palatine, 1953).

**Jean Cocteau,* special number of *Empreintes,* May–July, 1950.

Johannet, René, "Les Prédécesseurs de Proust," *Revue universelle* 22:487–491 (1925).

Johnson, C. W. M., "Tone in *A la recherche du temps perdu,*" *Forms of Modern Fiction,* ed. William Van O'Connor (Minneapolis, University of Minnesota Press, 1948), pp. 201–210.

*Jones, Stanley, "Two Unknown Articles by Marcel Proust, "*French Studies* 4:239–251 (1950).

Kinds, Edmond, *Marcel Proust* (Paris, Collection Triptyque, 1947).

Kolb, Philip, "A Lost Article by Proust," *Modern Language Notes* 53:107–109 (1938).

*——— "An Unknown Critical Item by Proust," *French Review* 24:105–110 (December, 1950).

——— *La Correspondance de Marcel Proust*: chronologie et *commentaire critique* (Urbana, The University of Illinois Press, 1949).

Krutch, Joseph Wood, *Five Masters* (London, Jonathan Cape, 1931).

*Lang, André, *Voyage en zigzags dans la Republique des Lettres* (Paris, La Renaissance du Livre, 1922).

*Lauris, Georges de, *A un Ami: correspondance inédite de Marcel Proust 1903–22* (Paris, Amiot-Dumont, 1948). English translation: *Letters to a Friend*, tr. Alexander and Elizabeth Henderson (London, Falcon Press, 1949).

Lavrin, Janko, "Dostoievsky and Proust," *Slavonic Review* 5:609–627 (1927).

Le Sage, Laurence, "Marcel Proust's Appreciation of the Poetry of Alfred de Musset," *French Review* 21:361–366 (March, 1948).

*Levin, Harry, "An Unpublished Dialogue by Marcel Proust," *Harvard Library Bulletin* 3:257–267 (Spring, 1949).

——— "Balzac et Proust," *Hommage à Balzac* (UNESCO) (Paris, Mercure de France, 1950), pp. 281–308.

Lindner, Gladys Dudley, *Marcel Proust: Reviews and Estimates in English* (Stanford University Press, 1942).

Luppé, R. de, "Proust et Schopenhauer," *Revue d'esthétique* 2:395–415 (1949).

Madaule, Jacques, *Reconnaissances*, I (Paris, Desclée, de Brouwer & Co., 1943).

Magny, Claude-Edmonde, *Histoire du roman français depuis 1918*, I (Paris, Editions du Seuil, 1950).

"Marcel Proust," special page in *Les Nouvelles littéraires*, July 25, 1936, p. 3.

Marcel Proust, Cahiers de la Quinzaine, XXe série, no. 5 (March 5, 1930).

March, Harold, *The Two Worlds of Marcel Proust* (Philadelphia, University of Pennsylvania Press, 1948).

———"The Artist as Seer: Notes on the Esthetic Vision," *Yale French Studies* 2:44–54.

Martin-Chauffier, Louis, "Proust and the Double I," *Partisan Review*, October, 1949, pp. 1011–1026.

Massis, Henri, *Le Drame de Marcel Proust* (Paris, Grasset, 1937).

Mauriac, Claude (ed.), *Marcel Proust par lui-même* (Paris, Aux Editions du Seuil, 1953).

Mauriac, François, *Du côté de chez Proust* (Paris, *La Table Ronde*, 1947). English translation: *Proust's Way*, tr. Elsie Pell (New York, Philosophical Library, 1949).

*Maurois, André, *A la recherche de Marcel Proust* (Paris, Hachette, 1949).
English translation: *Proust, Portrait of a Genius*, tr. Gerard Hopkins (New York, Harper & Brothers, 1950).

——— "Proust et Ruskin," *Essays and Studies by Members of the English Association* (Oxford, Clarendon Press, 1932), pp. 25–32.

Messières, René de, "Un Document probable sur le premier état de la pensée de Proust: Mystères, par Fernand Gregh," *Romanic Review*, April, 1942, pp. 113–131.

Meyerhoff, Hans, *Time in Literature* (Berkeley, University of California Press, 1955).

Milon, F.-J., *Proust, Valéry et le plaisir de la lecture* (Paris, Editions Fustier, n.d.).

Monnin-Hornung, Juliette, *Proust et la peinture* (Geneva, Librairie E. Droz, 1951).

Mouton, Jean, *Le Style de Marcel Proust* (Paris, Editions Corrêa, 1948).

Muller, Maurice, *De Descartes à Marcel Proust* (Neuchâtel, Editions de la Baconnière, 1947).

Murray, J., "Marcel Proust as a Critic and Disciple of Ruskin," *Nineteenth Century* 101:614–620 (1927).

———— "Marcel Proust et John Ruskin," *Mercure de France* 189:100–112 (1926).

Nicolson, Harold, "Marcel Proust et l'Angleterre," *Revue hebdomadaire* 45:7–21 (June 6, 1936).

O'Brien, Justin, "Albertine the Ambiguous: Notes on Proust's Transposition of Sexes," *Publications of the Modern Language Association* 44:933–952 (December, 1949). For a rejoinder and rebuttal, see also Harry Levin and Justin O'Brien, "Proust, Gide, and the Sexes," *Publications of the Modern Language Association* 45:648–653 (June, 1950).

———— (ed. and tr.), *The Maxims of Marcel Proust* (New York, Columbia University Press, 1948).

———— "La Mémoire involontaire avant Marcel Proust," *Revue de littérature comparée* 19:19–36 (January, 1939).

Peyre, Henri, *Hommes et oeuvres du XXe siècle* (Paris, Corrêa, 1938).

———— *The Contemporary French Novel* (New York, Oxford University Press, 1955).

*Pierre-Quint, Léon, *Comment parut "Du Côté de chez Swann"* (Paris, Kra, 1930).

*———— *Comment travaillait Marcel Proust* (Paris, Aux Editions des Cahiers libres, 1928).

———— *Marcel Proust, sa vie, son oeuvre* (Paris, Editions du Sagittaire, 1946).

Pommier, Jean, *La Mystique de Proust* (Paris, Droz, 1939).

*Porel, Jacques, *Fils de Réjane* (Paris, Plon, 1951–52). 2 vols.

Poulet, Georges, *Etudes sur le temps humain* (Edinburgh, Edinburgh University Press, 1949).

*Pouquet, Jeanne Maurice, *Le Salon de Madame de Caillavet* (Paris, Hachette, 1926).

Rambaud, Henri, "Le Premier Livre de Marcel Proust," *Revue universelle* 19:232–237 (October 15, 1924).

Raphael, Pierre, *Introduction à la correspondance de Marcel Proust. Répertoire de la correspondance de Proust* (Paris, Editions du Sagittaire, 1938).

Rivière, Jacques, *Nouvelles Etudes* (Paris, Gallimard, 1947).

———— "Marcel Proust et la tradition classique," *Nouvelle Revue française* 7:192–200 (February 1, 1920).

*Robert, Louis de, *Comment Débuta Marcel Proust* (Paris, Editions de la Nouvelle Revue Française, 1925).

*————De Loti à Proust (Paris, Flammarion, 1928).

Roche, A. J., "Proust as a Translator of Ruskin," *Publications of the Modern Language Association* 45:1214–1218 (1930).

Rossat-Mignod, Suzanne, "Proust et Sainte-Beuve," *Revue de l'Université de Lyon*, October, 1932, pp. 384–392.

Salvan, Albert J., "La Littérature dans l'oeuvre de Proust," *Courrier des Etats-Unis*, February 27, 1937.

Scott-Moncrieff, Charles Kenneth, *Marcel Proust: An English Tribute* (New York, T. Seltzer, 1923).

Seillère, Ernest, *Marcel Proust* (Paris, Editions de la Nouvelle Revue Critique, 1931).

Souday, Paul, *Marcel Proust* (Paris, Kra, 1927).

Soulairol, Jean "Marcel Proust et Madame de Sévigné," *Revue hebdomadaire* 35:385–389 (February 20, 1926).

Souza, Sybil de, *L'Influence de Ruskin sur Proust* (Montpellier, Imprimerie de la Manufacture de la Charité, 1932).

Spalding, P. A., *A Reader's Handbook to Proust* (London, Chatto & Windus, 1952).

Spitzer, Leo, *Stilstudien*, II (Munich, M. Hueber, 1928).

*Strauss, Walter A., "Twelve Unpublished Letters of Marcel Proust," *Harvard Library Bulletin* 7:145–171 (Spring, 1953).

Tauman, Leon, *Marcel Proust* (Paris, Collin, 1950).

Thibaudet, Albert, *Réflexions sur la critique* (Paris, Gallimard, 1939).

Tiedtke, Irma, *Symbole und Bilder im Werke Marcel Prousts* (Hamburg, Evert, 1936).

Turnell, Martin, *The Novel in France* (London, Hamish Hamilton, 1950).

Vigneron, Robert, "Genèse de Swann," *Revue d'histoire de la philosophie*, January 15, 1937, pp. 67–115. A condensed and undocumented translation of this article appeared in the *Partisan Review* 8:460–475 (November–December, 1941).

Vigneron, Robert, "Marcel Proust et Robert de Montesquiou," *Modern Philology* 30:159–195 (November, 1941).

———"Marcel Proust ou l'angoisse créatrice," *Modern Philology* 42:212–230 (May, 1945).

Wegener, Alfons, *Impressionismus und Klassizismus im Werke Marcel Prousts* (Frankfurt, Carolus Druckerei, 1930).

Wilson, Edmund, *Axel's Castle* (New York, Scribner, 1931).

——— "Proust and Yeats," *New Republic* 52:176–177a (October 5, 1927).

Zaeske, Käthe, *Der Stil Marcel Prousts* (Emsdetten, Verlags-Anstalt Lechte, 1937).

NOTES

The practice adhered to in the Notes is as follows: In the case of works by Proust or about Proust, bibliographical references have been given to the French texts as well as to the published English translations. In cases where translations of Proust do not exist, I have provided them myself. The translations from other authors are my own (unless otherwise specified).

For the accurate dating of letters I am indebted to Professor Kolb's indispensable *La Correspondance de Marcel Proust* (Urbana, The University of Illinois Press, 1949).

I. INTRODUCTION

1. L. A. Bisson, "Marcel Proust in 1947," *French Studies* 1:203 (1947).
2. Jacques Porel, *Fils de Réjane* (Paris, Plon, 1951), I, 328.
3. *Ibid.*, p. 321.
4. *A la recherche du temps perdu* (Paris, Bibliothèque de la Pléiade, 1954), I, ix.
5. *Remembrance of Things Past* (New York, Random House, 1932), II, 1024; *A la recherche*, III, 911.
6. Jacques-Emile Blanche, *Mes modèles* (Paris, Librairie Stock, 1928), p. 139.
7. Robert Vigneron, "Genèse de Swann," *Revue d'histoire de la philosophie et d'histoire générale de la civilisation*, 15 January 1937, pp. 67–115.
8. See Albert Feuillerat, *Comment Marcel Proust a composé son roman* (New Haven, Yale University Press, 1934).
9. Georges de Lauris, *A un ami* (Paris, Amiot-Dumont, 1948), p. 158; *Letters to a Friend*, tr. Alexander and Elizabeth Henderson (London, Falcon Press, 1949), p. 117. See also *Letters of Marcel Proust*, tr. Mina Curtiss (New York, Random House, 1949), p. 191, and *Correspondance générale* (Paris, Plon, 1930–1936), II, 45.
10. *Letters to a Friend*, pp. 135, 158; Lauris, *A un ami*, pp. 181, 217.
11. Jacques-Emile Blanche, *Propos de peintre: de David à Degas* (Paris, Emile-Paul, 1919). Both of the prefaces are included in *Marcel Proust: A Selection from his Miscellaneous Writings*, chosen and translated by Gerard Hopkins (London, Allen Wingate, 1948).
12. *Letters to a Friend*, p. 19; Lauris, *A un ami*, p. 22.

13. *M.P.: A Selection*, p. 107; *Pastiches et mélanges* (Paris, Gallimard, 1919), pp. 225–226.

14. *M.P.: A Selection*, p. 121; *Pastiches et mélanges*, p. 243.

15. John Ruskin, *Sesame and Lilies* (London, Cassell Co., 1909), p. 16.

16. John Ruskin, *Sésame et les lys*, tr. Marcel Proust (Paris, Mercure de France, n.d.), p. 71n.

17. *M.P.: A Selection*, p. 120; *Pastiches et mélanges*, p. 242.

18. *Sésame et les lys*, p. 70n.

19. *Ibid.*, pp. 70n.–71n.

20. *M.P.: A Selection*, p. 123; *Pastiches et mélanges*, p. 245.

21. *Jean Santeuil*, tr. Gerard Hopkins (New York, Simon and Schuster, 1956), pp. 229, 230; *Jean Santeuil* (Paris, Gallimard, 1951), I, 330.

22. *M.P.: A Selection*, pp. 123–124; *Pastiches et mélanges*, pp. 245–246.

23. *Jean Santeuil*, pp. 114–115; *Jean Santeuil*, I, 178.

24. *Jean Santeuil*, p. 115; *Jean Santeuil*, I, 178–179.

25. *M.P.: A Selection*, p. 125; *Pastiches et mélanges*, p. 248.

26. *Ibid.*

27. *Sésame et les lys*, p. 75n.

28. *M.P.: A Selection*, pp. 136–137; *Pastiches et mélanges*, p. 262.

29. *M.P.: A Selection*, p. 137; *Pastiches et mélanges*, p. 263.

30. *M.P.: A Selection*, p. 126; *Pastiches et mélanges*, p. 249.

31. *M.P.: A Selection*, p. 126; *Pastiches et mélanges*, pp. 249-250.

32. *M.P.: A Selection*, pp. 126–127; *Pastiches et mélanges*, p. 250.

33. *M.P.: A Selection*, pp. 127–128; *Pastiches et mélanges*, pp. 251–252.

34. *M.P.: A Selection*, p. 129; *Pastiches et mélanges*, p. 253.

35. *M.P.: A Selection*, p. 130; *Pastiches et mélanges*, p. 254.

36. *M.P.: A Selection*, p. 132; *Pastiches et mélanges*, p. 257.

37. *M.P.: A Selection*, pp. 133–134; *Pastiches et mélanges*, pp. 258–259.

38. *M.P.: A Selection*, p. 139; *Pastiches et mélanges*, pp. 265–266.

39. *M.P.: A Selection*, pp. 24n.–25n.; *Pastiches et mélanges*, pp. 108n.–109n. See also John Ruskin, *La Bible d'Amiens*, tr. Marcel Proust (Paris, Mercure de France, 1926), pp. 10–11.

40. *Lettres à André Gide* (Neuchâtel, Ides et Calendes, 1949), p. 13.

41. Léon Deffoux, *Le Pastiche littéraire des origines à nos jours* (Paris, Delagrave, 1932).

42. Léon Daudet, *Salons et journaux* (Paris, Grasset, 1932), p. 259.

43. Fernand Gregh, "Sur le pastiche," *Candide*, June 26, 1919, p. 3. See also Elisabeth de Clermont-Tonnerre, *Robert de Montesquiou et Marcel Proust* (Paris, Flammarion, 1925), p. 34.

44. Pierre Abraham, *Proust* (Paris, Rieder, 1930), p. 28.

45. Jean Mouton, *Le Style de Marcel Proust* (Paris, Corrêa, 1948), p. 41.

46. Benjamin Crémieux, *Vingtième Siècle*, Ière série (Paris, Gallimard, 1924), p. 29.

47. Georges Cattaui, *L'Amitié de Proust* (Paris, Gallimard, 1935), pp. 201–202.

48. Gregh, "Sur le Pastiche," p. 3.

49. Leo Spitzer, *Stilstudien* (Munich, M. Hueber, 1928), II, 484.

50. *Ibid.*, p. 429.

51. *Letters of Marcel Proust*, p. 330; *Correspondance générale*, III, 68.

52. *Letters to a Friend*, pp. 178–179; Lauris, *A un ami*, pp. 243–244.

53. Ralph Wright, "A Sensitive Petronius," in *Marcel Proust: An English Tribute*, ed. C. K. Scott-Moncrieff (New York, T. Seltzer, 1923), pp. 40–41.

II. PROUST AND THE SEVENTEENTH CENTURY

1. *M.P.: A Selection*, p. 142n.; *Sésame et les lys*, p. 55n.

2. *M.P.: A Selection*, p. 142; *Pastiches et mélanges*, p. 269. (Translation partly my own.)

3. *Letters of Marcel Proust*, p. 360; "Enquête sur le romantisme et le classicisme," *La Renaissance politique, littéraire, artistique* 9:13 (January 8, 1921).

4. *Letters of Marcel Proust*, pp. 360–361; "Enquête sur le romantisme," p. 14. (The translation of the last sentence is my own.)

5. *Correspondance générale*, III, 308.

6. *Letters of Marcel Proust*, p. 181; *Correspondance générale*, VI, 93.

7. *Correspondance avec sa mère*, 1887–1905 (Paris, Plon, 1953), p. 11.

8. *Letters of Marcel Proust*, 181; *Correspondance générale*, VI, 93–94.

9. *Jean Santeuil*, p. 241; *Jean Santeuil*, II, 15.

10. André Maurois, *Proust, Portrait of a Genius*, tr. Gerard Hopkins (New York, Harper & Brothers, 1950), pp. 317–319; unpublished text quoted by André Maurois, *A la recherche de Marcel Proust* (Paris, Hachette, 1949), pp. 33–35. The quotation is from Sainte-Beuve.

11. *M.P.: A Selection*, p. 143; *Pastiches et mélanges*, pp. 269–270.

12. *M.P.: A Selection*, p. 143n.; *Pastiches et mélanges*, pp. 269n.–270n.

13. *Letters of Marcel Proust*, p. 181; *Correspondance générale*, VI, 94.

14. *M.P.: A Selection*, p. 144n.; *Pastiches et mélanges*, p. 270n.

15. *Remembrance of Things Past*, II, 704, 705, *A la recherche*, III, 459–460, and Preface to *Tendres Stocks*, p. 31; *M.P.: A Selection*, p. 221.

16. *Remembrance of Things Past*, II, 126, 174, 275; *A la recherche*, II, 774, 843, 987.

17. *Remembrance of Things Past*, I, 577; *A la recherche*, I, 763.

18. *Remembrance of Things Past*, I, 68; *A la recherche*, I, 90. *Cf.* "Enquête sur le romantisme," p. 14: *Letters of Marcel Proust*, p. 361, and an earlier version of the same material in *Jean Santeuil*, p. 76 and *Jean Santeuil*, I, 128–129.

19. *M.P.: A Selection*, p. 219; Preface to *Tendres Stocks*, p. 27.

20. *M.P.: A Selection*, p. 219; Preface to *Tendres Stocks*, pp. 27–28.

21. Racine also serves Proust as a pretext for a mild satire on contemporary pedagogy. (See André Ferré, "Marcel Proust critique pédagogique," *Revue pédagogique* 95: 333–355 [1929].) The device which Proust uses is the discussion by the "jeunes filles en fleurs" of a school essay on the subject "Sophocle écrit des Enfers à Racine pour le consoler de l'insuccès d'*Athalie*." (*Remembrance of Things Past*, I, 682–685; *A la recherche*, I, 911–914.) Two of the girls relate their treatment of the subject — a procedure that gives Proust an opportunity to satirize lightly the absurd pedagogical devices current in the schools of his day. Proust's antidote to the academic approach is a genuine analysis of an author's materials, such as is found in Marcel's extended discourse (for Albertine's edification) on *phrases-types* in various authors. This draws the comment, "Regardez comme vous voyez la littérature d'une façon plus intéressante qu'on ne nous la faisait étudier . . ." from Albertine. (*Remembrance of Things Past*, II, 646; *A la recherche*, III, 381.)

22. *M.P.: A Selection*, p. 220; Preface to *Tendres Stocks*, pp. 29–30. There are several slight errors in Proust's quotation. *Cf.* Madame de Sévigné, *Lettres* (Paris, Hachette, 1863), II, 213. The translation of the Sévigné passage is my own.

23. *Remembrance of Things Past*, I, 496; *A la recherche*, I, 653–654. There are a few slight errors in Proust's quotation. *Cf.* Sévigné, *Lettres*, V, 60.

24. *Remembrance of Things Past*, II, 645; *A la recherche*, III, 379.

25. *Remembrance of Things Past*, I, 938; *A la recherche*, II, 312.

26. *Remembrance of Things Past*, II, 160; *A la recherche*, II, 771.

27. *Remembrance of Things Past*, I, 528–529; *A la recherche*, I, 697.

28. *Remembrance of Things Past*, II, 1120–1121; *A la recherche*, III, 1043–1044.

29. Abraham, *Proust*, pp. 58–64, and D. C. Cabeen, "Saint-Simon and Proust," *Publications of the Modern Language Association* 46:608–618 (1931).

30. "Marcel Proust et la tradition française," *Hommage à Marcel Proust, Les Cahiers Marcel Proust* (Paris, Nouvelle Revue Française, 1923), I, 136.

31. *Letters to a Friend*, p. 113; Lauris, *A un ami*, p. 154.

32. Mouton, *Le Style de Proust*, pp. 40–41.

33. Spitzer, *Stilstudien*, II, 485.

34. *Pastiches et mélanges*, pp. 66, 86, 60.

35. *Ibid.*, pp. 63–65.

36. Gaston Boissier, *Saint-Simon* (Paris, Hachette, 1892), p. 195.

37. *Letters of Marcel Proust*, p. 372; *Correspondance générale*, III, 94–95 (to Paul Souday, June 17, 1921).

38. *Remembrance of Things Past*, I, 581; *A la recherche*, I, 768.

39. *Remembrance of Things Past*, I, 420; *A la recherche*, I, 551.

40. *Remembrance of Things Past*, II, 260; *A la recherche*, II, 967.

41. *Remembrance of Things Past*, II, 967; *A la recherche*, III, 832.

42. *The Maxims of Marcel Proust*, ed. and tr. Justin O'Brien (New York, Columbia University Press, 1948), p. xiii; see also Germaine Brée, "Une Etude du style de Proust dans *Les Plaisirs et les jours*," *French Review* 15:401–409 (1942), and Henri Rambaud, "Le Premier Livre de Marcel Proust," *Revue universelle* 19:232–237 (October 15, 1924).

43. Ernst-Robert Curtius, *Französicher Geist im neuen Europa* (Stuttgart, Deutsche Verlags-Anstalt, 1925), p. 48.

44. Jacques Rivière, *Nouvelles Etudes* (Paris, Gallimard, 1947), p. 154.

45. *Correspondance générale*, II, 86–87.

46. *Letters of Marcel Proust*, p. 361; "Enquête sur le romantisme," p. 14.

III. PROUST AS A CRITIC OF THE NINETEENTH CENTURY

1. The Romantic poets — Baudelaire — other poets

1. *Correspondance générale*, II, 157–158.

2. Quoted by Maurois in *Proust, Portrait of a Genius*, p. 149; *A la recherche de Marcel Proust*, p. 160. (Maurois does not list this quotation as an *inédit*, although it has all the appearances of being from Proust's notebooks. In Maurois' book, the sentence is immediately followed by a passage dealing with Balzac found in *Remembrance of Things Past*, II, 491 — *A la recherche*, III, 160 — which the reader will find quoted in the Balzac chapter of this book, p. 86.)

3. *M.P.: A Selection*, p. 188; *Chroniques*, Paris, Gallimard, 1927, pp. 212–213.

4. *Chroniques*, p. 213.

5. *M.P.: A Selection*, p. 189; *Chroniques*, p. 213–214. (Proust has a tendency to quote from memory. He frequently makes minor errors in quoting or alters the punctuation. Whenever such errors require correction, the corrected version will be given in the note. Otherwise Proust's quotation will be given unchanged.)

6. *Sésame et les lys*, p. 95n. The poem "A l'Arc de Triomphe" is in *Les Voix intérieures.*

7. *Sésame et les lys*, p. 94n.; *cf.* André Lang, *Voyage en zigzags dans la République des Lettres*, p. 154.

8. *Sésame et les lys*, p. 95n. The poem alluded to is "Lettre," in Book II of *Les Contemplations*, and the "glorious ancestor" is Vergil in *Georgics* I, 470; but the correct form of the Latin is "importun*ae*que volucres."

9. *Sésame et les lys*, p. 95n.

10. "Quelques pensées inédites de Marcel Proust," *Le Figaro littéraire* 5:1 (November 18, 1950).

11. *Chroniques*, p. 208.

12. *Remembrance of Things Past*, I, 548; *A la recherche*, I, 723.

13. *Remembrance of Things Past*, I, 1068; *A la recherche*, II, 491–492.

14. *Remembrance of Things Past*, I, 1069; *A la recherche*, II, 493–494.

15. *Remembrance of Things Past*, I, 1107–1108; *A la recherche*, II, 549.

16. *M.P.: A Selection*, p. 193; *Chroniques*, p. 217.

17. *Remembrance of Things Past*, I, 1108; *Le Côté de Guermantes*, III, 202–203.

18. *M.P.: A Selection*, p. 190; *Chroniques*, p. 215.

19. *Ibid.* All these lines are found in the last four stanzas of Part III of the poem. The correct versions of lines 1 and 2 are as follows:

> Dans les balancements de *ta tête* penchée . . .
> Et dans ton pur sourire amoureux et souffrant . . .

20. *Remembrance of Things Past*, I, 547; *A la recherche*, I, 722.

21. *Remembrance of Things Past*, I, 550; *A la recherche*, I, 726–727.

22. *Cf.* Maurois, *A la recherche de Marcel Proust*, p. 18; *Proust, Portrait of a Genius*, p. 22.

23. *Remembrance of Things Past*, I, 68; *A la recherche*, I, 90. The line is from *La Nuit de Mai.*

24. *Remembrance of Things Past*, I, 580; *A la recherche*, I, 768.

25. *M.P.: A Selection*, p. 204; *Chroniques*, pp. 230–231. The quotation is from "A mon frère, revenant d'Italie."

26. *Correspondance générale*, VI, 9–10.

27. *Ibid.*, III, 139.

28. *Contre Sainte-Beuve* (Paris, Gallimard, 1954), p. 178. (Previously quoted by Maurois in *A la recherche de Marcel Proust*, pp. 148–149; *Proust, Portrait of a Genius*, p. 137. I have taken the liberty of changing Mr. Hopkins's translation slightly.)

29. René Galand, "Proust et Baudelaire," *Publications of the Modern Language Association* 65:1011-1035 (December, 1950).

30. See Margaret Gilman, *Baudelaire the Critic* (New York, Columbia University Press, 1943).

31. *M.P.: A Selection*, pp. 213-214; Preface to *Tendres Stocks*, p. 15.

32. *Contre Sainte-Beuve*, p. 181.

33. *Ibid.*, p. 182.

34. Walter A. Strauss, "Twelve Unpublished Letters by Marcel Proust," *Harvard Library Bulletin* 7:163 (Spring, 1953).

35. *M.P.: A Selection*, p. 188; *Chroniques*, p. 212.

36. *M.P.: A Selection*, p. 191; *Chroniques*, p. 215.

37. *Letters of Marcel Proust*, pp. 35-36; *Correspondance générale*, I, 4.

38. *Chroniques*, p. 227.

39. *M.P.: A Selection*, p. 197; *Chroniques*, p. 222.

40. *Letters of Marcel Proust*, p. 360; "Enquête sur le romantisme et le classicisme," *La Renaissance politique, littéraire, artistique* 9:14 (January 8, 1921).

41. *M.P.: A Selection*, p. 214; Preface to *Tendres Stocks*, p. 16.

42. *M.P.: A Selection*, p. 197; *Chroniques*, pp. 222–223.

43. *M.P.: A Selection*, p. 196; *Chroniques*, pp. 221-222.

44. *M.P.: A Selection*, p. 197; *Chroniques*, p. 223. The quotation is from *Femmes damnées: Delphine et Hippolyte. Cf.* Horace, *Odes*, I, 3 ("Sic te diva potens Cypri").

45. *M.P.: A Selection*, p. 194; *Chroniques*, p. 219.

46. *Chroniques*, p. 219.

47. J.-D. Hubert, *L'Esthétique des "Fleurs du Mal"* (Geneva, Pierre Caillier, 1953), p. 101.

48. *M.P.: A Selection*, p. 194; *Chroniques*, p. 219.

49. *M.P.: A Selection*, p. 195; *Chroniques*, p. 220.

50. *Chroniques*, p. 190.

51. *Contre Sainte-Beuve*, p. 185.

52. *Ibid.*, pp. 183, 184.

53. *Ibid.*, p. 187.

54. *Ibid.*, p. 189.

55. *Ibid.*, p. 190.

56. *M.P.: A Selection*, p. 198; *Chroniques*, pp. 223-224.

57. *M.P.: A Selection*, p. 195; *Chroniques*, p. 220.

58. *M.P.: A Selection*, pp. 195-196; *Chroniques*, pp. 220-224.

59. Hubert, *L'Esthétique des "Fleurs du Mal,"* pp. 273-274.

60. *Contre Sainte-Beuve*, p. 184.

61. *Ibid.*, p. 179. Previously quoted in Maurois, *Proust, Portrait of a Genius*, p. 137; *A la recherche de Marcel Proust*, p. 149.

62. *M.P.: A Selection*, pp. 202-203; *Chroniques*, pp. 228-229.

63. *M.P.: A Selection*, pp. 203-204; *Chroniques*, pp. 229-230. With respect to the "profound mystery" in Baudelaire, see Gide's conversation with Proust as reported in Gide's *Journal* (Paris, Bibliothèque de la Pléiade, 1948), p. 692, in which Proust expressed the conviction that Baudelaire was a "uranist." See also Justin O'Brien, "Albertine the Ambiguous: Notes on Proust's Transposition of Sexes," and the rejoinder by Harry Levin and Professor O'Brien's rebuttal under the title of "Proust, Gide, and the Sexes" in *Publications of the Modern Language Association*, 44:933-952 (December, 1949), and 45:648-653 (June, 1950).

64. *Remembrance of Things Past*, II, 1030; *A la recherche*, III, 920. The lines are from *La Chevelure* and *Parfum exotique*, respectively.

65. Letter to Rosny, quoted in André Lang, *Voyage en Zigzags*, pp. 154-155.

66. *M.P.: A Selection*, p. 199; *Chroniques*, p. 224.

67. *M.P.: A Selection*, p. 199; *Chroniques*, p. 225.

68. Paul Valéry, *Eupalinos* (Paris, Nouvelle Revue Française, 1924), p. 162.

69. *M.P.: A Selection*, p. 192; *Chroniques*, pp. 216-217.

70. *M.P.: A Selection*, p. 191; *Chroniques*, pp. 215-216. Actually, the first quoted line comes at the end.

71. *Correspondance générale*, I, 170.

72. *Chroniques*, p. 231. The second line should read: Vous ne paraissez pas heureuses.

73. *Chroniques*, p. 231. Lines 2 and 3 should read, respectively:

Leur visage est indifférent
Les anciennes ont l'air de veuves.

74. See letter to Jacques Porel, in Strauss, "Twelve Unpublished Letters of Marcel Proust," 156-157, and letter to S. Schiff (Stephen Hudson), *Correspondance générale*, III, 6.

75. *M.P.: A Selection*, p. 205; *Chroniques*, p. 231.

76. *M.P.: A Selection*, pp. 205-206; *Chroniques*, p. 232.

77. *Jean Santeuil*, p. 73; *Jean Santeuil*, I, 124.

78. *Jean Santeuil*, p. 75 (slightly modified), *Jean Santeuil*, I, 127.

79. *M.P.: A Selection*, pp. 207, 208; *Chroniques*, pp. 233, 234. The reference is to the opening stanzas of *La Ravine Saint-Gilles*:

La gorge est pleine d'ombre où, sous les bambous grêles
Le soleil au zénith n'a jamais resplendi,
Où les filtrations des sources naturelles
S'unissent au silence enflammé de midi.

De la lave durcie aux fissures moussues
Au travers des lichens l'eau tombe en ruisselant,
S'y perd, et, se creusant de soudaines issues,
Germe et circule au fond parmi le gravier blanc.

80. *Correspondance générale,* VI, 9.

81. Benjamin Crémieux, *Vingtième Siècle,* Ière série (Paris, Gallimard, 1924), p. 83.

82. *Chroniques,* pp. 137-138.

83. *Ibid.*, p. 140.

84. *Ibid.*

85. *Contre Sainte-Beuve,* p. 320 ("Contre la jeune école").

86. *Ibid.*, pp. 310-311.

87. *Chroniques,* p. 142.

88. *Ibid.*, pp. 140-141.

89. *Jean Santeuil,* p. 464; *Jean Santeuil,* II, 305-306.

2. Balzac

1. Abraham, *Proust: Recherches sur la création intellectuelle,* pp. 50-57.

2. Harry Levin, "Balzac et Proust," *Hommage à Balzac* (UNESCO) (Paris, Mercure de France, 1950), pp. 281-308.

3. Charles Daudet, *Répertoire des personnages de "A la recherche de temps perdu,"* preceded by "La Vie sociale dans l'oeuvre de Marcel Prouse," by Ramon Fernandez (Paris, Gallimard, 1928). See also P. A. Spalding, *A Reader's Handbook to Proust* (London, Chatto & Windus, 1952).

4. Anatole Cerfberr and Jules Christophe, *Répertoire de la Comédie Humaine de Honoré de Balzac* (Paris, Calmann-Lévy, 1887).

5. *Remembrance of Things Past,* II, 490; *A la recherche,* III, 160.

6. *Remembrance of Things Past,* II, 490–491; *A la recherche,* III, 160.

7. Henry James, *French Poets and Novelists* (London, Macmillan Co., 1919), pp. 79-80.

8. *Contre Sainte-Beuve,* p. 194.

9. *Ibid.*, p. 226.

10. Bernard de Fallois, in *Le Balzac de Monsieur de Guermantes* (Neuchâtel, Ides et Calendes, 1950), p. 16.

11. *Contre Sainte-Beuve,* p. 227.

12. *Le Balzac de Monsieur de Guermantes,* p. 21.

13. *Contre Sainte-Beuve,* p 227.

14. *Remembrance of Things Past*, II, 323–324; *A la recherche*, II, 1055.

15. *Contre Sainte-Beuve*, pp. 228 and 237.

16. *Proust, Portrait of a Genius*, pp. 144-147; *A la recherche de Marcel Proust*, pp. 155–159.

17. *Proust, Portrait of a Genius*, p. 146; *A la recherche de Marcel Proust*, p. 157.

18. *Remembrance of Things Past*, II, 320; *A la recherche*, II, 1050. See also *Contre Sainte-Beuve*, p. 218.

19. Honoré de Balzac, *Splendeurs et misères des courtisanes* (Paris, Bordas, 1948), p. 351.

20. See *Proust, Portrait of a Genius*, p. 208, and *A la recherche de Marcel Proust*, p. 221.

21. *Remembrance of Things Past*, II, 325; *A la recherche*, II, 1058.

22. *Contre Sainte-Beuve*, p. 241.

23. *Remembrance of Things Past*, I, 547; *A la recherche*, I, 722.

24. *Contre Sainte-Beuve*, p. 242.

25. *Ibid.*, p. 243.

26. *Jean Santeuil*, pp. 16, 17; *Jean Santeuil*, I, 52–53.

27. *Correspondance générale*, IV, 152.

28. *Remembrance of Things Past*, II, 881; *A la recherche*, III, 706.

29. *Le Balzac de Monsieur de Guermantes*, pp. 16–17.

30. *M. P.: A Selection*, p. 119n.; *Pastiches et mélanges*, p. 240n.

31. Levin, "Balzac et Proust," pp. 296, 282.

32. *Contre Sainte-Beuve*, p. 194.

33. *Ibid.*, p. 196.

34. *Ibid.*

35. Harry Levin, *Toward Balzac* (Norfolk, New Directions, 1947), p. 44.

36. James, *French Poets and Novelists*, p. 117.

37. *Contre Sainte-Beuve*, p. 197.

38. *Ibid.*, pp. 202-203.

39. *Le Balzac de Monsieur de Guermantes*, p. 17.

40. Balzac, *Splendeurs et misères*, p. 334.

41. *Contre Sainte-Beuve*, p. 207.

42. *Ibid.*

43. *Ibid.*, p. 208.

44. *Ibid.*, pp. 208-209.

45. *Ibid.*, p. 210.

46. *Ibid.*, pp. 215-216.

47. *Pastiches et mélanges*, p. 11.

48. *Ibid.*, p. 12.

49. *Ibid.*
50. *Ibid.*, pp. 12, 13, 14, 15.
51. *Ibid.*, p. 15.
52. *Ibid.*, p. 16.
53. *Ibid.*, pp. 17–18.
54. *Ibid.*, p. 17.
55. *Contre Sainte-Beuve*, p. 218.
56. Ernst-Robert Curtius, *Balzac*, tr. Henri Jourdain (Paris, Grasset, 1933), p. 326.
57. *Contre Sainte-Beuve*, p. 219.
58. Levin, *Toward Balzac*, p. 62.
59. *Contre Sainte-Beuve*, p. 222.
60. Curtius, *Balzac*, p. 340.
61. James, *French Poets and Novelists*, p. 116.
62. *Contre Sainte-Beuve*, p. 223.
63. *Ibid.*, p. 224.

3. Flaubert

1. Translated in *M. P.: A Selection*, pp. 224–240.
2. Robert de Billy, *Marcel Proust: lettres et conversations* (Paris, Edition des Portiques, 1930), p. 169.
3. Mouton, *Le Style de Marcel Proust*, p. 57.
4. See Douglas W. Alden, "Proust and the Flaubert Controversy," *Romanic Review* 38:230–240 (1937).
5. Jacques Boulenger, *Mais l'art est difficile!* 2ème série (Paris, Plon, 1921), p. 2.
6. Louis de Robert, *De Loti à Proust* (Paris, Flammarion, 1928), pp. 171–172.
7. *Chroniques*, p. 193.
8. *Ibid.*, p. 206; *M. P.: A Selection*, p. 235.
9. Jean Mouton (*Le Style de Marcel Proust*, pp. 52–57) gives a number of examples chosen from *Du côté de chez Swann* in which Flaubertian stylistic devices are used with similar effects by Proust, and Benjamin Crémieux (*Vingtième Siècle*, Ière série, p. 89) finds an example of imitation of Flaubert's style in *A l'ombre des jeunes filles en fleurs*.
10. *Correspondance*, 3ème série (1852–54) (Paris, Conard, 1926), p. 68 (to Louise Colet, December 17, 1852).
11. *Contre Sainte-Beuve*, p. 207.
12. *M.P.: A Selection*, pp. 224–225; *Chroniques*, pp. 193–194.
13. Martin Turnell, *The Novel in France* (London, Hamish Hamilton, 1950), p. 306.
14. *M.P.: A Selection*, p. 225; *Chroniques*, p. 194.

15. Albert Thibaudet, *Gustave Flaubert* (Paris, Plon, 1922), pp. 304–309.

16. *M. P.: A Selection*, p. 226; *Chroniques*, p. 195.

17. *Chroniques*, p. 196. Gustave Flaubert, *L'Education sentimentale* (Paris, Editions de Cluny, 1939), p. 2.

18. *M. P.: A Selection*, pp. 226–227; *Chroniques*, p. 196.

19. *M. P.: A Selection*, p. 227; *Chroniques*, p. 197. I have taken the liberty of altering Mr. Hopkins' translation somewhat.

20. *Chroniques*, p. 197. Flaubert, *L'Education sentimentale*, pp. 1–2. Proust quotes only the parts not in brackets.

21. Flaubert, *L'Education sentimentale*, p. 311.

22. *Ibid.*, pp. 339–340.

23. *Pastiches et mélanges*, p. 19.

24. *M. P.: A Selection*, pp. 228–229; *Chroniques*, pp. 198–199.

25. Charles Du Bos, *Approximations I* (Paris, Plon, 1922), p. 178.

26. *Pastiches et mélanges*, pp. 21–22.

27. *Chroniques*, p. 199.

28. Flaubert, *L'Education sentimentale*, p. 448.

29. Thibaudet, *Gustave Flaubert*, pp. 283–284.

30. *Chroniques*, p. 199. Flaubert, *L'Education sentimentale*, p. 450.

31. *Pastiches et mélanges*, p. 22.

32. *M.P.: A Selection*, pp. 229–230); *Chroniques*, pp. 199–200. (Translation slightly altered.)

33. Thibaudet, *Gustave Flaubert*, p. 299.

34. *M. P.: A Selection*, p. 230; *Chroniques*, p. 200. Flaubert, *L'Education sentimentale*, p. 308.

35. *M. P.: A Selection*, p. 230; *Chroniques*, p. 200. (Translation slightly altered.)

36. Boulenger, *Mais l'art est difficile!* 2ème série, p. 22.

37. *Pastiches et mélanges*, pp. 20, 21.

38. *M. P.: A Selection*, p. 232; *Chroniques*, pp. 202–203.

39. Flaubert, *L'Education sentimentale*, pp. 453 and 354, resp.

40. *Pastiches et mélanges*, p. 21.

41. *M. P.: A Selection*, p. 233; *Chroniques*, p. 204.

42. *M. P.: A Selection*, pp. 234–235; *Chroniques*, pp. 205–206. Flaubert, *L'Education sentimentale*, p. 448.

43. Turnell, *The Novel in France*, p. 296.

44. *M. P.: A Selection*, p. 231; *Chroniques*, p. 201.

45. *M. P.: A Selection*, p. 232; *Chroniques*, p. 202.

46. *Jean Santeuil*, p. 421; *Jean Santeuil*, II, 247–248.

47. *Correspondance*, 2ème série (1847–52), p. 344. (To Louise Colet, January 16, 1852.)

48. *Correspondance générale*, III, 207.

49. *M. P.: A Selection*, pp. 218–219; Preface to *Tendres Stocks*, pp. 25–26. The Flaubert quotation is from *L'Education sentimentale*, p. 2.

4. Other French Prose Writers

1. *Remembrance of Things Past*, II, 1030; *A la recherche*, III, 919. The quotations are to be found in the Biré edition of François Chateaubriand, *Mémoires d'outre-tombe* (Paris, Garnier, n.d.), I, 125 and 343.

2. *M.P.: A Selection*, p. 239; *Chroniques*, p. 210.

3. *Chroniques*, p. 209.

4. Albert Thibaudet, *Réflexions sur la critique* (Paris, Gallimard, 1939), p. 78. The quotation is from Chateaubriand's "Sur le voyage pittoresque et historique de l'Espagne par M. Alexandre de Laborde," *Voyages en Amérique, en Italie, au Mont-Blanc. Mélanges littéraires* (Paris, Garnier Frères, 1860), p. 512.

5. *M.P.: A Selection*, p. 238; *Chroniques*, p. 209.

6. *Letters to a Friend*, p. 113; Lauris, *A un ami*, p. 170.

7. *M.P.: A Selection*, p. 236; *Chroniques*, p. 207.

8. *Contre Sainte-Beuve*, p. 189.

9. Jacques Truelle, "Marcel Proust jugé de ses personnages," *Hommage à Marcel Proust, Les Cahiers Marcel Proust*, I, 86.

10. Gérard de Nerval, *Les Filles du feu* (Paris, Bordas, 1948), p. 108.

11. *M.P.: A Selection*, pp. 239–240; *Chroniques*, p. 211.

12. *M.P.: A Selection*, p. 240; *Chroniques*, p. 211.

13. *Contre Sainte-Beuve*, pp. 164–169, *passim*.

14. *Ibid.*, p. 166.

15. *Ibid.*, p. 158.

16. *M.P.: A Selection*, p. 221; Preface to *Tendres Stocks*, p. 32. *Cf.* Nerval, *Les Filles du feu*, p. 16.

17. *Contre Sainte-Beuve*, p. 160.

18. *Ibid.*, p. 159.

19. *Remembrance of Things Past*, II, 643; *A la recherche*, III, 376.

20. *Correspondance générale*, IV, 49.

21. *Remembrance of Things Past*, II, 644; *A la recherche*, III, 376.

22. *M.P.: A Selection*, p. 217; Preface to *Tendres Stocks*, p. 23.

23. *Contre Sainte-Beuve*, pp. 413–416.

24. *M.P.: A Selection*, p. 217; Preface to *Tendres Stocks*, p. 22.

25. *M.P.: A Selection*, p. 217; Preface to *Tendres Stocks*, p. 23.

26. *M.P.: A Selection*, pp. 217–218; Preface to *Tendres Stocks*, pp. 23–24.

27. Stendhal (Marie Henri Beyle), *Memoirs of an Egotist*, tr. T. W. Earp (London, Turnstile Press, 1949), p. 63.

28. *M.P.: A Selection*, p. 236; *Chroniques*, p. 207.

29. *M.P.: A Selection*, p. 212; Preface to *Tendres Stocks*, p. 12.

30. *Correspondance générale*, III, 109.

31. *Ibid.*, IV, 241–242.

32. *M.P.: A Selection*, p. 44n.; *Sésame et les lys*, p. 224n., and *Pastiches et mélanges*, p. 134n.

33. *M.P.: A Selection*, pp. 212–213; Preface to *Tendres Stocks*, pp. 12–13.

34. *M.P.: A Selection*, p. 213; Preface to *Tendres Stocks*, p. 14.

35. *M.P.: A Selection*, p. 213; Preface to *Tendres Stocks*, pp. 14–15.

36. See *Correspondance générale*, III, 284.

37. *Ibid.*, IV, 229–230.

38. Philippe Van Tieghem, *Renan* (Paris, Hachette, 1948), p. 184.

39. *Pastiches et mélanges*, p. 52.

40. *Ibid.*, pp. 53, 57.

41. *Ibid.*, p. 55. Jean Mouton (*Le Style de Marcel Proust*, p. 49n.) points out the similarity of this passage to a passage near the end of the preface to *Souvenirs d'enfance et de jeunesse*.

42. *Correspondance générale*, IV, 229.

43. *Pastiches et mélanges*, p. 41.

44. *Ibid.*, pp. 42–43.

45. *Remembrance of Things Past*, II, 882–887; *A la recherche*, III, 709–718.

46. *Pastiches et mélanges*, pp. 36 and 37.

47. *Ibid.*, p. 36.

48. Charles Du Bos, *Approximations*, IIe série, "Remarque sur les Goncourt" (Paris, Les Editions G. Crès et Cie, 1927), p. 62.

49. "Les Goncourt devant leurs cadets," *Le Gaulois*, 3ème série, 57:4 (May 27, 1922).

50. *A la recherche*, I, 42; *Remembrance of Things Past*, I, 32.

51. *Letters to a Friend*, p. 132; Lauris, *A un ami*, p. 178. See *Letters of Marcel Proust*, p. 199.

52. *Remembrance of Things Past*, II, 1006–1007; *A la recherche*, III, 1044.

5. Sainte-Beuve

1. *Contre Sainte-Beuve*, p. 53.
2. *Ibid.*, pp. 131–132.
3. *Ibid.*, p. 143.
4. *Ibid.*, p. 310.
5. *Chroniques*, p. 207.

6. *M.P.: A Selection*, p. 251; Preface to Jacques-Emile Blanche, *Propos de peintre* (Paris, Emile-Paul, 1919), I: *De David à Degas*, xix.

7. C.-A. Sainte-Beuve, *Causeries du lundi* (Paris, Garnier, n.d.), XIII, 276–277.

8. *M.P.: A Selection*, p. 250; Preface to *Propos de peintre*, I, xviii.

9. See Proust's letter to J.-E. Blanche (1917), *Correspondance générale*, III, 114, and *Letters of Marcel Proust*, p. 289.

10. *M.P.: A Selection*, p. 253; Preface to *Propos de peintre*, I, xxi.

11. *Pastiches et mélanges*, pp. 25–26. *Cf.* Sainte-Beuve, *Causeries du lundi*, XIII, 362.

12. *M.P.: A Selection*, p. 215; Preface to *Tendres Stocks*, pp. 17–18.

13. Fernand Vandérem, *Baudelaire et Sainte-Beuve* (Paris, Librairie Henri Leclerc, 1917).

14. *M.P.: A Selection*, pp. 214–217; Preface to *Tendres Stocks*, pp. 16–22.

15. *Pastiches et mélanges*, pp. 28–29.

16. Sainte-Beuve, *Causeries du lundi*, XIII, 276–277.

17. *Remembrance of Things Past*, II, 320–321; *A la recherche*, II, 1050–1051.

18. Sainte-Beuve, *Causeries du lundi*, II, 449.

19. *Contre Sainte-Beuve*, pp. 220, 225.

20. C.-A. Sainte-Beuve, *Portraits contemporains* (Paris, Calmann-Lévy, 1882), II, 353.

21. *M.P.: A Selection*, p. 236; *Chroniques*, p. 206.

22. Mouton, *Le Style de Marcel Proust*, p. 58.

23. *Pastiches et mélanges*, p. 28.

24. *Remembrance of Things Past*, II, 347; *A la recherche*, II, 1087.

25. *Pastiches et mélanges*, pp. 28, 29, 31.

26. *Ibid.*, p. 24.

27. *Ibid.*, p. 25.

28. *Ibid.*, p. 29.

29. *Correspondance générale*, III, 130 (to Jacques-Emile Blanche, 1919).

30. *Remembrance of Things Past*, II, 782; *A la recherche*, III, 570.

31. *Remembrance of Things Past*, I, 539; *A la recherche*, I, 711.

32. *Letters of Marcel Proust*, p. 330; *Correspondance générale*, III, 68.

33. See *Pastiches et mélanges*, pp. 266n.–267n., *Chroniques*, pp. 207–208, and *M.P.: A Selection*, pp. 140n. and 237; and "Un Professeur de Beauté," *Les Arts de la vie* 4:72 (July–December, 1905).

34. C.-A. Sainte-Beuve, *Chateaubriand et son groupe littéraire sous l'Empire* (Paris, Calmann-Lévy, 1889), II, 116n.

35. *M.P.: A Selection*, p. 236; *Chroniques*, p. 206.

36. *Chroniques*, p. 170.

37. *Contre Sainte-Beuve*, pp. 176–177.

38. C.-A. Sainte-Beuve, *Nouveaux lundis* (Paris, Calmann-Lévy, 1884), III, 15.

39. *Letters of Marcel Proust*, p. 289; *Correspondance générale*, III, 114.

40. *M.P.: A Selection*, p. 250; Preface to *Propos de peintre*, I, xvii.

41. *Contre Sainte-Beuve*, pp. 155–156.

6. Foreign Authors

1. Cattaui, *L'Amitié de Proust*, p. 192.

2. Porel, *Fils de Réjane*, I, 328.

3. Strauss, "Twelve Unpublished Letters of Marcel Proust," p. 151.

4. *Correspondance générale*, III, 64 (to Paul Souday, 1917).

5. *Contre Sainte-Beuve*, pp. 403–406. This is the source of the quotations that follow.

6. *Lettres à la NRF* (Paris, Gallimard, 1932), p. 174.

7. *Remembrance of Things Past*, II, 643; *A la recherche*, III, 376.

8. *A la recherche*, III, 378; *Remembrance of Things Past*, II, 644. The full text of this quotation is to be found only in the definitive edition. The translation of the additional sentence is my own.

9. *Remembrance of Things Past*, II, 645; *A la recherche*, III, 379.

10. *Ibid.*

11. *Remembrance of Things Past*, II, 646; *A la recherche*, III, 380.

12. *Remembrance of Things Past*, II, 646; *A la recherche*, III, 381. (Translation slightly altered.)

13. *Contre Sainte-Beuve*, p. 423. It is interesting to note that in speaking of dwelling places in Dostoevski, Proust used both *Crime and Punishment* and *The Brothers Karamazov* as examples. Cf. *A la recherche*, III, 1091, notes to p. 278.

14. *Contre Sainte-Beuve*, pp. 422–423.

15. *Remembrance of Things Past*, II, 646; *A la recherche*, III, 379.

16. *Contre Sainte-Beuve*, p. 420.

17. *Ibid.*, pp. 420–421.

18. *Chroniques*, p. 143.

19. *Remembrance of Things Past*, II, 645; *A la recherche*, III, 379.

20. *Contre Sainte-Beuve*, p. 421.

21. Strauss, "Twelve Unpublished Letters of Marcel Proust," p. 164.

22. *Remembrance of Things Past*, II, 646; *A la recherche*, III, 381.

23. *Letters of Marcel Proust*, p. 204; Robert de Billy, *Marcel Proust: Lettres et conversations* (Paris, Edition des Portiques, 1930), pp. 180–181.

24. Florence Emily Hardy, *The Later Years of Thomas Hardy: 1892–1928* (New York, Macmillan, 1930), p. 248.

25. *Remembrance of Things Past*, II, 1022; *A la recherche*, III, 909–910.

26. *Remembrance of Things Past*, II, 644; *A la recherche*, III, 377.

27. Possibly Hardy did not mean to be taken seriously every time. Albert J. Guerard suggest that Hardy's "impulse to comedy is likely to appear at highly inopportune moments. In *A Pair of Blue Eyes* Hardy finds it hard to decide whether Elfride's funeral train — with two suitors on board, ignorant of her marriage and death, and for a while ignorant of each other — should be considered more ludicrous than tragic or more tragic than ludicrous." *Thomas Hardy: the Novels and Stories* (Cambridge, Mass., Harvard University Press, 1949), p. 7.

28. *Hommage à Marcel Proust, Les Cahiers Marcel Proust*, I, 146.

29. Maurois, *Proust, Portrait of a Genius*, p. 22; *A la recherche de Marcel Proust*, p. 29.

30. L. A. Bisson, "Proust, Bergson and George Eliot," *Modern Language Review* 40:109 (1945).

31. *Jean Santeuil*, p. 377; *Jean Santeuil*, II, 190–191.

32. *M.P.: A Selection*, p. 21n.; *Pastiches et mélanges*, pp. 104n. and 105n.

33. *Contre Sainte-Beuve*, pp. 417–419.

34. Joan Bennett, *George Eliot: Her Mind and Her Art* (Cambridge, Cambridge University Press, 1948), p. 84.

35. Henry James, *Partial Portraits* (London, Macmillan and Co., 1911), p. 62.

36. *The George Eliot Letters*, ed. Gordon S. Haight (New Haven, Yale University Press, 1954), I, 278.

37. *Correspondance générale*, I, 123.

38. *La Nouvelle Nouvelle Revue française* 1:763–767 (October, 1953).

39. *Lettres à une amie* (Manchester, Editions du Calame, 1942).

40. See Bibliography, under the following entries: L. A. Bisson, André Maurois, J. Murray, A. J. Roche, and Sybil de Souza.

41. *M.P.: A Selection*, pp. 11–16 and 97–106; *Pastiches et mélanges*, pp. 91–99 and 198–209 and *Chroniques*, pp. 145–169.

42. *La Chronique des arts et de la curiosité* 18:146–147 (1906).

43. *Sésame et les lys*, p. 62n.

44. *Ibid.*, pp. 62n.–63n.

45. *M.P.: A Selection*, p. 89; *La Bible d'Amiens*, p. 85, and *Pastiches et mélanges*, pp. 187–188.

46. *La Bible d'Amiens*, pp. 235n.–236n.

47. *Sésame et les lys*, pp. 102n.–103n.

48. *M.P.: A Selection*, p. 91; *La Bible d'Amiens*, p. 88, and *Pastiches et mélanges*, p. 190.

49. John Ruskin, *Lectures on Art* (New York, Charles E. Merrill & Co., 1891), p. 71.

50. *M.P.: A Selection*, p. 83; *La Bible d'Amiens*, pp. 78–79, and *Pastiches et mélanges*, p. 181.

51. *M.P.: A Selection*, p. 84; *La Bible d'Amiens*, p. 80, and *Pastiches et mélanges*, p. 182.

52. *M.P.: A Selection*, p. 88; *La Bible d'Amiens*, p. 84, and *Pastiches et mélanges*, pp. 186–187.

53. *M.P.: A Selection*, p. 88; *La Bible d'Amiens*, p. 85, and *Pastiches et mélanges*, p. 187.

54. *M.P.: A Selection*, p. 82; *La Bible d'Amiens*, p. 77, and *Pastiches et mélanges*, p. 179.

55. *M.P.: A Selection*, p. 88; *La Bible d'Amiens*, p. 85, and *Pastiches et mélanges*, p. 187.

56. *M.P.: A Selection*, p. 89; *La Bible d'Amiens*, p. 86, and *Pastiches et mélanges*, p. 188.

57. *M.P.: A Selection*, pp. 93–94; *La Bible d'Amiens*, pp. 90–91, and *Pastiches et mélanges*, pp. 192–194.

58. Quoted in Clermont-Tonnerre, *Robert de Montesquiou et Marcel Proust*, pp. 148–149.

59. *Letters to a Friend*, p. 110; *A un ami*, p. 149.

60. *Letters of Marcel Proust*, p. 59; *Lettres à une amie*, p. 5.

61. L. A. Bisson, "Proust and Ruskin: Reconsidered in the Light of *Lettres à une amie*," *Modern Language Review* 39:35 (1944).

62. *M.P.: A Selection*, pp. 94–95; *La Bible d'Amiens*, p. 93, and *Pastiches et mélanges*, pp. 195–196.

IV. PROUST AND HIS CONTEMPORARIES

1. *Correspondance générale*, I and II, and *Lettres à André Gide*, Paris, Ides et Calendes, 1949.

2. Jeanne-Maurice Pouquet, *Le Salon de Madame Arman de Caillavet* (Paris, Hachette, 1926), p. 194. Professor Kolb dates this letter about February–March, 1899.

3. Quoted in Maurois, *Proust, Portrait of a Genius*, p. 124; *A la recherche de Marcel Proust*, pp. 135–136.

4. *M.P.: A Selection*, p. 212; Preface to *Tendres Stocks*, p. 10.

5. *Contre Sainte-Beuve*, p. 305.

6. *Pastiches et mélanges*, pp. 32, 33, 34.

7. *Ibid.*, p. 35.

8. *Contre Sainte-Beuve*, pp. 436–437.

9. A reference to another (?) Régnier and to a Maeterlinck pastiche is to be found in M. de Fallois' preface to *Contre Sainte-Beuve*, p. 15n.

10. *Letters to a Friend*, p. 126; *A un ami*, p. 170.

11. *Sésame et les lys*, p. 80n.

12. *Chroniques*, p. 183.

13. *Letters to a Friend*, p. 162; *A un ami*, p. 222.

14. *Chroniques*, p. 183.

15. *Sésame et les lys*, pp. 81n.–82n.

16. *Correspondance générale*, II, 93–94, 121, 155. See also *Letters of Marcel Proust*, p. 152.

17. *Correspondance générale*, II, 66.

18. *Remembrance of Things Past*, II, 1008; *A la recherche*, III, 888.

19. Germaine Brée, "Marcel Proust et Maurice Barrès," *Romanic Review* 40:98 (April, 1949).

20. Maurice Barrès, *Mes Cahiers* (Paris, Plon, 1935), IX (1911–12), 161–162.

21. Maurice Barrès, *Un Discours à Metz (15 août 1911)* (Paris, Emile-Paul, 1911); Mrs. [Margaret] Oliphant, *La Ville enchantée*, tr. H. Bremond (Paris, Emile-Paul, 1911).

22. Barrès, *Mes Cahiers*, IX, 162–163.

23. *Correspondance avec sa mère 1887–1905* (Paris, Plon, 1953), p. 267.

24. Proust wrote another pastiche, which he misplaced, of Faguet for the benefit of his friend Jacques Boulenger; the opening sentences of his pastiche, quoted by Proust from memory, may be found in a letter to Boulenger of May 17, 1921. (*Correspondance générale*, III, 245.)

25. Mouton, *Le Style de Marcel Proust*, p. 60.

26. *Letters of Marcel Proust*, pp. 35–36; *Correspondance générale*, I, 4.

27. *Correspondance générale*, I, 148.

28. *Ibid.*, p. 170.

29. *Contre Sainte-Beuve*, pp. 426–435.

30. *Les Arts de la vie* 4:76–77 (July, 1905).

31. *Chroniques*, p. 189.

32. *Ibid.*, pp. 188–189.

33. Charles Du Bos, *La Comtesse de Noailles et le climat du génie* (Paris, La Table Ronde, 1949), p. 221.

34. *Chroniques*, p. 188.

35. *Ibid.*, p. 190.

36. *Correspondance générale*, II, 75–76.

37. *Ibid.*, pp. 85–86.

38. *Ibid.*, p. 121. This discussion of *Domination* seems actually to have

been stimulated by a review of the book by Gaston Rageot in *La Renaissance latine* of June 15, 1905, in which Rageot spoke of Madame de Noailles as having "des dons de sensibilité passionnée et de clairvoyante analyse barrésiste."

39. *Correspondance générale,* II, 143–144.

40. *Ibid.*, p. 7.

41. *Ibid.*, V, 139. (The date of this letter is 1908 or 1909.)

42. *Lettres à André Gide,* pp. 24–25.

43. *Ibid.*, pp. 25–26.

44. *Ibid.*, pp. 34–35.

45. *Ibid.*, p. 60.

46. *Ibid.*, p. 61.

47. *Ibid.*, p. 63.

48. *Ibid.*, p. 61.

49. *Correspondance générale,* III, 139 (to Jacques-Emile Blanche).

50. *Ibid.*, 238.

51. *M.P.: A Selection,* p. 223; Preface to *Tendres Stocks,* p. 36.

52. *Bulletin de la Société des Amis de Marcel Proust et des Amis de Combray,* no. 2 (1951–52); (Illiers, 1952), p. 15.

53. *M.P.: A Selection,* pp. 222–223; Preface to *Tendres Stocks,* p. 35.

54. Cattaui, *L'Amitié de Proust,* pp. 205–206.

55. Louis de Robert, *Comment débuta Marcel Proust* (Paris, Editions de la Nouvelle Revue Française, 1925), p. 41.

56. *Ibid.*, pp. 40–41.

57. *Contre Sainte-Beuve,* p. 308.

58. *Ibid.*, p. 425.

59. Strauss, "Twelve Unpublished Letters of Marcel Proust," 162–171; and one letter in *Jean Cocteau,* special number of *Empreintes* (May–July 1950), p. 115.

60. Strauss, "Twelve Unpublished Letters," p. 163.

61. *Ibid.*, pp. 163–164.

V. CONCLUSION

1. *Lettres à André Gide,* pp. 60–61.

2. Léon Pierre-Quint, *Marcel Proust* (Paris, Editions du Sagittaire, 1946), pp. 254–255.

3. *Remembrance of Things Past,* I, 71–72; *A la recherche,* I, 94.

4. *Ibid.*, III, 187, and *Remembrance of Things Past,* II, 509, *A la recherche,* III, 187.

5. Curtius, *Französischer Geist im neuen Europa,* p. 66.

6. *Contre Sainte-Beuve,* p. 193.

7. *M.P.: A Selection*, p. 193; *Chroniques*, p. 218.

8. *Contre Sainte-Beuve*, p. 352 ("La Contemplation artistique").

9. *Remembrance of Things Past*, I, 1054; *A la recherche*, II, 471.

10. Harry Levin, Introduction to *Letters of Marcel Proust*, p. xvi.

11. Quoted by M. de Fallois in his preface to *Contre Sainte-Beuve*, p. 35.

12. *Jean Santeuil*, II, 29–30; *Jean Santeuil*, p. 253. *Cf.* also *Jean Santeuil*, p. 426, *Jean Santeuil*, II, 253.

13. *Jean Santeuil*, pp. 204 and 239; *Jean Santeuil*, I, 296–297, and II, 12.

14. *Contre Sainte-Beuve*, p. 303.

15. *Remembrance of Things Past*, II, 1001; *A la recherche*, III, 880.

16. *Remembrance of Things Past*, II, 1001; *A la recherche*, III, 879.

17. *Remembrance of Things Past*, II, 1005; *A la recherche*, III, 885. (The original edition contained an inadvertent repetition of this passage, which can be found on p. 1009. In the definitive edition, this duplication has been eliminated.)

18. *Remembrance of Things Past*, II, 1016; *A la recherche*, III, 900.

19. *Letters of Marcel Proust*, pp. 382–383; quoted in Lang, *Voyage en zigzags dans la République des Lettres*, pp. 154–155.

20. In "Sommes-nous en présence d'un renouvellement du style? . . . ," *La Renaissance politique, littéraire, artistique* 9:6 (July 22, 1922).

21. *M.P.: A Selection*, p. 242; Preface to *Propos de peintre*, I, ii.

22. *M.P.: A Selection*, pp. 221–222 (translation slightly altered); Preface to *Tendres Stocks*, pp. 32–34.

23. *Letters of Marcel Proust*, pp. 405–406; *Correspondance générale*, III, 195 (to Camille Vettard, 1922).

24. *M.P.: A Selection*, pp. 222–223; Preface to *Tendres Stocks*, pp. 35–36.

25. "Sommes-nous en présence d'un renouvellement du style?" p. 6.

26. *Letters of Marcel Proust*, pp. 180–181; *Correspondance générale*, VI, 93 (to Madame Straus, 1908).

27. *Jean Santeuil*, p. 163; *Jean Santeuil*, I, 244.

28. *Correspondance générale*, II, 86–87. (For complete text, see Chapter II, Note 45.)

29. Quoted in Robert Dreyfus, *Souvenirs sur Marcel Proust* (Paris, Grasset, 1926), p. 292.

30. *Remembrance of Things Past*, II, 1008–1009; *A la recherche*, III, 889.

31. *Remembrance of Things Past*, II, 1013; *A la recherche*, III, 896.

32. *Remembrance of Things Past*, I, 628; *A la recherche*, I, 835.

33. "Un Professeur de Beauté," p. 74.

34. *M.P.: A Selection*, pp. 24n.–25n.; *La Bible d'Amiens*, pp. 10–11; and *Pastiches et mélanges*, pp. 108n.–109n.

35. *Remembrance of Things Past, II*, 1002; *A la recherche*, III, 881.

36. *M.P.: A Selection*, pp. 233–234; *Chroniques*, pp. 204–205.

37. André Malraux, *The Psychology of Art*, II, *The Creative Act*, tr. Stuart Gilbert (New York, Pantheon, 1949), p. 145.

38. *M.P.: A Selection*, p. 234; *Chroniques*, p. 205.

39. *Sésame et les lys*, p. 93n.

40. *Contre Sainte-Beuve*, p. 50.

INDEX OF NAMES

This is an index of composers, painters, philosophers, and writers. The names of critics and scholars mentioned in the text have not been indexed unless they fall into one of those categories.

Aeschylus, 168
Althon Shée, Edmond d', 153
Andrea del Sarto, 102

Babou, Hippolyte, 72
Balzac, Honoré de, 2, 3, 4, 7, 8, 9, 10, 11, 12, 15, 24, 27, 37, 40, 49, 50, 58, 73, 84–105, 107, 108, 109, 119, 121, 123, 128, 129, 132, 136, 140, 142, 146, 148, 150, 151, 154, 156, 168, 169, 172, 179, 189, 195, 201, 211, 212, 213, 224, 226
Barbey d'Aurevilly, Jules, 123, 128–130, 226
Barrès, Maurice, 189, 194–195, 200, 216
Baudelaire, Charles, 2, 3, 4, 8, 11, 30, 37, 40, 49, 52, 57, 58, 60, 61–76, 77, 84, 115, 125, 126, 128, 143, 146, 149, 155, 156, 159, 199, 212, 213, 214, 217, 226
Beausergent, Madame de, 41
Beethoven, Ludwig van, 3, 70, 120, 212, 219
Bélugou, Léon, 184
Béranger, Pierre-Jean de, 145, 147
Bernstein, Henry, 196
Berthelot, Philippe, 137
Billy, Robert de, 106, 172
Bion, 152
Blanche, Jacques-Emile, 4, 12, 59, 134, 146, 157, 218
Boigne, Madame de, 147, 154
Boilleau-Despréaux, Nicolas, 38, 39, 48, 217
Bossuet, Jacques-Bénigne, 25, 31, 156, 220
Boulenger, Jacques, 107, 116, 122, 136, 204
Bourget, Paul, 144, 217
Boylesve, René, 93
Broglie, Duchesse de, 147

Carlyle, Thomas, 160
Carpaccio, Vittore, 164
Chaix d'Est-Ange, 152
Chardin, Jean-Baptiste, 40, 96, 222
Chateaubriand, François-René de, 2, 3, 58, 73, 81, 123–125, 128, 145, 146, 147, 152, 157, 159, 192, 194, 212
Chénier, André, 159
Claudel, Paul, 203–204
Cocteau, Jean, 63, 171, 187, 189, 207–208
Coleridge, Samuel Taylor, 20
Colet, Louise, 122
Corneille, Pierre, 33, 34, 35, 56, 78
Courbet, Gustave, 110
Cousin, Victor, 134

Dante Alighieri, 20
Daudet, Léon, 25, 205
Daudet, Lucien, 139
Deffand, Madame du, 32
Descartes, René, 14
Dickens, Charles, 3, 160
Diderot, Denis, 32
Dostoevski, Fedor, 2, 3, 40, 41, 45, 75, 131, 132, 160, 163–168, 169, 170, 171, 202, 211, 213, 224, 226
Dreyfus, Robert, 134, 136
Dumas, Alexandre, 127

Eliot, George, 2, 9, 160, 169, 172, 174–177, 212
Emerson, Ralph Waldo, 20, 160, 172

Faguet, Emile, 24, 195–196
Fantin-Latour, Ignace, 157, 158
Fénelon, François de, 92
Feuerbach, Ludwig, 176
Flaubert, Gustave, 3, 7, 11, 24, 31, 32, 40, 88, 99, 105–123, 124, 132, 142, 146, 147, 148, 149, 151, 152, 153,

154, 155, 156, 172, 192, 195, 208, 211, 213, 214, 220, 224, 226
Fontanes, Louis de, 20
France, Anatole, 5, 26, 38, 39, 61, 62, 122, 134, 159, 187, 189–190, 196, 218
Freud, Sigmund, 166

Gautier, Théophile, 17, 18, 28, 38, 68, 78, 141, 176
Gide, André, 60, 187, 189, 201–203, 210
Giotto, 177
Goethe, Johann Wolfgang von, 103, 146, 160, 161–163
Gogol, Nicolai, 165
Goncourt, Edmond and Jules de, 12, 24, 138–140, 154, 195
Guizot, François, 134

Hardy, Thomas, 2, 160, 171–174, 213, 226
Homer, 17, 25, 152
Horace, 65
Hugo, Victor, 3, 21, 31, 38, 49–57, 58, 62, 68, 69, 71, 75, 76, 78, 81, 84, 86, 137, 145, 154, 192, 212, 217, 220
Huxley, Aldous, 27

Ingres, Dominique, 217

James, Henry, 87, 97, 104, 160, 176
Jammes, Francis, 189, 205–206, 212
Joyce, James, 164

Kant, Immanuel, 109
Kock, Paul de, 165
Koestler, Arthur, 27

La Bruyère, Jean de, 46
La Fontaine, Jean de, 48, 78
Lamartine, Alphonse de, 49, 145
Lamennais, Félicité de, 145
La Rochefoucauld, François de, 46
Lauris, Georges de, 14, 27, 43, 141, 192, 193
Leconte de Lisle, Charles, 76, 77–79, 84, 192
Leonidas of Tarentum, 152
Loménie, Louis de, 58

Maeterlinck, Maurice, 21, 31, 189, 192–193, 212, 220
Malherbe, François de, 64
Mallarmé, Stéphane, 60, 68, 79, 128
Malraux, André, 224, 225
Manet, Edouard, 110, 157, 158, 217
Mantegna, Andrea, 36
Martial, 152, 153
Martin-Chauffier, Louis, 31
Mendelssohn, Felix, 219
Mendès, Catulle, 82
Meredith, George, 3, 160
Mérimée, Prosper, 147
Michelet, Jules, 16, 24, 25, 86, 137–138, 195
Mill, John Stuart, 160
Molé, Louis-Mathieu, 58, 147, 155, 156
Molière, 45, 48, 60
Monet, Claude, 3
Montaigne, Michel de, 3, 31, 47
Montesquieu, Charles de, 32
Montesquiou, Robert de, 25, 63, 177, 187, 188, 189, 196–197
Morand, Paul, 12, 106, 130, 146, 189, 190, 205
Moréas, Jean, 82
Morris, William, 160
Moschus, 152
Musset, Alfred de, 58–61, 77, 154

Nerval, Gérard de, 2, 8, 68, 73, 123, 125–128, 142, 146, 159, 212
Nicole, Pierre, 39
Nietzsche, Friedrich, 160
Noailles, Anna de, 48, 49, 136, 137, 187, 188, 189, 193, 197–201
Nordlinger, Marie, 178, 183, 185

Offenbach, Jacques, 135

Pascal, Blaise, 39, 42, 212
Pasquier, Etienne-Denis, 155, 156
Péguy, Charles, 204–205
Plato, 15, 16, 20, 158, 173, 214
Poe, Edgar Allan, 160

Racine, Jean, 2, 3, 12, 15, 29, 30, 33–39, 45, 48, 49, 58, 61, 64, 65, 68, 78, 115, 125, 143, 155, 156, 184, 212, 217
Ramond de Carbonnières, 153

Raphael, 86, 87, 97, 102
Regnard, Jean, 217
Régnier, Henri de, 24, 27, 189, 190–192, 195
Rembrandt van Rijn, 164, 166, 222, 223
Renan, Ernest, 24, 108, 134–137, 138, 154, 195, 223
Renard, Jules, 207
Renoir, Auguste, 218
Rimbaud, Arthur, 60
Robert, Louis de, 106, 107, 205
Rolland, Romain, 207
Rosny, J.-H., 217
Rousseau, Jean-Jacques, 31, 32, 128, 131, 192, 220
Royer-Collard, Pierre-Paul, 147
Ruskin, John, 2, 3, 5, 6, 7, 8, 9, 13, 14, 15, 16, 18, 19, 20, 22, 23, 80, 121, 125, 142, 160, 172, 174, 177–186, 199, 212, 214, 221, 225

Sainte-Beuve, Charles-Augustin, 8, 9, 10, 11, 12, 23, 24, 26, 27, 59, 60, 61, 68, 85, 87, 93, 95, 96, 100, 123, 134, 141–160, 177, 185, 212, 214, 225, 226
Saint-Simon, Duc de, 2, 3, 12, 15, 24, 29, 37, 41–46, 115, 136, 154, 189, 192, 195, 224
Sand, George, 2, 13, 28, 140, 147, 176, 226
Sarcey, Francisque, 195
Sartre, Jean-Paul, 27
Schopenhauer, Arthur, 21, 22, 160
Sénac de Meilhan, Gabriel, 153
Sévigné, Madame de, 12, 37, 39–41, 48, 57, 165
Shakespeare, William, 81, 160
Sophocles, 168
Souday, Paul, 26, 106
Stendhal, 3, 123, 128, 130–134, 144, 146, 156, 172, 202, 226
Stevenson, Robert Louis, 160, 172, 201, 224
Straus, Madame Emile, 32, 36, 59, 79
Strauss, David Friedrich, 176
Sully Prudhomme, Armand, 68, 76–77, 196

Taine, Hippolyte, 8, 59, 134, 142, 143, 144, 145
Thackeray, William Makepeace, 160
Thibaudet, Albert, 42, 106, 107, 109, 114, 115, 120, 124
Thiers, Adolphe, 134
Titian, 97, 194
Tocqueville, Alexis de, 147
Tolstoi, Leo, 3, 100, 160, 168–171, 202, 211, 212

Valéry, Paul, 60, 74
Vaudoyer, Jean-Louis, 129
Verlaine, Paul, 78
Vermeer, Jan, 3, 40, 159, 165, 211, 222, 223
Vigny, Alfred de, 2, 3, 27, 49, 57–58, 63, 64, 72, 84, 154, 157
Villemain, Abel-François, 134
Vinci, Leonardo da, 70, 97
Virgil, 9, 20, 155, 192
Vogüé, Eugène-Melchior de, 217
Voltaire, 131, 136

Wagner, Richard, 33, 56, 85, 86, 128, 179, 211, 217, 219
Wilde, Oscar, 90, 91

Xenophon, 16

Zola, Emile, 104, 140